Dominant Trojan Coaching Eras

Russ Goodenough

Copyright, Content, Printing, & Fair Use Doctrine

All Profits from sales of this book will be donated to the Athletic Department of the University of Southern California (USC).

Dominant Trojan Coaching Eras

Copyrighted in 2023 by Russ Goodenough
Printed in the United States
Published and First Printed in 2023

U.S. Copyright Office Case Number: In process
Library of Congress Control Number: In Process
International Standard Book Number (ISBN): 9798863996653

About the Book

Much has been written about the very successful football program at the University of Southern California (USC). Throughout its football history, starting in 1888, USC has given meaning to the word excellence. Every team has its ups and downs and USC is no exception. But down through the years it has forged an enviable reputation throughout the college football world for excelling.

As with any university, success at the athletic level starts with the university administration. If the leaders are not on board, then any program is doomed to failure. The leaders for USC have always been on board. They have understood that the prestige and desirability of the University of Southern California are tied to the success of its athletic programs.

Due to a variety of factors, the top three universities in the United States for the number of NCAA athletic championships, both men's and women's sports, are all located here in California: Stanford, UCLA, and USC. Southern California has more men's national champions (98) and more men's NCAA national champions (86) than any other university. It stands for athletic excellence.

The Track and Field teams from USC have always set the American standard and have won 28 National Championships as well as placing 12th among all competing countries in the number of earned gold medals in the history of the Summer Olympic Games. Consider the implications of that statement: It has won more Olympic gold medals than any other university in the world and all but eleven other nations.

Trojan football has been the hallmark of USC athletics and its success is recognized nationally. The Athletic Department of USC has provided the capabilities for its football success, but the real cause has been the coaching staff. Going back over 100 years to 1919, three dominant Trojan coaching eras stand out. Together, they have been responsible for a record 34 Rose Bowls appearances, winning a record 25 of them. The next highest win total is Ohio State with 9. They have won 11 National Championships and an astounding 39 Conference Championships. Its overall athletic teams have won 135 national championships, including NCAA championships, the most of any university in the United States. Please note that this is the number of total championships, which includes those not affiliated with the NCAA.

The first chapter of this book deals with the early years of development of the standards that led to football success. Part-time coach Dean Cromwell was the one who set the standards and who guided USC in both football and track & field. His was the introduction to the first era of coaching excellence.

It was after Cromwell that the Trojans hired, for the first time, a full-time coach who brought them fame. That first year of Elmer Henderson's coaching reign, 1919, was also the beginning of Trojan dominance in college football. Henderson still has the highest winning percentage of football coaching in Trojan history, but he was fired for the guilt of never beating California.

Henderson was replaced after his 1924 season by Coach Howard Jones. Between Henderson and Jones, from 1919 to 1940, they created a program that won 166 football games, four national championships, and seven conference championships. In seven post-season appearances, including six Rose Bowls, they never lost. It was just the beginning.

The Henderson-Jones Era was soon followed by the Cravath-Hill Era, from 1942 through 1956. It would have been longer had Jess Hill stayed on as coach. He was moved up to Athletic Director after the 1956 season. Both managed to win a combined 100 games.

For this book, Cravath-Hill is not considered a dominant era, but it was a successful and significant era, just the same. When Hill moved to Athletic Director, he developed all the other athletic teams under his control. The measure of his success is that he won 29 national championships for USC in all sports. Hill's winning percentage in football was .722, placing him among the more successful coaches at USC.

The most successful of the three dominant eras is that of John McKay and John Robinson. The record speaks for itself. Together they won 231 victories with only 75 losses. Together they won five National Championships, often coming in second, and 14 Conference Championships. Together they won nine Rose Bowls and only lost three.

The third dominant era was that of a single coach, Pete Carroll. He won two National Championships and lost a third to a last-minute Rose Bowl touchdown by Texas in overtime. He won four Rose Bowls and only lost the one to Texas. He won two Orange Bowls out of two played. At one point, he won 34 straight games. He also won five Pacific Coast Conference Championships in the years between 2001 and 2009. His was the very definition of success.

Statistics can tell a very telling story. The author can tell you what happened, but that process can be greatly shortened and better understood by just printing the factual charts and leaving judgment in the hands of the reader. That is what the author has attempted to do throughout this book.

The current coaching era belongs to new coach Lincoln Riley. It is way too early to pass judgement on his performance. His first year was certainly promising. Riley's record at Oklahoma was 55-10. His first year at USC was marred by losing his last two games. But, two of the three losses were by only one point. His first year was also encumbered by inheriting a team that had posted a 4-8 record the year before. Riley did a commendable job in restructuring his 2022 team, which he did largely by using the NCAA Transfer Portal. He has also created an outstanding group of assistant coaches, which will bode well for the immediate future. With that staff and a group of players from all over the country who had never played together, he crafted an 11-3 season. While the two consecutive losses at the end of the season did tarnish the season, it should not have tarnished what was an amazing turnaround. Both coaches and players should be happy at creating a very successful season.

The promise of this period might result in another dominant era. It could even exceed past Trojan eras. Coach John McKay famously stated that he could win continual national championships with just the high school talent available within 60 miles of the USC Campus. Riley has extended that reach to the national level, as did Pete Carroll before him.

For high school talent, Riley had previously made huge inroads into Oklahoma and Texas recruitment. Since coming to USC, he has continued to recruit both states heavily, while expanding his target areas to include Nevada and Arizona as well as California.

The Trojans have lost any exclusivity, which they had into the 1980s, in the recruitment of talent-rich Southern California. Riley is starting to re-establish that dominant recruitment of the Greater Los Angeles areas. If he re-establishes the lock that John McKay had in local area recruiting, there is no limit on what Riley might do.

During the last ten to fifteen years, Greater Los Angeles has become the best development area for high school football in the nation, especially for skilled positions such as quarterbacks, tailbacks, and wide receivers. The powerhouse parochial schools can provide an unbeatable group of athletes.

If Riley can field national-championship-caliber teams, his inroads to those great high school programs can again be successfully rebuilt, perhaps on the scale of the McKay-Robinson Era or, perhaps on an even greater scale. It promises to be an interesting ride.

About the Book Cover

TROJAN WARRIORS:

The Trojan War that pitted the Greeks against the Anatolian City of Troy, was wrapped up in myth that includes wild tales that feature stories that include the Greek Gods. That the Trojan War existed seems to have been proven by recent archaeological findings. That it was a massive, brutal, and long-lasting war (ten years), there now seems no doubt. It was of such importance that the Greeks interwove the stories of warfare with tales of the Gods is self-evident. Additionally, the sheer number of Roman writers who wrote of the Trojan War and their fascination with it, bears strong evidence that their tales eulogizing the courage of the Trojan warriors are true.

The ruins of Troy lie on the western coast of the modern state of Turkey. Perched next to the Trojan Plain, which lies between the ruins of Troy and the Aegean Sea facing Greece, the City of Troy has a history that takes it back thousands of years. More recent archaeological diggings have unearthed strong evidence of Greek influence in pottery design, architecture, and language. There are so many unearthed layers of past civilizations on the site of Troy that they have numbered them from Troy I to Troy IX.

Across the Aegean, the Greek city-states were in a constant state of war between each other. It seems that they only united against a common threat. One such threat originated with the Persian Empire that sent great armies against the Grecian city-states. The Battle of Marathon was the result of and culmination of one such war.

The irony seems to be that Troy VI, which fought the Trojan War against the Greeks, was itself a Greek city-state.

USC STATUES in HONOR of the WARRIORS of ANCIENT TROY:

The classic, helmeted figure of a Trojan Warrior is emblazoned on the front cover. It stands in tribute to the fighting spirit of both the ancient Trojans and the modern-day Trojans of the University of Southern California (USC). The statue of an ancient Trojan, historically called "Tommy" by students, that stands in the center of the USC campus is one such tribute. Another statue in honor is the centerpiece of the Heritage Hall of Champions.

Chapter Contents

continued

THIRD DOMINANT ERA:

SUPPORT INFORMATION:

Chapter One

The Early Years

1888 - 1918

The history of USC football started in 1888. It was a case of hit-or-miss in fielding a team with a coach for the period from that 1888 start until a full-time coach, Elmer "Gus" Henderson, was hired in 1919. The chart below is graphic evidence of the disorganized state of Trojan football.

Starting in 1888 for the first 15 years ending in 1902, USC had only three years that they fielded a team with a coach. The other twelve years they either had no team or played without. The records for those years played without a coach are not included below.

The overall record for the three years in which there was a coach, was 7-2-0. In only one year was any record kept of spectator attendance, and that was a lonely estimated "crowd" of 500. The game of American football, derived from rugby, had yet to excite audiences.

YEAR	COACH	RECORD	SCORING	MAX ATTENDANCE
1888	Henry Goddard & Frank Suffel	2-0	20-0	No record
1889	None			
1890	No Varsity			
1891	None			
1892	No Varsity			
1893-1896	None			
1897	Lewis Freeman	5-1-0	100-18	500
1898-1900	None			
1901	Clair Tappaan	0-1-0	0-6	No record
1902	None			

Starting in 1903, the Trojans were never without a coach. During the five-year period from 1903 through 1908, there were two coaches, with one, Coach Harvey Holmes, lasting for four years: His 19 victories and a .792 winning percentage set an early standard. Audiences started to swell and hit a maximum of 4,000 for two games in 1906.

The quality of the competition was not great. In fact, they played Los Angeles High School in each of the six years from 1903 to 1908. Other teams included Cal Tech, Occidental, Pomona, Loyola, and Stanford. In 1907, USC played Los Angeles High twice and Santa Ana High once. That year they even played Whittier Reformatory and the crew of the USS Colorado.

YEAR	COACH	RECORD	SCORING	MAX ATTENDANCE
1903	John Walker	4-2-0	58-27	600
1904	Harvey Holmes	6-1-0	199-27	1,600
1905	Harvey Holmes	6-3-1	211-45	800
1906	Harvey Holmes	2-0-2	36-0	4,000 (Occidental)
1907	Harvey Holmes	5-1-0	182-20	2,200
1908	Bill Traeger	3-1-1	63-18	2,500

Starting in 1909, the Trojans finally got a coach who did not seem interim. He was still part-time, but coached teams that played exciting, physical ball. Spectators were curious and attendance continued to rise. Dean Cromwell coached football plus track and field at USC. His record in two different football coaching periods was 21-8-5 for a very respectable winning percentage of .724. The last high school played was Long Beach Poly in 1910, which was an undefeated season. From then on, the competition started to get better. During the years 1911 through 1913, USC did not play football, but played rugby instead.

When USC stopped playing football, Coach Cromwell went on to other endeavors. His record for those first two years was 10-1-3. His replacement for the two years after they resumed playing was Ralph Glaze who went 7-7-0. The administration wanted Cromwell back.

Under Cromwell, maximum attendance at football games rose to 5,000, then 7,000 under Ralph Glaze, and finally leveling off at 10,000 for Glaze's final year and for the remainder of Cromwell's reign as USC head coach.

Attendance figures were estimates. The final four years of the period from 1909 and 1918 (shown below), which encompassed Cromwell's two stints as head coach, saw that their opponent California-Berkeley garnered the most fan interest of any of the USC opponents.

YEAR	COACH	RECORD	SCORING	MAX ATTENDANCE
1909	Dean Cromwell	3-1-2	133-13	3,500 (Occidental)
1910	Dean Cromwell	7-0-1	189-24	5,000 (Occidental)
1914	Ralph Glaze	4-3-0	116-88	7,000 (Oregon State)
1915	Ralph Glaze	3-4-0	132-119	10,000 (California)
1916	Dean Cromwell	5-3-0	129-80	10,000 (California)
1917	Dean Cromwell	4-2-1	127-47	10,000 (California)
1918	Dean Cromwell	2-2-2	61-61	10,000 (California)

In 1919, USC hired Coach Elmer Clinton "Gus" Henderson who came from the high school coaching ranks in Seattle, Washington. Those selecting their first full-time coach saw something in Henderson. They took a gamble and found a gem.

That year marked the start of the first dominant coaching era for which this book is dedicated.

Henderson was simply a great coach. It was he who started the Trojans on their uphill climb to the top of the collegiate football world.

His tenure will be more fully explained in the following chapter and is included herein to show the virtual explosion in Trojan victories, Trojan scoring, and Trojan game attendance under Henderson's leadership. Football had finally captured the imagination of Southern Californians. Winning has a way of doing that. It was a habit that would remain to this day.

Another innovation that captured football fans, was the start of intersectional competition. The Rose Bowl, described by announcer Mel Allen as the "Granddaddy of them all," was the first post-season bowl game and would remain the only bowl game until 1936. The name Rose Bowl describes the game itself as well as the stadium structure. The Rose Bowl Stadium was completed in 1922 in time for the first Rose Bowl game, won by USC, on New Year's Day, 2023.

It was a rather audacious plan envisioned by the City of Pasadena. The original Rose Bowl structure was built to contain over 100,000 customers. Later seating improvements reduced the number of customers allowed inside.

Not to be outdone, the City of Los Angeles built a football stadium that was completed the following year, in 1923. The Los Angeles Memorial Coliseum, which was built to contain over 100,000 fans, became USC's football home and would continue as such for the next 100 years. This year, 2023, marks the 100th anniversary of the stadium and USC's period of usage.

YEAR	COACH	RECORD	SCORING	MAX ATTENDANCE
1919	Gus Henderson	4-1-0	87-21	9,000 (Cal)
1920	Gus Henderson	6-0-0	170-21	20,000 (Oregon)
1921	Gus Henderson	10-1-0	362-52	25,000 (Cal)
1922	Gus Henderson	10-1-0	236-31	35,000 (Cal
January 1 — 1st Rose Bowl Game Played: USC 14, Penn State 3				**43,000**
1923	Gus Henderson	6-2-0	173-62	72,000 (Cal)
1924	Gus Henderson	9-2-0	269-44	60,000 (Cal)
December 25, the Christmas Festival: USC 20, Missouri 7				**47,000**

Overall Henderson Record: 45-7-0 (an outstanding .862)

COACH DEAN CROMWELL:

Cromwell was born Dean Bartlett Cromwell in Turner, Oregon. He attended Occidental Prep School and graduated from Occidental College in Eagle Rock, California. While at Occidental, "he was a multi-sports standout athlete, playing football, baseball, cycling, and track and field."

"In 1901, the Helms Athletic Foundation named him the most outstanding athlete in Southern California." He later was inducted into the Helms Athletic Hall of Fame and the Occidental College Athletic Hall of Fame, both along with the author's father.

The author's father later attended USC to earn a certificate for school administration and for

Coach Dean Cromwell, an austere man, set standards of excellence.

two years attended the USC School of Law. He held Dean Cromwell in high regard and apparently knew him well, based on Cromwell's attempt to recruit him to USC. Because of the times he favorably mentioned Cromwell, it was all-the-more disturbing to read of Cromwell's actions and words regarding Jewish and black athletes.

While Cromwell did coach USC football for five years, as described earlier in this chapter, he was better known as the USC Track & Field Coach. With-the-exception of 1914 and 1915, he coached USC Track & Field from 1909 to 1948, a period of 38 years.

During that period, he won NCAA National Titles in Track & Field in 1926, 1930, 1931, 1935, 1936, 1937, 1938, 1939, 1940, 1941, 1942, and 1943. Nicknamed the "Maker of Champions" he also coached athletes to 34 individual NCAA titles.

Cromwell was named assistant head coach for the United States Olympic Track team in 1928 at Amsterdam, in 1932 in Los Angeles, and in Berlin in 1936. He was instrumental in American victories in each Olympics he coached, with the exception of Berlin in 1936. In the 1948 Olympic Games held in London, he was named head coach for the American track team, which also won the Olympic Games that year.

Cromwell was known for developing star athletes. "His many outstanding pupils included Fred Kelly, 1912 gold medalist in the 110m hurdles; Charley Paddock, 1920 gold medalist in the 100m and 4X100 relay; Bud Houser, 1924 gold medalist in the shot put and discus and gold medalist in the discus in 1928; Jess Mortensen, 1929 NCAA javelin champion, plus held the world record, 1931, in the decathlon; Frank Wykoff, gold medalist in the 4X100 relay in the 1928, 32 and 36 Olympics; Ken Carpenter, gold medalist in the 1936 Olympics in the discus; Earle Meadows, 1936 gold medalist in the pole vault; Louis Zamperini, collegiate record-holder in the mile from 1938 to 1953; Wilbur Thompson, 1948 gold medalist in the shot put; Cliff Bourland, 1948 gold medalist in the 4X100 relay; Bill Sefton, two-time world record holder in the pole vault; and (Pel) Mel Patton, world record holder in the 100m dash and the 1948 gold medalist in the 200m and the 4X100 relay. "Athletes coached by Cromwell at USC eventually set individual world records in 14 events and relay world records in three others. They also won 12 Olympic gold medals during his time at USC."

Cromwell tarnished his reputation by voicing comments that were racist regarding black athletes and in 1936 removing Jewish athletes from relay teams, in accordance with the wishes of Adolph Hitler, during the 1936 Berlin Olympics.

In January 2023, the USC Track and Field Stadium, then named Cromwell Field, was renamed for Allyson Felix, who is an 11-time Olympic medalist and graduate of USC.

The number of gold medals won in all the modern Summer Olympic Games by America is 1022, followed by the Soviet Union at 589. The U.S. also leads in silver medals with 795 followed by the Soviet Union (Russia) at 486, It won 796 bronze medals, with Russia also coming in second with 481.

Following is a listing of the nations that have won the Summer Olympics:

YEAR	CITY	WINNER
1896	Athens	United States
1900	Paris	France
1904	**St. Louis**	United States
1908	London	Great Britain
1912	Stockholm	United States
1916	Cancelled due to World War I	—
1920	Antwerp	United States
1924	Paris	United States
1928	Amsterdam	United States
1932	**Los Angeles**	United States
1936	Berlin	Germany
1940 & 1944	Cancelled due to World War II	—
1948	London	United States
1952	Helsinki	United States
1956	Melbourne	Soviet Union
1960	Rome	Soviet Union
1964	Tokyo	United States
1968	Mexico City	United States
1972	Munich	Soviet Union
1976	Montreal	Soviet Union
1980	Moscow	Soviet Union

YEAR	CITY	WINNER
1984	**Los Angeles**	**United States**
1988	Seoul	Soviet Union
1992	Barcelona	Unified Team (Russia)
1996	**Atlanta**	**United States**
2000	Sydney	**United States**
2004	Athens	**United States**
2008	Beijing	China
2012	London	**United States**
2016	Rio de Janeiro	**United States**
2020	Tokyo	**United States**
2024	Paris	(pending)
2028	**Los Angeles**	(pending)
2032	Brisbane	(pending)

USC Track and Field teams have won 28 NCAA titles. The university has sent 511 athletes to Olympic Summer Games in 773 different events. Trojan athletes have won 326 Olympic medals, "153 of them gold, including at least one gold in every Olympics since 1912." They have also won 96 silver and 77 bronze.

The Olympic record for USC is, by far, more than any other university in the world. If USC were a county competing in the Summer Olympics, it would place as follows against all Olympic countries in the world for the total history of the modern games since the start of record keeping in 1904.

RANK	COUNTRY	GOLD	SILVER	BRONZE	TOTAL
1	**United States**	**1,022**	**795**	**706**	**2,523**
2	Russia / Soviet Union	589	486	481	1,556
3	Germany	428	444	474	1,346
4	Great Britain	263	295	293	851
5	France	212	241	263	716
6	Italy	206	178	193	577
7	China	224	167	155	546
8	Australia	147	163	187	497
9	Sweden	145	170	179	494
10	Hungary	175	147	169	491

RANK	COUNTRY	GOLD	SILVER	BRONZE	TOTAL
11	Japan	142	136	161	439
12	**USC**	**153**	**96**	**77**	**326**
Numbers included with United States numbers (above)					
13	Romania	89	95	122	306
14	Finland	101	85	111	303
15	Canada	64	102	136	302
16	Netherlands	85	92	108	285
17	Poland	68	84	132	284
18	South Korea	90	87	90	267
19	Cuba	78	68	80	226
20	Bulgaria	51	87	80	218

The author cannot verify the accuracy of the medal counts listed above and on the previous page. Counts vary from various sources for both the number of American Olympic medals and those earned by Trojan athletes. The numbers listed are from historical records compiled by USC. To put the numbers in a different perspective, 11.4% of all American Summer Olympic medals were won by athletes who attended USC.

The Olympics are individual competitions and accounting on a national basis is unofficial. However, it is of interest that USC has been so outstanding in its Olympic participation. Coach Dean Cromwell, in addition to his five years as Trojan football coach, did an admirable job in representing USC as a team and individual coach for Track and Field. His Trojan coaching participation lasted from 1909 to 1948, a period during which the University of Southern California became known worldwide for athletic excellence.

It is no coincidence that the home stadium for USC football is the same stadium that hosted two Summer Olympic Games, in 1932 and 1984, and will again host the games in 2028. The lighting of the Coliseum Olympic torch in the 4th quarter of every USC home game in football is symbolic of much more than a simple torch. It stands for a standard of excellence in all athletics for which Trojans from all eras can be justly proud.

Chapter Two
Setting The Standard
1919 - 1940

THE FIRST DOMINANT USC FOOTBALL COACHING ERA:

The first championship coaching era at USC started with Coach Elmer "Gloomy Gus" Henderson. He was a very upbeat guy and did not deserve to be called gloomy. Paul Lowry, Sports Editor of the *Los Angeles Times* named Gus "Gloomy" due to his penchant to downgrade the Trojan chances before any football game.

Henderson started it all in 1919. For five years, from 1919 to 1924, Henderson won games at a .865 clip, getting 45 wins with only 7 losses. The problem for Coach Henderson was not how many he won, but how many he lost to California. Cal won several national championships from 1920 through 1923, a period when they did not lose a game, going 36-0-2 (ties). The administrators at USC wanted victories and losing for five straight years to Cal was too much. It did nothing to sway the administrators that Coach Gus went 47-2 in all the rest of his games; he was fired. His .865 percentage turned out to be the highest winning record in USC history, up to the present day.

When Gus coached, there was only the Rose Bowl and no other bowl games. When the Rose Bowl was created, it was the first actual bowl game ever played in the world, and stayed that way until 1935. It did, however, borrow its name from the Yale Bowl, which was not national. Following is the history of bowl creation for the first 10 bowls in the United States:

EVENT	ESTABLISHED	PLAYED IN
Rose Bowl	Established in 1902 and played annually since 1916	Pasadena, California
Orange Bowl	Established in 1935	Miami Gardens, Florida
Sugar Bowl	Established in 1935	New Orleans, Louisiana
Sun Bowl	Established in 1935	El Paso, Texas
Cotton Bowl	Established in 1937	Arlington, Texas
Gator Bowl	Established in 1946	Jacksonville, Florida
Citrus Bowl	Established in 1947	Orlando, Florida
Liberty Bowl	Established in 1959	Memphis, Tennessee
Peach Bowl	Established in 1968	Atlanta, Georgia
Fiesta Bowl	Established in 1971	Glendale, Arizona

Coach Henderson did not win any Pacific Coast Conference titles, which contributed to his demise as a West Coast coach. He did win five conference championships in three different conferences in the ten years he coached after leaving USC.

After Henderson, USC hired Coach Howard Jones. Together, they set the standard for others to follow. Jones coached from 1925 to 1940 and won four national championships and seven conference championships. His National Championships came in 1928, 1931, 1932 and 1939. His Pacific Coast Conference Championships came in 1927, 1928, 1929, 1931, 1932, 1938, and 1939.

Together, their coaching era amassed a record of 166 wins, 43 losses, and 13 ties over 21 years. Howard Jones coached in five Rose Bowls, winning all five against Pittsburg twice, Duke, Tulane, and Tennessee. However, the first Rose Bowl ever played in the actual Rose Bowl Stadium was won by Coach Henderson. He beat Penn State 14-3. The following year the Christmas Festival took the temporary place of the Rose Bowl and was played on Christmas Day 1924 in the new Los

---

National Championships (4): 1928, 1931, 1932, 1939
Pacific Coast Conference Championships (7): 1927, 1928, 1929, 1931, 1932, 1938, 1939.
Rose Bowl Victories (6): 1922, 1930, 1932, 1933, 1939, 1940
Rose Bowl Losses: 0
Heisman Trophy Winners: 0 *(Heisman Trophy winners were first selected in 1935)*
Combined Record: 166 victories, 43 defeats, 13 ties (.772)

Gus Henderson: 45-7 (.865)

1919: 4-1-1	1922: 10-1-0
1920: 6-0-0	1923: 6-2-0
1921: 10-1-0	1924: 9-2-0

Undefeated seasons: 1920
Ten-win or more seasons: 1921, 1922

Howard Jones: 121-36-13 (.750)

1925: 11-2	1933: 10-1-1
1926: 8-2	1934: 4-6-1
1927: 8-1-1	1935: 5-7
1928: 9-0-1	1936: 4-2-3
1929: 10-2	1937: 4-4-2
1930: 8-2	1938: 9-2
1931: 10-1	**1939: 8-0-2**
1932: 10-0	1940: 3-4-2

(National Championship years in blue)
Undefeated seasons: 1928, 1932, 1939
Ten-win or more seasons: 1925, 1929, 1931, 1932, 1933

Angeles Memorial Coliseum. Henderson won that game, played in the SC home stadium, by beating Missouri 20-7.

Construction of the Rose Bowl stadium started on February 27, 1922, and was being built at the same time as the Los Angeles Memorial Coliseum. Construction of the Rose Bowl was completed in October 1922. The original design of the Rose Bowl was a horseshoe. Later, the open end was closed off to make a complete bowl in appearance.

Construction on the Coliseum started on December 21, 1921, was finished on May 1, 1923, and USC has played all its home games in that stadium since 1923.

Coach Howard Jones' tenure at SC can be divided into two separate periods. His first nine years were extraordinary. In those nine years (1925-1933), he went 84-11-3 for a .8842 winning percentage, which is truly extraordinary. In his final seven years, he dropped off significantly to 37-25-10 for a .5968 winning percentage. Still, he won a national championship during that later period and he must be judged by his overall achievement and that was certainly excellent.

The combined era amassed a bowl record of 7-0. The Trojans won seven Conference Championships, and four National Championships. Henderson and Jones set the standard and USC became the premier football university in the Western United States.

The first year that USC played under Howard Jones' coaching was a wild one. It was highlighted by seven shutouts against Whittier College, Cal Tech, Pomona, Arizona, Iowa, Oregon State, and St. Mary's. In Jones' first four games there were only two points scored against the Trojans, while SC scored 214 points. It was wild. Then they ran up against Stanford and in front of an estimated crowd of 70,000, USC lost 9-13. The next five games were again an explosion as the Trojans scored 181 points against only 23. Then they lost their second game of the season against Washington State 12-17. They finished out with two shutouts.

Howard Jones' team scored an incredible 456 points with only 55 scored against. His record was 11 wins and only 2 losses. It was an amazing performance and the crowds continued to grow in numbers.

The second year under Jones really solidified his legacy. He again lost only two games, but both by identical scores of 12-13 against Stanford and Notre Dame. They shut out four teams and scored 317 points against only 52 against. The Trojans averaged 31.7 points per game, continuing the scoring onslaught of the first year when they averaged 35.1 points per game.

The Los Angeles Memorial Coliseum proved a blessing in many ways. Of the ten games played that year, eight were in the Coliseum. The loss to Stanford in the Coliseum was in front of 78,500 fans. The loss to Notre Dame was also in the Coliseum in front of 74,378 fans. The only games played outside of the Coliseum were to Oregon Agricultural College at Multnomah Stadium in Portland and to Cal at California Memorial Stadium in Berkeley. Oregon Agricultural later became Oregon State.

It was the Notre Dame game that really galvanized the public. It was the culmination of the work first started by Gus Henderson to schedule Knute Rockne's team. The game was played on December 4th, which must have played a part in Notre Dame agreeing to play in much warmer Southern California. The revenue derived from such a game played in front of so many paying customers also had to have an effect. The reported crowd that lined the streets of Los Angeles to laud the strong showing of USC against a national power such as Notre Dame, was an estimated 300,000, which was the total population of Los Angeles at that time.

Some colleges made the decision to grow and others to stay small. That was the case for little Occidental College. The first game that Jones coached against Oxy was in 1926 and it was the last time that Oxy scored against USC. The scores kept mounting: 1926 28-6; 1927 33-0; 1928 19-0; 1929 64-0. Nobody wants to get beaten 64-0.

For the next three years, USC did not schedule Occidental. In two of those three years, they won the National Championship. It is curious why they again scheduled Oxy, but they did in 1933 and 1934. The results were the same: 39-0 and 20-0. That was mercifully the last.

UCLA managed to schedule USC for two years: 1929 and 1930. It was a rough start for the Bruins. They lost 76-0 and 52-0. UCLA returned to the schedule in 1936 with a vastly improved team, tying USC 7-7. The results of the following games were: 1937 19-13, 1938 42-7, 1939 0-0, 1940 28-12, 1941 7-7 under Coach Sam Berry, and their first loss to UCLA was 7-14 in 1942, the first year under new Coach Jeff Cravath.

During Howard Jones' coaching tenure, he never lost to UCLA. The other rivalries of consequence were the Northern California powers: Stanford and Cal Berkeley plus Notre Dame. Jones' record against Stanford was 8-7-1 with scores as follows: 9-13, 12-13, 13-13, 10-0, 7-0, 41-12, 19-0, 13-0, 7-13, 0-16, 0-3, 14-7, 6-7, 13-2, 33-0, 7-21.

His record against Cal Berkeley started in 1926 with an avenging score of 27-0 to compensate for the five losses under Henderson. California did not score on USC until 1929, when they won 15-7. Next year was another avenging one as they crushed Cal 74-0. Cal again did not score until 1932, when they lost 27-7. Overall Jones' record against Cal was 8-6-1, with five shutouts.

Against mighty Notre Dame, Jones' scoring record was: 1926 12-13, 1927 6-7, 1928 27-14, and 1929 12-13. In other words, during the first four games, Jones went 1-3 with each loss by just one point. In 1930 0-27, 1931 16-14, 1932 13-0, 1933 19-0, and 1934 0-14. In 1935, the Trojans played a frigid game in South Bend 13-20, 1936 13-13, 1937 6-13, 1938 13-0, 1939 another very cold game in South Bend 20-12, 1940 6-10. Overall, 6-8-1 with three shutouts.

An interesting note about the second Notre Dame game played in 1927. A tackle named Marion Morrison was moved up to varsity his sophomore year (1927) and played for USC in November against Notre Dame. Unfortunately, in December, Morrison was surfing at Newport Beach and fell, breaking his collarbone. Morrison lost his football scholarship to USC due to his injury. He later took the toughness he learned playing on the Trojan offensive line to the movie sets of Fox and started acting under the stage name of John Wayne.

COACH ELMER CLINTON "GUS" HENDERSON:

Coach Elmer Clinton "Gus" Henderson is the most underrated coach in the long and legendary history of USC Trojan football. Born in Oberlin, Ohio, he graduated from Oberlin College destined to be a coach. Among other notable alumni from Oberlin was football coach John William Heisman, for whom the Heisman Trophy is named.

Coach Elmer Clinton "Gus" Henderson (1919-1924); wikipedia.com

During Henderson's time at USC, the Sports Editor of the *Los Angeles Times* named Gus Henderson, "Gloomy Gus," due to his penchant for always telling the media that his teams had little chances in games he coached. It was one of several psychological habits he developed to gain advantage for his teams.

Henderson's first coaching opportunity out of college came in Seattle, Washington at Broadway High School. Broadway High started as Seattle High School, which opened in 1902. It was the only high school in Seattle for five years, until a second school, Lincoln, was opened in 1907, at which time the name was changed from Seattle to Broadway High.

His high school coaching record is lost to history. However, in 1912, during his tenure at Broadway, they were one of the original teams assigned to the top prep football league in Washington State, the Metro League. While his record at Broadway was lost, it was significant enough that Henderson jumped directly from high school to head coach at the rising football power in Los Angeles, the University of Southern California.

HENDERSON'S IMPACT on BLACK HISTORY at USC:

What is of note is that Metro League rival Franklin High had a standout Black player that played against the Broadway Tigers team coached by Elmer Henderson. His name was Brice Taylor, and in 1925, he went on to become the first All-American at USC. Taylor was born without a left hand and obviously rose above his disability. His ancestry included African slaves and he was a direct descendent of the famous Shawnee Indian Chief Tecumseh. From a high school rival to a member of Henderson-coached teams at Southern Cal, Taylor was the start of a rich tradition of Black player

Brice Taylor, guard & 1ˢᵗ Trojan All-American (1925).
He was born without a left hand, as shown above. e-bay photo.

excellence at USC.

While the listing of Heisman winners and runners-up is only a part of the Trojan Black players who excelled, the listing is impressive: Mike Garrett, O.J. Simpson, Charlie White, Marcus Allen, Rodney Peete, Anthony Davis, Ricky Bell, Reggie Bush, and the 2022 Heisman winner, Caleb Williams. All quarterbacks and tailbacks. From Garrett to Williams, the greatest listing of Black Heisman footballers in NCAA history and Taylor started it all in 1925.

Howard Jones, the coach who followed Henderson at USC, is often given credit for helping make Taylor an All-American during Jones' first year at USC. Credit is also due Henderson for coaching him during his undergraduate years up until his senior year in 1925. In fact, it is assuredly Henderson who brought Taylor to USC after watching freshman Brice Taylor's Franklin team play his own Broadway High School team. In the days that Taylor played, footballers were two-way and he stood out as a defensive as well as offensive guard.

Henderson set the tone for integration in football at USC. Early on, he ensured that the Trojans disregarded the absurdity of segregated football, then predominant in much of the United States.

From Taylor's freshman season in 1922, which was three years into Henderson's tenure at USC, until the USC-Alabama football game on September 12, 1970, the Trojans had stood out as a colorblind team as well as a colorblind school.

It was the game in September 1970, that really put the Trojans on the integration map. Starting in 1965, Mike Garrett, a Trojan Black tailback, won the Heisman. Then in 1967, Simpson, another Black tailback, was runner-up. In 1968, Simpson won the trophy outright. In 1969, another Black tailback, Sam Cunningham, joined the Trojans. He finished his USC football career on the undefeated 1972 unanimous national champions, who some consider the finest team in the history of NCAA football. Cunningham went on to play nine years for the New England Patriots of the NFL. As of 2023, he holds the all-time rushing record for the Patriots of 5,453 yards and 43 touchdowns.

While his collegiate and professional football career has many noteworthy accomplishments, it was the September 1970 game that probably stands as his greatest deed. It was certainly one of the Trojans' greatest. Perhaps the best description of what happened and its importance was stated in the excellent book by Don Yaeger titled Turning the Tide, How One Game Changed the South. A direct quote from that book follows:

"In 1970, legendary University of Alabama coach Bear Bryant met his good friend and USC coach John McKay in the Los Angeles Airport. Their handshake set the stage for an event that would resonate in history: the first fully integrated football game to be played in Alabama. The teams that met on Crimson soil in September represented two distinct faces of college football: Bear Bryant's Tide was the all-white national powerhouse in the SEC, and the USC Trojans, (were) a diverse team featuring a nearly all-Black starting backfield, reflected the social changes that were sweeping the nation. Though he and the (Crimson) Tide were revered in the South, Bryant knew that he was signing on for a certain loss at the hands of Southern Cal, a fearfully dominant force that had featured in the past Black players like Heisman winners O.J. Simpson and Mike Garrett. Alabama's resounding 42-21 loss broke down the last stronghold of segregation in college football."

Sam Cunningham was one of 18 Black players on the Trojans that year. He ran for 250 yards and scored four touchdowns in a game-shattering performance. A year later, Alabama won the rematch 17-10. In that game, Alabama featured four standout Black stars with other Black players as backup. It showed the rest of the Southeast Conference (SEC) that they needed to integrate to be able to field similarly outstanding teams. McKay, Cunningham, and the Trojans, on that September Saturday, went a long way toward the eventual integration of the entire South.

The continuation of Black significance at USC, after that Alabama game, was embodied in stars Anthony Davis, Ricky Bell, Charles White, Marcus Allen, Rodney Peete, Reggie Bush, Caleb Williams, and a host of other outstanding Black athletes. Heisman-winning white quarterbacks Carson Palmer and Matt Leinart have helped balance out the Trojan riches.

FROM OBERLIN COLLEGE (OC) to SC:

Those early years in college football were formative in creating things, such as school colors, banners, logos, mascots, etc. Note the similar interlocking logo styles and school colors of Oberlin and SC. Henderson may have been more influential at USC than we are aware.

Oberlin College has official colors described as "cardinal red and gold." Henderson's first college experience after Oberlin was at USC. Did Henderson possibly influence the official color selection at USC, which are also cardinal and gold?

According to www.about.usc.edu, "In 1895, USC adopted cardinal and gold as its official colors." So, the identical colors at Oberlin are only a coincidence. But what about logos, decals, and banners? Did Henderson's knowledge of Oberlin possibly influence development at USC?

CREATOR of the SPREAD FORMATION:

According to Wikipedia, former *Los Angeles Times* Sports Editor Paul Zimmerman noted, "Until someone proves otherwise, it must be assumed that Henderson invented the spread formation, variations of which have become an important form of attack in modern day football." Although he may be unaware, the current USC football coach, Lincoln Riley, employs a variation of Henderson's spread offense.

FIRST FULL-TIME COACH:

Henderson was the first USC full-time football coach starting in 1919 and led USC to an undefeated record in 1920. He also coached the first Trojan Rose Bowl and the first Rose Bowl game ever played, a 14-3 victory over "heavily favored" Penn State. "Gordon Campbell, a halfback on USCs 1923 Rose Bowl team, said of Henderson, "He put the Trojans on the map. He was a great coach when we needed one most because we were just growing up." Henderson was also the instigator of the USC-Notre Dame intersectional game when he wrote a letter to Norte Dame Coach Knute Rockne asking for a game between the Trojans and the Fighting Irish. The first game, played in 1926, resulted in a one-point defeat of USC by a score of 13-12. Rockne later said that it was the best football game he had ever witnessed. That recognition by the then-greatest American football coach, was instrumental in the Trojans becoming a nationally-known power.

Henderson led the Trojans in joining the Pacific Coast Conference in 1922 and in 1923 moved from the on-campus Bovard Field to play in the Los Angeles Memorial Coliseum. He also coached the USC baseball team in 1920 and 1921, going 18-7-1, and coached the USC basketball team in 1919, 1920, and 1921, going 18-6 in that sport. Overall, his college football coaching career, which included USC, Tulsa, and Occidental, was 126-42-7. His USC football record was 45-7.

In 1925, his first year after being fired by USC, Gus Henderson coached the University of Tulsa to the Oklahoma Intercollegiate Conference Championship. Then the Tulsa Golden Hurricane changed conferences to the Big Four, and Henderson won championships in that conference in 1929, 1930, and 1932. Tulsa again changed conferences and Coach Henderson won another championship in the Missouri Valley Conference in 1935, his last year with Tulsa. His eleven-year record at Tulsa was 70-25-5 (.737). The Tulsa University Hall of Fame coach won more games for Tulsa than any other football coach, which included ten straight winning seasons. The number of his victories at Tulsa is a record that still stands.

Like famed USC coach John McKay, Henderson decided to move on to coach professional football and returned to Los Angeles to coach the Los Angeles Bulldogs of the American Football League. The Bulldogs, under his leadership in 1937, went undefeated with an 8-0 record and capturing another conference title for Coach Henderson. In 1938, the AFL folded.

In 1939, Henderson's coaching excellence was rewarded by becoming coach of the Detroit Lions of the NFL. The Lions went 6-5 his first year under the ownership of Dick Richards, who also owned the Los Angeles radio station KMPC. After the end of that 1939 season, Richards sold the Lions and the new owner had his own plans. In spite-of Henderson's three-year contract, he released Henderson.

Richards must have been impressed by Gus. He and others coaxed Henderson back to Los Angeles to coach at the small, liberal arts Occidental College, located in Eagle Rock, 15 miles from the USC campus. Despite going 7-4 in SCC conference play, the talent was just not there during his three-year coaching stint at Oxy.

After his 1942 season, when World War II was transforming the Los Angeles region, Gus Henderson decided to "hang it up" and left the coaching ranks for good.

His outstanding legacy is intact. His achievements at USC went largely unnoticed by those that followed. Those achievements include:

(1) He was USCs first full-time football coach.

(2) While USC Coach John McKay is well known for being the instigator of the I formation, USC Coach Elmer "Gus" Henderson is largely unknown for being the instigator of the spread formation.

(3) He has the winningest football coaching record in USC history (.865).

(4) Other than those games played against the then-perennial National Champion Cal Bears, Henderson's record against other opponents was 45-2 for an unheard-of winning percentage of .957.

(5) He coached the first USC winner of the Rose Bowl, beating "heavily favored" Penn State 14-3. It was also the first Rose Bowl game ever played in Rose Bowl Stadium. That year, USC went 10-1 and outscored their opponents by a combined total of 236 to 31.

(6) With his 1924 letter to Notre Dame Coach Knute Rockne, he instigated the USC-Notre Dame

football rivalry, which started with a game in 1926 between USC Coach Howard Jones and Notre Dame Coach Rockne.

(7) In 1923, Coach Henderson led the Trojans to victory over Pomona College in the first varsity football game ever played in the Los Angeles Memorial Coliseum.

(8) Former High School Coach Henderson was responsible for the recruitment of the first USC All-American and first Black All-American. Henderson graduated from Oberlin College, which in 1835 was the first college in America to "adopt a policy to admit Black students."

(9) Possible instigator of multiple Trojan traditions as follows:

In 1922, during Henderson's tenure, the official fight song "Fight On" was created. Did he influence the iconic fight song? Also in 1922, Henderson led the Trojans to join the Pacific Coast Conference, which has later-become the PAC-12 Conference.

In 1923, also during Henderson's tenure, the USC alma mater, "All Hail" was composed by a member of the Trojan Marching Band. In 1924, the last year of Henderson's time, the university held its first formal observance of homecoming.

Trojan Coach Gus Henderson

Gus Henderson was a quiet, taciturn man, not given to boasting. Others were often credited for his innovations and actions, which is epitomized by Coach Howard Jones usually given credit for starting the traditional Notre Dame football rivalry, when it was Henderson who instigated it before he left for Tulsa. Gus would not have claimed credit for the many innovations that occurred at USC during the time he was coaching.

His excellence in the games that the Trojans played has marked him as the coach who began the development of what later became the powerhouse of West Coast football. Even though he was fired and replaced by Howard Jones, both coaches have excellent records, and both, together, created the first of the eras of excellence that have been a hallmark of USC football. It is worth mentioning again: against teams other than California, USC, under Henderson's coaching, won 45 games and lost only two, a phenomenal record.

The Henderson record in college football for three different colleges was 126-42-7, which was a total of 175 games and a winning percentage of .750. That was comparable to that of Howard Jones at USC, which was 121-36-13 for a total of 173 games with a winning percentage of .756. The other college games coached by Gus were at the University of Tulsa and Occidental College, located in the Eagle Rock section of Los Angeles.

Henderson's record for coaching 11 seasons for the University of Tulsa was 70-25-5 for a winning percentage of .737. He was not so successful during his three years at Occidental, with an overall record of 11-10-2 for a winning percentage of .524. It was the termination of a brilliant coaching career.

Occidental is not known for its football. It is a small, liberal-arts campus with only a few thousand students. However, it has a rich tradition of athletic excellence in track and field. For years, it was the second strongest track and field university in the West and came extremely close to beating the Trojan National Championship Track and Field teams on more than one occasion.

Prior to Howard Jones' time at USC, he served as coach for the following universities: Syracuse (1 year: 1908) 6-3-1; Yale (2 years: 1909 & 1913) 15-2-3; Iowa (8 years: 1916-1923) 42-17-1; Duke (1 year: 1924) 4-5-0, for an overall 67-27-5, a winning percentage of .713.

As mentioned, Henderson not only excelled in football, but he also coached a record of 18-6 in college basketball and 18-7-1 in college baseball while at USC. He went on to coach the Los Angeles Bulldogs in the professional AFL, where he had no defeats and eight victories. He coached the Detroit Lions to a 6-5 record in his only year with them. He won the only Rose Bowl he coached, including the first ever played in the new (1923) Rose Bowl Stadium. Finally, he won six conference championships: OIC, 1925; Big Four, 1929, 1930 & 1932; MVC, 1935; and the SCC (Southern California Conference) with Occidental in 1942.

HENDERSON'S OUTSTANDING RECORD AT USC		
1919	4-1	First year as first USC full-time football coach.
1920	6-0	
1921	10-1	
1922	10-1	Won the Rose Bowl in the first year it was played in its brand-new Pasadena stadium.
1923	6-2	
1924	9-2	Won the Christmas Festival.
Overall:	45-7	Rose Bowl Record: 1-0

Howard Jones — First USC coach to win National Championships. newsday.com

COACH HOWARD JONES:

After Henderson, USC hired Coach Howard Jones. Together, they set the standard for others to follow. Jones coached from 1925 to 1940 and won four national championships and seven conference championships. His National Championships came in 1928, 1931, 1932 and 1939. His Pacific Coast Conference Championships came in 1927, 1928, 1929, 1931, 1932, 1938, and 1939.

Together, their coaching era amassed a record of 166 wins, 43 losses and 13 ties over 21 years. Howard Jones coached in five Rose Bowls, winning all five against Pittsburg twice, Duke, Tulane, and Tennessee. Prior to 1935, there were no other bowl games other than the Rose Bowl.

The era amassed a bowl record, exclusively Rose Bowl, of 7-0, won seven Conference Championships and four National Championships. Henderson and Jones set the standard and became the premier football university in Southern California, if not the entire West.

Jones had an extraordinary career before coming to USC.

He was another Ohio-born coach, coming from Excello, Ohio. His college of choice was Yale, and he lost no time in making a name for himself.

He was an exceptional athlete. From 1905 to 1907, he played football for the Yale Bulldogs, and they never lost a game, going 28-0-2 in the process. Yale won the national championship in all three years that Jones played.

On the advice of the famous Walter Camp, Jones became head coach at Syracuse University at the unheard-of young age of 23. As soon as he graduated from college, he became head coach at a major university. He led the Orangemen to a 6-3-1 record that first year and must have convinced his alma mater, as Yale hired him back as head coach the following year. Howard's brother, Tad, then became head coach at Syracuse.

National Championships (4): 1928, 1931, 1932, 1939
Pacific Coast Conference Championships (7): 1927, 1928, 1929, 1931, 1932, 1938, 1939.
Rose Bowl Victories (7): 1923, 1924, 1930, 1932, 1933, 1939, 1940
Rose Bowl Losses: 0
Heisman Trophy Winners: 0 *(Heisman Trophy winners were first selected in 1935)*
Record: 166 victories, 43 defeats, 13 ties (.772)

Gus Henderson: 45-7 (.865)
Howard Jones: 121-36-13 (.750)

1925: 11-2	1933: 10-1-1
1926: 8-2	1934: 4-6-1
1927: 8-1-1	1935: 5-7
1928: 9-0-1	1936: 4-2-3
1929: 10-2	1937: 4-4-2
1930: 8-2	1938: 9-2
1931: 10-1	1939: 8-0-2
1932: 10-0	1940: 3-4-2
(eight-win seasons in red)	

Yale went 10-0 that first year and they claimed another national championship, Coach Jones' 4th in five years. When he led his team to a 15-0 victory over Syracuse in that year, it was the "first time that two brothers had ever faced off against each other as opposing head coaches."

Now 25, Jones' next stop was as head coach of Ohio State University, which he led to a one-loss season with a 6-1-3 record. He must have had wanderlust, because after that one year as Ohio State Head Coach, he left coaching for private business, only returning to Yale for one year as coach of a 5-2-3 squad in 1913.

In 1916, after deciding that the business world could not match the excitement of the football world, he left his budding business career. His next stop was as head coach of the University of Iowa.

It was a terrible start for someone used to winning national championships. His Iowa team lost to Minnesota 67-0 in his first year and to Nebraska 47-0 in 1917. He vowed never to lose by those margins again, and he never did. In 1918 and 1919, Iowa fell just short of the Big Ten title, losing each year by one game. By 1920, Iowa had the top two scorers in the Big Ten and posted a 5-2 record.

Jones was recruiting Iowans, which had never been done to any extent before at Iowa. He recruited them and coached them as never before. By 1921, Iowa went undefeated and won the Big Ten title. During the season, Iowa defeated Notre Dame and ended Notre Dame Coach Knute Rockne's 20-game win streak. It would be Rockne's longest win streak of his illustrious career.

The relationship established between Rockne and Jones would flourish with the help of Henderson's 1924 letter requesting a game between USC and Notre Dame. Five years after that 10-7

Jones' victory over Notre Dame, Rockne avenged it with a 13-12 victory over the Jones' coached Trojans in 1926.

In 1922, Iowa again went undefeated and again won the Big Ten. A notable win in 1922 was against his alma mater, Yale, then coached by his brother Tad. The Iowa winning streak reached 20 games in 1923, which covered a period of almost three years.

His time in Iowa ended after that 1923 season. Jones' wife did not like Iowa City and Jones demanded changes to his contract with the Iowa Athletics Board, which were refused. It led to his resignation as both Head Football Coach and Athletic Director.

After a brief stint at Duke University, he became head coach at USC.

Howard Jones was an aloof coach who did not relate to his players. He also disliked recruiting, allowing his assistants to do the chores. Because he had what was described as a stone face, he intimidated those who met him. He was also a terrible speaker. Despite those deficiencies, he was a dynamic coach. He "lived and breathed football." He also favored hard-nosed football and his teams were noted for their "physicality."

He was also a very fair man. Once, before a game with Stanford, he visited the Stanford locker room and found that the Stanford running back had an injured knee. He returned to the Trojan locker room and instructed his team to avoid hitting him on that injured knee. It was a reminder to all that football is still just a game and victory should be gained with honor and respect for opponents. Jones was an ethical man. One may wonder if today's college coaches would use that knowledge to gain a victory or would they try to protect opposing players from greater injury by doing the same as Jones?

Notable victories during his time included: a Rose Bowl victory against Duke that relied on a Trojan touchdown with only a minute left in the game. It was the first points scored against Duke during their entire season. "In the 1940 Rose Bowl, the Trojans defeated the Tennessee Volunteers 14-0, ending a 23-game win streak and scoring the first points scored against the Volunteers all season." In 1951, Jones was one of the original inductees (posthumously) into the College Football Hall of Fame.

HOWARD JONES' HEAD COACHING RECORD:

SCHOOL	YEAR	RECORD
Syracuse	1908	6-3-1
Yale	1909	10-0
Ohio State	1910	6-1-3
Yale	1913	5-2-3
Iowa	1916-1923	42-17-1
Duke	1924	4-5
USC	1925-1940	121-36-13
Total		194-64-21

NATIONAL CHAMPIONSHIPS (As a player- 3; As a coach- 6):

As a player:	Yale in 1905 Yale in 1906 Yale in 1907	As a Coach:	Yale in 1909 Iowa in 1921	USC in 1928 USC in 1931 USC in 1932 USC in 1939

CONFERENCE CHAMPIONSIPS (10):

Claimed national championships for USC highlighted in yellow. Conference championships are earned by won-loss records and thus are unquestioned. That is the benefit of a national championship playoff as currently constituted.

As a Coach:	Yale in 1909 Iowa in 1921 Iowa in 1922 USC in 1927 USC in 1928 USC in 1929 USC in 1931 USC in 1932 USC in 1938 USC in 1939			
	USC in 1929	Won Rose Bowl	USC 47	Pittsburgh 14
	USC in 1931	Won Rose Bowl	USC 21	Tulane 12
	USC in 1932	Won Rose Bowl	USC 35	Pittsburgh 0
	USC in 1938	Won Rose Bowl	USC 7	Duke 3
	USC in 1939	Won Rose Bowl	USC 14	Tennessee 0
Rose Bowl Scoring: 124-29; 56-3 in last 3 games.				

Photo Gallery 1

Football, Baseball, & Soccer Stadiums, plus Horse & Auto Racing Tracks

Greater Los Angeles, Sports Capital of the World

Left: USC's Los Angeles Memorial Coliseum and its Olympic Torch, the only stadium that was host to two Olympics and soon to be a third. Home to USC Football. *Adobe Stock image*

Below: The Rose Bowl, built in 1923, with the San Gabriel Mountains in the background. Host to many classic Rose Bowl games and home of UCLA Football. *sbnation.com*

Above: Baseball's Friday Night Lights. Los Angeles Dodger Stadium in Chavez Ravine, which elevated it closer to the top of the LA skyline. *wallpapercave.com photo*

Below: Angel Stadium, Anaheim, Orange County. Home of the Los Angeles Angels. *thegreatgame.com*

Above: SoFi Stadium in Inglewood. Home of the Los Angeles Rams and Los Angeles Chargers professional football teams. Airliner in upper left is on final approach for landing at nearby Los Angeles International Airport (LAX). *photo by teazilla.com*

Below: The state-of-the-art interior of SoFi Stadium for professional football. *photo by stadionwelt.de*

Above: Dodger Stadium. *photo by abcnew.delaugher.org*

Below: Banc of California Soccer Stadium in Exposition Park, next to the L.A. Memorial Coliseum (to the left of photo) with the Los Angeles skyline in the distance. *reddit.com photo*

SPORTS VENUES in the LOS ANGELES AREA:

Exposition Park, home to the Banc of California Stadium, the Olympic Swim Stadium, and the Los Angeles Memorial Coliseum. Inglewood Sports Complex, home of the Forum, SoFi Stadium, and the future Intuit Dome, which is under construction. The Sports Park in Carson, home of Dignity Health Soccer and Tennis Stadiums, plus the individual Rose Bowl, Dodger, and Angel Stadiums. For horse racing enthusiasts, there is Santa Anita.

Artist Rendering of Exposition Park in Los Angeles. *cnu.org photo*

Exposition Park with the Memorial Coliseum (top center) and the Banc of California Stadium (lower right). The Olympic Swim Stadium is to the left of the Coliseum. The USC campus is shown on upper right. The Park is also home to: The Discovery Center, the *Endeavour* Space Shuttle, the Museum of Science & Industry, L.A. County Museum of Natural History, the Rose Garden, and the African-American Museum, among other venues.

Dignity Health Sports Park in Carson. *dignityhealthsportspark.com*

Formerly Home Depot Stadium, has 27,000 seats for both soccer and football. It is home to the LA Galaxy professional soccer team and former home to the Los Angeles Chargers. The Tennis Stadium is on right side. Carson is located 16.8 road miles from downtown Los Angeles.

Santa Anita Racetrack in Santa Anita Park, Arcadia. *courtesy of Off-Track Betting California*

Located 14 miles to the east of downtown Los Angeles, Santa Anita is nestled at the base of the beautiful San Gabriel Mountains. "The Santa Anita Handicap has been the biggest and best-known race on the West Coast since its inception in 1935."

Auto Club Speedway in Fontana. *courtesy of San Bernardino Sun*

Fontana is located 50 miles to the east of downtown Los Angeles and is part of Greater Los Angeles, which includes five SoCal counties with accompanying populations: Los Angeles County 9,861,224 (2022), Orange County 3,168,000 (2021), Riverside County 2,458,000 (2021), Ventura County 839,784 (2021), and San Bernardino County 2,195,000 (2021) for a total of 18,522,000 residents in **Greater Los Angeles, Sports Capital of the World.**

Chapter Three

Conference Champions and the "Conference of Champions"

The USC Trojans have won an incredible 39 conference championships in what started out to be the PCC or Pacific Coast Conference. Through several changes, the PCC is now the PAC-12.

One might conjecture that was a national record. One would be wrong.

That honor belongs to the University of Oklahoma with 50 conference championships, followed by Nebraska with 46, Michigan with 44, and Ohio State with 41, 39 of those earned in the Big 10, which ties USCs 39 gained in the Pac-12. After Ohio State and the Trojans, comes Tulsa University with 35, which was helped along by former USC coach Gus Henderson. After Tulsa it is Alabama, Texas, Fresno State, and Utah to finish off the top ten.

Yet the total of 39 Trojan conference championships in football is a significant number and good for 5th in the United States. What the author has claimed are the "forgotten years" has denied USC a higher national placement. Since the last conference championship under Pete Carroll in 2008, the Trojans have only won one other, and that was in 2017 under the under-performing Clay Helton. It remains to be seen if Lincoln Riley will get the Trojans back on a winning track and resume their domination in league play. However, he only has one more year in the Pac-12, and then it is on to the Big Ten.

USC is entering a large unknown. Not only are they being coached by someone who is only in his second year at the university, but they will be entering a new conference that is foreign to the experience of both USC and Lincoln Riley. The final chapter of this book will deal with Riley and the Trojan move to the Big Ten.

The unknown can be interesting and sometimes very productive. It can also be very exciting and that is what all Southern California can be waiting for as its two internationally- known universities are looking east for their future competition in a wide range of NCAA sports. It might be a wild and crazy ride.

CONFERENCE CHAMPIONSHIPS WON by USC:

PACIFIC COAST CONFERENCE (PCC):

The Pacific Coast Conference was started in 1916, 28 years after USCs first football game. It lasted until 1958. The teams that eventually became part of the conference included: Washington, Washington State, Oregon, Oregon State, Stanford, California, UCLA, and USC.

Conference championships won by USC in the new PCC were: 1927, 1928, 1929, 1931, 1932, 1938, 1939, 1943, 1944, 1945, 1947, and 1952. Twelve Trojan championships in the 43 years of PCC existence: 27.9% success rate.

ATHLETIC ASSOCIATION OF WESTERN UNIVERSITIES (AAWU):

The reason for changing the name is unknown. The same universities that were part of the PCC became part of the AAWU. The only apparent change was the name. USC conference championships continued at an accelerating pace: 1959, 1962, 1964, 1966, 1967. Five conference championships in 9 years of conference existence: 55.6% success rate.

PACIFIC EIGHT CONFERENCE (Pac-8):

Changing the name of a business can be expensive. Signage needs to change as well as all written forms and documents. It can also be time-consuming. Why they again decided to change the name without any changes in membership is not understood. The change did not seem to matter to USC, as it again won championships in 1968, 1969, 1972, 1973, 1974, 1976. Six championships in 11 years of conference existence: 54.5% success rate.

PACIFIC TEN CONFERENCE (Pac-10):

Finally, they made a change that made sense. After the 1976 football season, on December 14, 1976, the Pac-8 Conference extended an invitation to Arizona and Arizona State to join the conference. USC continued winning conference championships: 1978, 1979, 1984, 1987, 1988, 1989, 1993, 1995, 2002, 2003, 2004, 2005, 2006, 2007, 2008. Fifteen championships in 34 years of conference existence: 44.1% success rate.

PACIFIC TWELVE CONFERENCE (Pac-12):

In 2011, the Pac-10 asked Colorado and Utah to join the conference. Since that date, USC has only won one conference championship in 2017. One championships in 12 years of the conference: 8.3% success rate.

Thirty-nine championships earned during 109 years of competition in five different West Coast conferences amount to a 35.8% overall success rate. That is a very significant achievement and one for which all Trojan students, athletes, faculty, administration, families, friends, and fans can be justly proud. This author salutes those teams, coaches, athletes and support personnel who participated directly in that success.

BIG TEN "CONFERENCE of CHAMPIONS" in 2024: (written when the Pac-12 had only 4 schools: Washington State, Oregon State, Stanford, and the University of California, Berkeley):

The Pac-12 often advertises that it is the "Conference of Champions," yet they have never seemed to have offered any televised numbers to back up that claim. Below is the back up:

In 29 NCAA sports, the Pac-12 has won 550 NCAA National Championships compared to 330 for the Big Ten. The four California universities (in blue) account for 407 of those 550 West Coast championships.

In 2024, when UCLA, USC, Oregon, and Washington leave the Pac-12 for the Big Ten, the Pac-12 will no longer be able to make the claim that it is the "Conference of Champions" as its total, with the loss of eight schools, will become irrelevant. The Big Ten can then lay claim to the title as their total will jump from 330 to 605.

The following numbers of NCAA national championships are current as of 2022. There are discrepancies in reported data from several different sources. The data included on the next pages was extracted from the following articles: "List of Big Ten Conference National Championships" by Wikipedia; "List of Pac-12 Conference (and National) Football Champions" by Wikipedia; "Pac-12 Championships" by the PAC-12; "Ranking Big Ten Schools by Most NCAA Championships Across All Sports" and "College Football Championship History" by the NCAA.

The figures listed in the following chart are close to being exact for the PAC-12. However, the figures for the Big Ten were wildly different. No two listings, of those checked, were identical. The final figures for football championships were extracted from *USA Today*.

NCAA NATIONAL CHAMPIONSHIPS EARNED by BIG TEN and PAC-12 by 2023:

BIG TEN		In Football	PAC-12		In Football
Illinois	22	3	Arizona	19	-
Indiana	24	-	Colorado	27	-
Minnesota	26	6	Utah	25	-
Nebraska	19	5	Oregon	34	-
Iowa	28	1	Washington	8	2 (1960, 1991)
Michigan St.	18	3	Arizona St.	24	-
Rutgers	1	-	California	42	5 (1920, 1921, 1922, 1923, 1937)
Purdue	4	-	USC	112	11 (1928, 1931, 1932, 1939, 1962, 1967, 1972, 1974, 1978, 2003, 2004)
Ohio State	41	8	UCLA	121	-
Penn State	52	3	Stanford	132	1 (1926)
Maryland	6	1	Oregon St.	4	-
Northwestern	9	-	Washington St.	2	-
Totals	**330**	**9**		**550**	**19**

NCAA NATIONAL CHAMPIONSHIPS EARNED by BIG TEN by 2024 with the addition of the PAC-12 schools:

Totals (from p.35)	330	9 (in football)
USC	112	11
UCLA	121	1
Oregon	34	-
Washington State	8	2
Totals	**605**	**23**

Author's Note: *As mentioned above, the totals for each university in the Big Ten for total NCAA titles and football championships are approximate, but overall they are unreliable. The author apologizes for his inability to determine which set of data for the Big Ten was reliable. Each set examined was significantly different than the others.*

With the additions of the four Pac-12 universities to the Big 10, the total number of NCAA championships in all sports earned by the Big Ten will increase from 330 to 605, an 83% increase. The football championships will increase from 39 to 53, with 11 of those 14 additional titles added by USC alone.

It is a shame that Stanford and the University of California-Berkeley will not be joining the Big Ten, as that would have added two of the finest academic universities in the country as well as the winningest NCAA champion in America (Stanford), with its 132 titles. It would also have simplified traveling in a Western Division for all sports.

However, the numbers do add up and by gaining the four Pac-12 additions, the Big Ten will truly become the new "Conference of Champions."

Chapter Four
Effective Interim Years
1942 - 1956

The period from 1942 through 1956 could have been considered for dominant era status if not for some glaring deficiencies. There were no national championships during that period and the Rose Bowl record was a pedestrian 3 wins and 3 losses.

Jeff Cravath started slow and ended slower. His first year in 1942 was 5-5-1 and his in 1950 was 2-5-2. However, in between were seven years with winning records.

THE JEFF CRAVATH RECORD — Yellow highlight denotes Pacific Coast Conference Champions		
YEAR	RECORD	CONFERENCE CHAMPS
1942	5-5-1	UCLA
1943	8-2	USC
1944	8-0-2	USC
1945	7-4	USC
1946	6-4	UCLA
1944	8-0-2	USC
1948	6-3-1	California / Oregon
1949	5-3-1	California
1950	2-5-2	California

Overall Jeff Cravath Record: 54-28-8 (.659)

THE JESS HILL RECORD — Yellow highlight denotes Pacific Coast Conference Champions		
YEAR	RECORD	CONFERENCE CHAMPS
1951	7-3	Stanford
1952	10-1	USC
1953	6-3-1	UCLA
1954	8-4	UCLA
In 1954, UCLA under Coach Red Sanders, won the national championship.		
1955	6-4	UCLA
1956	8-2	Oregon State
1948	6-3-1	California / Oregon

Overall Jess Hill Record: 46-17-1 (.730) • Combined Cravath-Hill Record: 100-45-9 (.690)

Jess Hill compiled an envious record in his six short years coaching the Trojans. His .730 winning percentage is favorably compared to the best of the USC coaches. His problem was the dominance of UCLA during his coaching period and his lack of championships, either national or conference. After his 1956 season, Hill was elevated to Athletic Director of USC. As Athletic Director, USC won 29 NCAA championships in many of the athletic teams under Hill's control.

Hill will be long remembered as the coach of the Trojan team that won the Rose Bowl in 1953 and salvaged a little honor for the PCC against a much more effective conference in the Big-10.

In 1959, Don Clark coached the Trojans to a share of the Conference Title, with UCLA and Washington, in the inaugural year of the Athletic Association of Western Universities. It was the only bright spot in three years (1957-1959) of ineffectual leadership.

After Clark, John McKay took over the reins. It took McKay two years (1960 & 1961) to form the basis for the dynasty that lasted until John Robinson coached his last USC year in 1997.

USC Coach Jeff Cravath. *wikipedia photo*

COACH JEFF CRAVATH:

Jeff Cravath was born in Breckenridge, Colorado. His mother died in childbirth and his father died when he was only six. He was raised in Santa Ana, California by his maternal grandparents and it is from them that he got his surname Cravath.

Young Jeff got his first name from James J. Jeffries, who was a champion American prizefighter. Young Jeff was a fighter like Jeffries and was called "little Jeffries."

Cravath graduated from Santa Ana High School and entered USC. He starred as center for the Trojans from 1924 to 1926, and was on the same offensive line as renowned Western movie stars, Ward Bond, and John Wayne.

His first-year coach was Gus Henderson and then Howard Jones for his final two years as player. In his senior year (1926) he played against Notre Dame in the inaugural of that classic intersectional game. The team went 8-2 in 1926, with the only two losses to Stanford and Notre Dame by identical scores of 13-12.

All-American teammate Jesse Hibbs later noted, "I played with Jeff the year we opened the series against Notre Dame. He should have made All-American Center. That year the Notre Dame center made the All-America team and Jeff completely outplayed him. He was a champ on and off the field." Cravath played the 1927 East-West Shrine Game, which was a large event in the early years of the PCC.

After graduation from USC, Cravath served as an assistant to Howard Jones in 1927 and 1928, a year when the Trojans won a national championship. In 1929, he was head coach at the University of Denver at the age of 26. For three years his teams went 11-9-1. He spent one year as an assistant at Chaffey College before Howard Jones again called him "asking him to assist." He served under Jones as a line coach from 1933 to 1940. When Jones left USC, Cravath was appointed as head coach for the University of San Francisco and compiled a record of 6-4.

Howard Jones died in 1941, and one of his assistants, Sam Berry, took over that year. However, international events took precedence. Japan attacked the US in December and two days after we declared war on Japan, Germany declared war on us. There was a rush to enlist and Sam Berry entered the Navy. "Cravath was rejected for military service due to poor eyesight." Barry recommended Cravath for the head coaching position at USC as they had served together as assistants under Jones. Cravath thus became the first USC alumnus to lead the football program. His buddy Sam Berry returned after the end of the war and served as assistant to Cravath from 1945 to 1950.

"In nine seasons Cravath led USC to the Rose Bowl four times, after the 1943, 1944, 1945, and 1947 campaigns." The Trojans went undefeated and unscored upon for his first two Rose Bowls, when he led USC to triumphs over Washington 29-0 and Tennessee 26-0. Then they met Alabama and Michigan in the next two Rose Bowls and the Trojans ended up 2-2 in the Bowl during the Cravath years. They marked the first losses for USC in the Rose Bowl since its inception, after eight straight victories.

Cravath led his 1943 team to six consecutive shutout victories. His 1944 team was undefeated and ended the season ranked 7th in the nation. After the 1945 season, Cravath was offered a five-year contract to coach the Washington Redskins, which he eventually turned down for a five-year extension with USC.

Cravath coached standout players such as Ralph Heywood, Jim Hardy, John Ferraro, who later became a Los Angeles politician of long-standing, and Frank Gifford. Even though his final two years showed a decline in effectiveness, his final game with USC was a 9-7 victory over archrival Notre Dame. His record against the other archrival, UCLA, was 8-3-1.

Like Gus Henderson, Cravath was fired in 1950 in large part due to losing to California his final three years, each by six points. That and a 2-5-2 mark in 1950 after being ranked 12th in the nation to start the season did him in. He retired and became a horse racing official at Santa Anita Park, which he did for two winters. He served as a technical advisor on the 1953 football film titled *Trouble Along the Way,* starring his old teammate John Wayne.

When he was advising on the film, Cravath was living in El Centro and working his own ranch. Shortly after working on the film, Cravath was driving his ranch pickup in Calexico, California when he collided with a dump truck. He underwent an emergency tracheotomy, but never regained consciousness. He died at age 50, just three short years after leaving the Trojans.

COACHES as INNOVATORS:

Jeff Cravath can be considered a successful coach. He was also an innovator. One of several during USCs long football tradition. He introduced the "T" formation to Trojan football. in the 1940s and 1950s. The "T" was the preferred type for most major colleges and for most high schools. During the 1950s, cross-town UCLA coach Red Sanders was one of the top innovators of the single-wing formation and he rode it to a national title for UCLA.

While the T formation was not created by Cravath, several other formations were created by Trojan coaches. Gus Henderson created the first version of the spread formation ever used in America. The spread is used by many coaches today, including Lincoln Riley's own version of the spread.

John McKay invented the "I" formation, where the tailback lines up directly behind the quarterback who is directly behind the center. Sometimes, McKay employed a fullback who lined up directly in front of the tailback, all in a line, which gave the I formation its name. In the I, the fullback would lead the tailback into the line, blocking for the tailback. Marcus Allen initially played in the backfield as a fullback, blocking for Heisman winner Charles White in 1979. That blocking helped make Allen a complete back, leading to his own Heisman in 1981.

Allen branched out in the Hawaiian Aloha Stadium during a post-season All-Star game and was the leading receiver for the game, as witnessed by the author. Excellence in receiving and blocking, in addition to running, helped make Marcus Allen one of the finest NFL backs in history.

Football Coach and later Athletic Director Jess Hill in 1951. *Wikipedia photo*

COACH JESS HILL:

Many know Jess Hill as a fine Trojan football coach and athletic director. Few realize that he was an outstanding athlete, who was world-class in track.

Hill attended Corona High School and Riverside City College before transferring to USC where he excelled in baseball, football, and track. At USC he lettered in football, track, and baseball. "He played fullback on the 1928 USC national champion football team," as a junior and during his senior year he was on the 1929 team that won the 1930 Rose Bowl.

He led the Pacific Coast Conference with an average of 8.2 yards per carry. "As a junior, he won the national title in the broad jump (now called the long jump) with a leap of 25 feet 7/8 inch, breaking the intercollegiate record by 2.5 inches. He also won the baseball conference (PCC) batting championship with a .389 average as a senior in 1930." He was the leading ground gainer for the PCC in football, a national record holder in track, and PCC batting champion in baseball. Pretty heady stuff.

PROFESSIONAL ATHLETE:

After graduation, Hill signed with the Hollywood Stars of the Pacific Coast League. In his first professional at-bat, he hit a home run against crosstown rivals the Los Angeles Angels (minor league). "He played as an outfielder (for three different teams) in Major League Baseball from 1935 to 1937" In 1935, his contract was sold to the New York Yankees where he batted .293 in 107 games. The following year he played for the Washington Senators and batted .305 as a reserve. He was then sent to the Philadelphia Athletics (who later moved to Oakland) and hit .293 for the year. He was then sent to the Oakland Oaks of the Pacific Coast League where he played two more years. Over his major league career, he batted .289, hit six homers, scored 175 runs, drove in 108 RBIs, had 277 hits, and stole 43 bases.

USC's SUPPORT for the MILITARY:

The military played a large part in Jess Hill later becoming a Trojan coach. "USCs unbroken partnership with the U.S. Military began in 1914 when USC hosted a training school for U.S. Army officers." This was at the start of the First World War in Europe. The military knew that it might have to eventually join the war, which became a reality three years later when the United States started fighting in 1917.

With the advent of World War II in the early 1940s, the USC Price School of Public Policy began hosting "Reserve Officer Training Corps (ROTC) programs, with unwavering support and commitment to produce the next generation of officers."

USC ranks #4 among private research universities in Department of Defense-sponsored research with over $200 million in active research grants. USC is one of 60 universities nationwide to house all three (Air Force, Army, and Navy) ROTC programs on campus. The Navy ROTC program on campus also includes the Marine Corps. The long-term program has been hugely successful as more than 200 USC ROTC alumni attained the rank "of a flag officer or senior civilian in the Department of Defense."

JESS HILL's MILITARY CONNECTION at USC:

While playing baseball, the ambitious Hill began coaching California high schools and colleges in track and football during baseball off-seasons. With the national patriotic surge of those enlisting in the military at the commencement of World War II, Jess Hill joined the Navy.

One of the USC programs in support of the U.S. Military during World War II was an aviation cadet program for the U.S. Army's burgeoning Air Corps. They assigned USC Athletic Director Willis O. Hunter to head up the program.

It appears that Hill's short-lived Navy career was as successful as everything else he ever did. He rose to the rank of Lieutenant Commander and was assigned by the Navy to work with Hunter and USC in the Av-Cad. (aviation cadet) program.

JESS HILL BECOMES a TROJAN COACH:

Willis Hunter must have been impressed with what he saw in Hill. After all, with Hill's outstanding background in track and football at USC, and his obvious organizational skills shown when in the Navy, Hunter hired Hill in 1946 and immediately made him coach of the freshman football and track teams. A few short months later, Hill was an assistant coach on USC's 1947 Rose Bowl team. From that hiring in 1946 through 1948, Hill studied under and was assistant to Jeff Cravath.

In 1949 and 1950, Hill became USCs head track coach succeeding Dean Cromwell, and won national titles both years. In 1962, he returned for one season as track coach after the sudden death of Coach Jess Mortensen.

With the firing of Jeff Cravath after his terrible 1950 football season, Jess Hill was selected to be head football coach. As earlier mentioned, Hill served as USCs head football coach for six years and compiled a very successful record of 45-17-1 (.730). His teams went 1-1 in the Rose Bowl in 1952 and 1954. "His 1952 squad finished the year ranked 5th in the nation with a 10-1 record, outscoring their opponents 254-47 and leading the nation in scoring defense at 4.7 points (allowed) per game." Their only loss was an end-of-the-season defeat 9-0 to perennial national power Notre Dame.

"Hill's players included Frank Gifford, Rudy Bukich, Jim Sears," and the electrifying tailback, Jon Arnett. Arnett was clearly the best white tailback in Trojan history in a university with such a rich tradition of so many outstanding black tailbacks, five of whom won the Heisman. Arnett was the heart of the team and his moves were very exciting to watch.

Trojan fans have long remembered the exploits of Mike Garrett, O.J. Simpson, Ricky Bell, Anthony Davis, Charles White, Marcus Allen, and Reggie Bush. Arnett was electrifying in every sense of that word and belongs in that group.

Elsewhere in this book is the story of Coach John McKay leading his team to Alabama to play Bear Bryant's Crimson Tide. McKay's Trojans trounced Alabama and Sam Cunningham, a black fullback, crushed the Tide defense. That was after McKay changed hotels on finding that the assigned hotel, in segregated Alabama, did not allow blacks. That Trojan victory was a deciding factor in the integration of SEC football and, eventually, the integration of the segregated South.

McKay was not the first Trojan coach to make that decision to change hotels due to Jim Crow traditions in the South. Jess Hill's 1956 season opener was against Texas and the game was scheduled for Austin, Texas. "Hill made the decision to change hotels (for his team) after discovering that USCs integrated team could not stay at the segregated Austin hotel that had been booked: USC went on to win the game 44-20, as fullback C.R. Roberts, an African American, ran for a school-record 251 yards" in a performance reminiscent of Sam Cunningham's years later. "USC ended the year with wins over UCLA and Notre Dame, the only time in Hill's six years that they won both games."

HILL BECOMES ATHLETIC DIRECTOR:

The Trojans tied for second in the PCC in 1956. It turned out to be Hill's last as USC coach. College administrators are always on the lookout for those with proven organizational and people skills. That was the case for Jess Hill. The USC president picked the successful football and track coach to become USC Athletic Director.

Hill succeeded Athletic Director Willis O. Hunter, with whom he worked so successfully in the Navy Aviation Cadet Program at USC. Hunter served as AD for the entire coaching period of Howard Jones, Sam Berry, Jeff Cravath, and Jess Hill. It was Hunter who, as much as anyone, created the foundation for the broad athletic success of USC.

The USC track and football athlete; the successful professional baseball player; the successful Naval Commander; the successful USC track and football coach; also became one of the most successful Athletic Directors in the storied history of USC sports. As he had learned from Cravath, he learned from Hunter.

Jess Hill served as Athletic Director for 16 years (1957-1972). During his time he helped direct the following coaches to winning the following national titles:

- Tennis Coach George Toley: 1958, 1962, 1963, 1964, 1966, 1967, 1968, and 1969
- Baseball Coach Rod Dedeaux: 1958, 1961, 1963, 1968, 1970, and 1971
- Track Coaches Jess Mortenson & Vern Wolfe: 1958, 1961, 1963, 1965, 1967, and 1968
- Swimming Coach Peter Daland: 1960, 1963, 1964, 1965, and 1966
- Football Coach John McKay: 1962 and 1967
- Indoor Track Coach Vern Wolfe: 1967
- Gymnastics Coach Jack Beckner: 1962

Twenty-nine national championships under Hill's direction. That is an unqualified success in any form of evaluation. At the end of 1972, Hill stepped down as Athletic Director and accepted the prestigious job of Commissioner of the Pacific Coast Athletic Association (PCAA). In 1978, Hill stepped down from that position and finally entered retirement.

Jess Hill is another in a long line of Trojan greats who probably deserve better recognition for their accomplishment. As can be seen, Hill's accomplishments were extraordinary.

His legacy is somewhat of a mixed bag. A mixed bag that was created by his success. His success as first an outstanding student-athlete, then a successful multi-sport coach, leading to a final success as Athletic Director created a false sense of "family" success that has plagued USC of late.

Success as an athlete does not necessarily lead to success as an athletic director. Based on past

Willis O. Hunter served as USC Athletic Director for 33 years (1925-1957). *Wikipedia photo*

success, such as that of Jess Hill, USC was lulled into a sense that they should always select athletic directors from within the Trojan "family." That has created difficulties. The recent decision to go outside of the Trojan family to pick athletic directors is a good change of direction.

USC is BECOMING the "MECCA" of COLLEGIATE SPORTS:

Mike Bohn's recent firing did not diminish his success as athletic director. He was "from the outside" and brought in fresh blood and fresh ideas. He also brought in Lincoln Riley. Riley is one smart dude. Years before his hiring, his recruiting trips to the rich Southern California prep football environment enlightened him on "what is wrong with USC." When he first came to Los Angeles to evaluate his newly-found situation, he was blown away by finding all "that is right with USC."

Sometimes it takes an outside vision of what we have here in Southern California. In the words of Lincoln Riley himself, "It is a Mecca." The best high school football in the nation is played right here in the Greater Los Angeles area, especially in the skilled positions. What university in the country has on-campus and off-campus athletic facilities, led by the USC-controlled Los Angeles Memorial Coliseum, that are as good as we have at USC? The USC programs in support of student-athletes are as good as found anywhere. What recruit would not like what he sees in and around USC?

The Southern California community is filled with many generations of Trojan graduates who support USC in many ways, including as huge financial backers. Their business power and influence have helped many Trojan athletes.

Los Angeles is the entertainment capital of not only the United States, but the world. The USC

School of Cinematography is one of the best in an area that thrives on motion picture support. Its graduates populate the highest regions of the entertainment world as well as the SoCal business world. USC is one of only a handful of universities with such alumni support. The importance of which cannot be overestimated in a NIL athletic world.

Southern California offers some things that others cannot. One of those things is unequaled weather. Unequaled weather that is not only good for quality of life but for almost unlimited outdoor athletic practice. Southern Cal offers its Pacific beaches and snow-capped mountains in excess of 10,000 feet. What other area of our country offers some of the best water and snow sports and both within easy reach?

Los Angeles is filled with museums and myriad cultural amenities. It hosts more professional sports teams than any other area. It has the richest tradition of Summer Olympics of any other city in the world. It is the gateway to an expanding Asia and its twin seaports account for almost half of all American imports and exports to Asia.

With over 100 languages spoken in the Los Angeles City School System, we are a true American melting pot. Visitors and recruits find a laid-back lifestyle and an equality-based acceptance. We have a vibrant California economy that is easy to see. As the leading agricultural and industrial state in the Union, Bloomberg predicts that the California economy will eclipse that of Germany in 2023 and become the 4th largest economy in the world, only topped by the United States, China, and Japan.

With all the positives mentioned above, the most important is what we have so close to the USC campus, and that is our Coliseum. Recruits know its reputation, but nothing can compare to stepping onto the grass at the base of the iconic stadium. It can be awe-inspiring and magnificent with the roar of an adoring Trojan crowd.

Life is good in Greater Los Angeles. What is there not to like? It is a Mecca. With proper coaching, it will once again draw the needed recruits and propel USC back to the top of intercollegiate football.

Chapter Five

The Golden Era

1962 - 1982

Left to Right: Quarterback Pat Haden, Assistant Coach John Robinson, and Head Coach John McKay discuss strategy during the 1974 National Championship season. Future USC Athletic Director Haden lived with Coach McKay and together with McKay's son, J.K. McKay, formed one of the most effective quarterback-receiver combos in Trojan history. *insider.espn.go.com.*

Coach turned Athletic Director Jess Hill started it all in 1951 when he assumed the football head coaching position at USC. From then until becoming Athletic Director in 1957, Hill's teams went 45-17-1, which was one of the more successful coaching tenures in the long, storied history of Trojan football.

COACH JOHN McKAY:

However, Hill's greatest contribution to the program was after he became Athletic Director. He was responsible for luring Oregon Assistant Coach John McKay down to SC. Head Coach McKay's tenure started inauspiciously in 1960. His was an example that it takes more than one season to turn a program around. His predecessor, Coach Don Clark, had some bright moments and coached a few brilliant players, but his mark was that his three-year coaching stint bridged the time between Hill and McKay.

John McKay was born in West Virginia to Scots-Irish parents. His father was a coal-mine superintendent who died when John was only thirteen. He starred on his high school football team and gained a scholarship to Wake Forest, graduating in 1941, mere months before the start of World War II. He was enrolling at Wake Forest when his widowed mother became ill. He had to return to West Virginia and work to support her. For her support, he worked as an electrician's assistant in a coal mine for a year.

In 1942, McKay enlisted in the U.S. Army Air Corp and fought the Pacific portion of the war flying as a tail gunner. He later flew in the most advanced bomber of the war, the B-29. During World War II, enlistments did not mean returning to the United States after serving for a year, as was the case for many in the Vietnam War. It meant that those enlisting would spend the duration of the war fighting and would not return until victory was achieved.

After the war, "he entered college at Purdue University in 1946 at the age of 23, then transferred to the University of Oregon in 1947. At Purdue, he was a halfback" and played the same at Oregon alongside quarterback Norm Van Brocklin, who would later star for the Los Angeles Rams.

As a junior, his Oregon Duck team went undefeated in the Pacific Coast Conference and 9-1 overall. They tied with Cal for co-champions with Cal going to the Rose Bowl and Oregon to the Cotton Bowl.

As a senior, McKay took over the offense from the departed Van Brocklin and called audibles from his stance as halfback. Without the future hall of famer, Van Brocklin, and without their halfback McKay, who graduated in 1950, the Ducks temporarily slipped back to mediocrity.

McKay graduated shortly before his 27th birthday. After graduation, he decided to become a coach. For nine seasons, he worked as the Duck's assistant. Eight of those years were under famed head coach Len Casanova. The Ducks improved during the 1950s and tied for the PCC title in 1957, ending up giving Coach McKay his first taste of playing in the Rose Bowl at the start of 1958.

After the 1958 season at Oregon, McKay moved south to USC as assistant to third-year Trojan coach Don Clark. He teamed up with Trojan line coach, Al Davis, who would later be inducted into the NFL Hall of Fame as successful coach and owner of both the Los Angeles and Oakland Raiders.

Clark had a very rocky start coaching USC. His first two seasons were 1-9 in 1957 and 4-5-1 in 1958. In 1959, with Davis and McKay helping, things turned around and the Trojans won their first eight games. Then disaster struck. They lost their last two games, which were to UCLA and Notre Dame.

Coaches at USC are still regarded by how well they play against the Trojan arch-rivals Notre Dame and the UCLA Bruins. Clark was unable to beat either in his three years and he ended up resigning at the end of the 1959 season.

McKay had apparently shown something to the USC administration, and he was hired as Trojan head coach going into the 1960 season.

His first two seasons were losing ones, going 4-6 in 1960 and 4-5-1 in 1961. He felt he was on the verge of being fired after his second season, but University President Norman Topping resisted calls for his firing. Topping had seen the results of McKay's recruiting and cautioned patience. He was rewarded with a National Championship in the 1962 season.

On January 1, 1963, USC nearly lost the championship in the Rose Bowl. Leading comfortably in the fourth quarter, 42-14, the future national champs were cruising. The author had just graduated from college in 1962 and was home with his parents listening to the game on their radio.

It had been an even ten years since the Trojans played Wisconsin. That was in the 1953 Rose Bowl and USC brought honor back to the Pacific Coast, winning the first Rose Bowl against the Big Ten, 7-0 over Wisconsin.

Ten years later, it was an entirely different story. Instead of one touchdown scored, it was many. Earl Gustkey, a *Los Angeles Times* staff writer, stated decades later that "the memory of what was probably the greatest of all Rose Bowl games still burns brightly." Some of the fans in the Rose Bowl stands began to file out of the stadium and others switched off the telecast for something more interesting or exciting.

In Gustkey's words, "Then it began. The greatest show in Rose Bowl history. In the final quarter, Wisconsin and USC fought each other like two prizefighters, with Wisconsin much the fresher at the finish. The Badgers simply ran out of time against the Trojans, who had run out of gas."

Two-way USC defensive lineman Marv Marinovich recalled that McKay ran out of defensive players that afternoon. Marinovich stated, "We had several defensive guys hurt before the game and a couple more (were hurt) during the game. I remember two guys playing defense in the second half who hadn't been in a game all year."

The Trojans, who entered the game #1 in the nation, had also been a 2-point underdog to Wisconsin to start the game, based on #2 Wisconsin's strong offensive performance during the regular season where they beat teams with scores such as 69-13, 30-6, 42-14, 37-6 and 35-6.

John Robinson, Golden Era coach, along with John McKay.
sports.usatoday.com photo

The architect of the memorable comeback was Wisconsin quarterback Ron Vanderkelen. Wisconsin scored 23 points in that 4th quarter in the greatest comeback the author had ever heard or witnessed, other than later watching from the stands the Trojan 1974 comeback against the #1 ranked Notre Dame defense. In that game, USC came back from being down 24-0 to winning in the second half 55-24. Those witnessing Wisconsin's exploding, including the author, were convinced that given a few more minutes, Wisconsin would have won the game.

That stirring Rose Bowl victory started the Trojans on a 20-year run (1962-1982) that was the greatest period of gridiron success in the storied history of Trojan football.

COACH JOHN ROBINSON:

John Robinson was born in Chicago in 1935 but moved to Daly City, California when he was only nine years old. He attended a Catholic parochial school with future pro football Hall of Famer John Madden. Robinson graduated from high school in 1954. He then attended the University of Oregon "where he played tight end on Oregon's 1958 Rose Bowl team," along with Oregon Assistant Coach John McKay.

Robinson started coaching as an assistant to Len Casanova in 1960 and served at Oregon until 1972, when he then joined McKay at USC. His first year with McKay was coaching the 1972 team that went undefeated, won the National Championship, and was considered one of the best, if not the best, college football team to ever play the game.

He was Offensive Coordinator at USC for three years (1972-1974), going 31-3-2, winning two National Championships, three Pac-8 Conference Championships, and appearing in three Rose Bowls, winning two of them.

In 1975, Coach Robinson then left USC to serve as running backs coach for the Oakland Raiders. At the end of 1975, Coach McKay decided to leave USC to become the first head coach of the new Tampa Bay Buccaneers of the NFL He was later quoted as regretting leaving the Trojans.

In 1976, Robinson was named to succeed McKay. "Robinson would coach at USC from 1976 to 1982, during which he led the Trojans to three conference titles and five bowl games. He won the Rose Bowl in 1977, 1979, and 1980, earning a National Championship in 1978." He went 67-14-2 in seven seasons at USC before stepping down to coach the Los Angeles Rams. His 1979 team was exceptional but did not win a portion of the National Championship that it richly deserved. More will be written about that 1979 team later in this chapter.

Robinson returned to coach USC after leaving the Rams, where he was head coach for the Trojans from 1993 to 1997, winning another Rose Bowl (1995) and winning Pac-8/ Pac-10 championships in 1993 and 1995. As head coach, he won four Rose Bowls, while losing none. He also won two Rose Bowls as an assistant, while losing one. He was inducted into the Rose Bowl Hall of Fame in 2003.

Later, he was coach and athletic director of UNLV (1999 to 2004). In 2010, he served as defensive coordinator at San Marcos High School in California. At the request of his good friend, LSU head coach Ed Orgeron, he served as senior consultant for LSU (2019-2021).

Can the reader imagine what it must have been like in 2010, playing defense for San Marcos High? To be coached by a former nine-year Ram coach and a 12-year Trojan coach must have

Coach John Robinson led the Trojans and L. A. Rams. *thetowntalk.com photo*

seemed a dream. It surely was an unpaid position and it showed how much Robinson had a love for the game and a love for developing young men.

Taking the job at LSU was the result of a long friendship between Robinson and Ed Orgeron. The gravelly-voiced Cajun Orgeron was the only holdover from Coach Paul Hackett to Coach Pete Carroll and Orgeron was Carroll's Defensive Coordinator while Robinson was his Offensive Coordinator.

Orgeron loved USC. During the "Turmoil Years," he took over as interim head coach for the Trojans while they searched for a permanent replacement for one of the three fired coaches. Orgeron went 6-2 during that time and was totally loved by the team. It broke his heart when USC chose another after Orgeron had done such a good job as interim.

He finally gave up on his long-held hope to be the head coach for USC and took the head coaching job at LSU. With Orgeron coaching and with Robinson advising, LSU won an undisputed National Championship. The intense Orgeron was a giving man and more than once gave talks to the Southern California Trojan Clubs. He always had a ready smile for anyone, a real cheerleader for the Trojans.

THE BEST TAILBACKS NEVER to WIN a HEISMAN — ANTHONY DAVIS:

Coach McKay was responsible for USC being called "Tailback U." Under McKay, tailback Anthony Davis was runner-up for the Heisman. He was a terrific runner and a total nemesis to fabled Notre Dame. The Irish have never, before or since, experienced such a devastating tailback and the results speak for themselves.

It all started in December 1972, when the Trojans were on the march that destroyed all their

Coach John McKay and Notre Dame nemesis, tailback Anthony Davis. *pinterest.com photo*

opponents that year. Closing out their final three games of that memorable season, in November they destroyed arch-rival UCLA 24-7. Their final game of the regular season was at the Coliseum on December second. They crushed number 10 ranked Notre Dame by a score of 45-23.

The headlines in the Los Angles Times after the game did not extol USC for its victory. They were all about the Trojan tailback, Anthony Davis. Long before the Los Angeles Laker's Anthony Davis came on the scene, the USC Davis was electrifying the football world. The headline bannered at the top of the *Times'* Sports Section declared "Davis! Davis! Davis! Davis! Davis! Davis!"

As the *Times* later reflected, "The six touchdowns scored (by Anthony Davis) on Notre Dame that day in December 1972 would go down as one of the greatest single-game performances in college football history, the piece de resistance of a storybook '72 season for USC that still ranks among the best the sport has ever seen."

In 2020, the Times again reflected on Davis, only this time it was about the greatest game the author has ever seen. The venue was the same as in 1972, the Los Angeles Memorial Coliseum. This time it was in late November.

In a year that saw the Lakers win their 17th NBA title, the Times wrote: "The most famous Anthony Davis in Los Angeles is the one who plays for the Los Angeles Lakers, but the most famous Anthony Davis in the history of college sports in Los Angeles is the man who authored one of the most famous and furious rallies in the 150-year history of college football."

Year's after that '72 game, the author's season tickets were right in front of Davis's season ticketed seats, not far from the famous Coliseum tunnel which was witness to the fury of the Trojan Band in its "ramping up" for the intensity of the Carroll-era game. Davis was always reflective when it came to remembrances of that 1974 comeback. He always felt that, while the 1972 season was "probably the greatest in college football history," the 1974 season was worthy of another championship year, highlighted by the Notre Dame game.

The *Times'* Matt Zemek continued: "The Notre Dame Fighting Irish won the 1973 college football national championship…Coach Ara Parseghian, and the rest of the Fighting Irish were college football royalty, at the height of their powers. Notre Dame was ranked No.5 (in the nation) that late-November game in 1974. A win would have given the Irish a chance to repeat as national champions, though Oklahoma and Alabama had more favorable positions."

Given the prowess and proven nature of Notre Dame at that point in history, the fact that the Fighting Irish rolled to a 24-0 lead (over the Trojans) late in the second quarter suggested this game was over. College football was not nearly as pass-centric as it became two decades later. The sport was still the province of running backs.

Yet from the rubble of a 24-point deficit, Anthony Davis carried the Trojans back, as part of a truly remarkable rally which is still resonant 46 years after it happened. It will still be talked about 246 years after it happened.

With only 10 seconds left in the first half, and with USC deep in Irish territory, Davis broke around left end and crossed the goal line untouched. That last-second score gave hope to those watching from the stands. The feeling was not that the game might be over. It was one of anticipation. In that 1972 game, Davis had run back two kickoffs the length of the field for touchdowns. The anticipation was that another magic Davis moment might happen.

"He then took back the opening kickoff of the second half" (for a touchdown). The Coliseum went crazy. "In roughly 20 seconds of scoreboard clock time, the 24-point deficit had been halved, to 24-12. Davis kept piling on the points. He scored two more touchdowns and added a 2-point conversion. USC had wiped away its 24-point deficit in roughly half a quarter, taking a 27-24 lead." From the stands, it appeared as though the Irish players were stunned. Their body language was a giveaway. That Notre Dame defense was rated the best in the nation. The Notre Dame reserves that lined the sidelines, seemed to be saying "how can this be happening?"

"Those 27 points, 26 of them scored by Davis, were hardly the last volleys USC would fire at the stunned Fighting Irish. The Trojans scored four more touchdowns in a heartbeat. With just over 13 minutes left in the 4th quarter, USC had amassed a 55-24 lead." The fact that it had been accomplished against the vaunted ND defense cannot be overlooked.

Wherever Notre Dame plays, a large portion of every stadium crowd roots for the Irish. They have a truly national fan base. It was no different that November day in the Coliseum. Trojan fans on the press-box side of the stadium were interspersed with very vocal Irish fans. That second-half atmosphere was more than electric. It was indescribable. The collective energy was not just heard, it was felt deeply by every Trojan in the stands and on the field. It was a power that was not to be denied and that power was reflected by the Trojans on the field.

The powerfully-felt energy seemed to sweep in waves throughout the crowd. The Irish fans were in disbelief. "The Trojans scored 55 points in 17 minutes of scoreboard-clock time, one of the most unfathomable barrages of brilliance and brutality in college football history." The Irish players on the field seemed numb and their measured steps across the field grass mirrored that numbness. Fifty-five points in only 17 minutes against the greatest defense in college football. It was an incomprehensible feat engineered by one man, Anthony Davis.

Anthony Davis was second to Archie Griffin of Ohio State in the Heisman voting in the year of that magical Notre Dame game of 1974.

RICKY BELL "THE BULL":

Ricky Bell was a different type of tailback than Davis. His teammates called him "Bulldog, because he growled when he carried the ball." He was as brutal on the field as he was kind off the field. Coach John Robinson said, "He punishes tacklers like no one I've ever seen."

Bell started his Trojan career in 1973, but on defense. "As a freshman in 1973, he lettered as an outside linebacker on a Rose Bowl team. As a sophomore, he started as a fullback for the 1974 national champion" Trojans. He normally blocked for the tailbacks but was a fullback when he carried the ball, averaging a huge 6.6 yards on every carry. "Moved to tailback by Coach John McKay, who was in his final season, Bell led the nation in rushing with what was then the second-highest total in NCAA history of 1,957 yards, while only a junior.

Like Anthony Davis, who was voted second in the Heisman to Archie Griffin of Ohio State the year before, Ricky Bell was voted third in the 1975 Heisman balloting behind the same Archie Griffin.

Beset by injuries, that kept him completely out of one game and out of most of four others, he still managed to rush for 1,433 yards, an incredible feat during his senior season. Tony Dorsett of Pittsburg got most of the media attention that year and that carried him to victory in the Heisman

Ricky Bell was a terrifying visage charging through defensive lines. *trojanswire.usatoday.com*

balloting. But it was Bell, who was second to Dorsett that year in the Heisman, who electrified the college football world.

"Bell turned in perhaps the greatest single-game performance in USC history as he literally carried the Trojans to a victory" over Washington State. He was invincible in that game. Washington nose guard, Dean Pedigo, bore the brunt of the Bell attack in the middle of the Washington State defensive line. Pedigo said of the game: "We had to gang tackle him on every carry. It usually took three or four of us to wrap him up. It was the worst, as a team, we've ever been beaten up."

Bell carried an incredible 51 times. Robinson took him out of the game in the 4th quarter, thinking he had beaten the national single-game record. The stadium scoreboard flashed the news that the record had been broken. Charlie White, a freshman who won the Heisman three years later, replaced Bell.

A statistical error left him three yards short of the record. But he still ran an unbelievable 347 yards before they pulled him from the game. Coach Robinson said after the game that "As far as I am concerned, he is the best football player of all time. I have never been around a man to equal him. The tougher the game got, the tougher he got. I don't remember a better performance from a guy."

John McKay was privileged to coach Bell as a Trojan in 1975 and later coached him at Tampa Bay of the NFL. Even after Dorsett won the Heisman, Bell was selected #1 in the NFL draft. Bell's mid-season injury seemingly kept him from his rightful place as a Heisman winner. McKay reportedly agreed with Robinson, saying that Bell was the greatest player he had ever coached.

Football great and Trojan legend O.J. Simpson said, after Bell's untimely death at age 29, that "He only wished that people had known Ricky like he did." Although Simpson's legacy has been severely tarnished, his football wisdom and accomplishments on the field cannot be denied. Simpson held Ricky Bell in the greatest esteem: "He was a man with as much dignity and courage as any I have known. He was the Noble Trojan."

THE BEST TEAM NEVER to WIN a NATIONAL CHAMPIONSHIP:

While the best team ever, the 1972 Trojan National Champions, won accolades everywhere and included 13 All-Americans and 33 players that later played for the NFL, the 1979 Trojan team might have been as great.

Too many evaluators in college football are stuck in canonizing teams with undefeated, untied records. They do not place enough attention to the quality of their opponents. USC is the only university in the nation that has never scheduled a non-Division One team. Until very recently, UCLA and Notre Dame could also boast the same, but have succumbed to the siren call of an undefeated season and have scheduled lesser teams. .

The 1979 Trojans beat #20 ranked LSU. They beat #15 ranked Washington. They crushed #9 ranked Notre Dame in Notre Dame stadium and they finally beat then #1 ranked Ohio State in the Rose Bowl. The only blemish on their season was a 21-21 tie with rival Stanford.

Although they defeated the #1 team in their final game, they were only awarded a #2 ranking in both the Coaches and the AP final polls.

Let us look at the roster of that 1979 team. The following players all later played in the NFL, but that is just a footnote to their exploits and their individual accomplishments and awards:

TEAM ROSTER for the 1979 USC TROJANS:

Marcus Allen, tailback, sophomore

- Super Bowl MVP
- NFL Most Valuable Player 1985
- NFL Offensive Player of the Year 1985
- NFL Offensive Rookie of the Year 1982
- NFL Comeback Player of the Year 1993
- Two-time 1st Team All-Pro 1982, 1985
- Second team All-Pro 1984
- Six-time Pro Bowl (1982, 1984, 1985, 1986, 1987, 1993)
- NFL rushing leader 1985
- NFL scoring leader 1982
- National Champion (USC) 1978
- Heisman Trophy winner 1981
- Maxwell Award winner 1981
- Walter Camp Award winner 1981
- Pac-10 Player of the Year 1981
- Unanimous All-American 1981
- Second Team All-American 1980
- USC Trojans No 33 retired
- NFL Hall of Fame

Hoby Brenner, tight end, junior
- New Orleans Saints, NFL

Brad Budde, guard, senior
- Unanimous All-American
- Lombardi Award winner 1979
- Kansas City Chiefs, NFL
- USC Football Hall of Fame 1999
- College Football Hall of Fame

Scott Tinsley, quarterback
- Los Angeles Rams, NFL

Ray Butler, wide receiver, senior
- Professional Football Writers Association All-Rookie Team 1980
- Baltimore Colts, NFL

Chris Foote, center, senior
- Baltimore Colts, NFL

Roy Foster, guard, sophomore
- Pro Bowl in 1985 and 1986
- Miami Dolphins, NFL
- Morris Trophy winner in 1980 and 1981

Bruce Mathews, center, freshman
- Seven-time 1st Team All-Pro (1988, 1989, 1990, 1992, 1998, 1999, 2000)
- Second team All-Pro (1991,1993)
- 14 ties Pro-Bowl
- Bart Starr Award 2001
- NFL 1990s All-Decade Team
- HFL 100th Anniversary All-Time Team
- PFWA All-Rookie Team 1983
- Titans/Oilers Ring of Honor
- Houston Oilers, NFL
- Tennessee Titans No. 74 retired
- Morris Trophy 1982
- Consensus All-American (USC) 1982
- 1st Team All-Pacific-10 in 1981, and 1982
- Texas Sports Hall of Fame
- USC Hall of Fame
- NFL Hall of Fame, most career starts with one Team 293, an NFL record.

Paul McDonald, quarterback, senior
- Second Team All-American (USC) 1979
- All-Pac-10 1979

Don Mosebar, offensive tackle, freshman
- Super Bowl Champion XVIII
- 1st Team All-Pro 1991

Anthony Munoz, offensive tackle, senior
- NFL Man of the Year 1991
- 1st Team All-Pro 1981, 1982, 1983, 1985, 1986, 1987, 1988, 1989, 1990
- 11-time Prowl Bowl (1981-1991)
- NFL 1980s All-Decade Team
- NFL 75th Anniversary All-Time Team
- NFL 100th Anniversary All-Time Team

Keith Van Horne, offensive tackle, junior
- Super Bowl XX Champion 1978
- USC National Champions 1978
- PFWA All-Rookie Team 1981

Charles White, tailback, senior
- College Football Hall of Fame
- USC #121 retired
- Heisman Trophy winner 1979
- Maxwell Award winner 1979
- Chic Harley Award 1979
- Walter Camp Award 1979
- UPI Player of the Year 1979
- Sporting News Player of the Year 1978 and 1979

Michael Harper, wide receiver

Kevin Williams, wide receiver

- Cleveland Browns, NFL
- Second Team All-Pac-10 1978
- NCAA Silver Anniversary Award 2005

- Los Angeles Raiders, NFL
- 2nd Team All-Pro 1990
- Pro-Bowl 1986, 1990, 1991

- Cincinnati Bengals, NFL
- PFWA All-Rookie Team 1980
- Cincinnati Bengals Ring of Honor
- National Champion (USC) 1978
- Bart Starr Award 1990
- California Sports Hall of Fame
- USC Hall of Fame
- NFL Hall of Fame

- Chicago Bears, NFL
- Consensus 1st Team All-American 1980
- Started 169 games for Chicago
- 100 Greatest Bears of All Time

- Cleveland Browns, NFL
- Pac-10 Player of the Year 1978 and 1979
- Unanimous All-American 1978 and 1979
- National Champion (USC) 1978
- NFL rushing touchdowns co-leader 1987
- NFL rushing yard leader 1987
- Pro Bowl 1987
- NFL Comeback Player of the Year 1987
- USC Running Backs Coach 1993 to 1997 under Coach Robinson.

- New York Jets, NFL

- Baltimore Colts, NFL

Called by Anthony Davis "the fastest wide receiver ever at USC." He caught 71 passes for 1,358 yards with 25 touchdowns, still a Trojan record. Williams scored 151 points his senior year in high school football and was California State Champion in the 100-yard dash. "Holds NCAA record for highest percentage of passes caught for touchdowns, scoring 24 times on 68 receptions." He was a member of two USC NCAA 400-meter relay teams. He was in the same San Fernando High School backfield as Charles White and Kenny Moore (below). He was killed at 38 years old in a train wreck in the Cajon Pass.

Kenny Moore, defensive back   • Baltimore Colts, NFL

Brother of USC players Manfred and Malcolm Moore, played quarterback for San Fernando High School in the same backfield as USC standouts Kevin Williams and Charles White. White, Williams and Moore were named Los Angles City tri-players of the year.

Vic Rakhshani, wide receiver   • Los Angeles Express (USFL)

Retired from the Express due to severe injury in 1983. Started all four years at USC, member of USC 1978 National Champions; Rose Bowl Champion 1978 and 1979; established the Rakhshani Institute for Pain and Regenerative Surgery.

Malcolm Moore, wide receiver   • Dallas Cowboys, NFL
Brother of Kenny Moore (above).

James Hunter, tight end   • Pittsburgh Steelers, NFL

Dennis Edwards, defensive end   • Buffalo Bills, NFL

Myron Lapka, defensive tackle   • New York Giants, NFL

George Achica, defensive tackle, freshman   • Indianapolis Colts, NFL
• Consensus 1st Team All-American 1982   • Morris Trophy 1982

Byron Darby, defensive line, freshman   • Philadelphia Eagles, NFL

Chip Banks, linebacker, sophomore   • Cleveland Browns, NFL
• NFL Defensive Rookie of the Year 1982   • SEA 2nd Team All-Pro 1983
• AP 1st Team All-Pro 1983   • Pro Bowls 1982, 1983, 1985, 1986
• PFWA 1st Team All-Pro 1983

Riki Gray (Ellison), linebacker   • San Francisco 49ers, NFL
• Rose Bowl Champion (USC) 1979 and 1980   • National Champion (USC) 1978
• Super Bowl Champion, XIX, XXIII, and XXIV.

Eric Scoggins, linebacker junior   • Baltimore Colts, NFL
• National Champion (USC) 1978

Joey Browner, safety, freshman   • Minnesota Vikings, NFL
• 1st Team All-Pro 1987, 1988, 1990   • Minnesota Vikings Ring of Honor
• 2nd Team 1989   • Member 50 Greatest Vikings
• Pro-Bowl 1985 to 1990   • Minnesota Vikings 40th Anniversary Team
• NFL 1980s All-Decade Team

Steve Busick, linebacker, junior   • Denver Broncos, NFL

Jeff Fisher, cornerback, junior
- National Champion (USC) 1978
- Coach of the Following NFL Teams: Chicago Bears, Philadelphia Eagles, Los Angeles Rams, San Francisco 49ers, Los Angeles Rams, Houston Oilers, Tennessee Oilers, St. Louis Rams, Tennessee State 2021, and Michigan Panthers 2022.
- Super Bowl XX Champion as coach
- Maxwell Club NFL Coach of the Year 2008
- Tennessee Titans Ring of Honor as coach

- Chicago Bears, NFL

Dennis Johnson, linebacker, senior
- Minnesota Vikings, NFL

Ronnie Lott, safety, junior
- San Francisco 49ers, NFL
- College Football Hall of Fame
- NFL Hall of Fame
- In NFL: 63 interceptions, 17 fumble recoveries, 16 forced fumbles
- NFL Record: Most interceptions returned for a touchdown in a season by a rookie
- Consensus All-American 1980
- National Champion (USC) 1978
- San Francisco 49er Hall of Fame
- NFL 75th Anniversary All-Time Team
- 10-time Pro Bowl 1981-1984, 1986-1991
- NFL 100th Anniversary All-Time Team
- NFL interceptions leader 1986 and 1991
- PFWA All-Rookie Team 1981
- NFL forced fumble leader 1982
- San Francisco 49ers No 42 retired
- NFL 1980s All-Decade Team
- National Champion (USC) 1978
- NFL 1990s All-Decade Team
- Consensus All-American 1980
- Super Bowl Champion in XVI, XIX, XXIII, XXIV
- 1st Team All-Pro 1981, 1983, 1986, 1987 1988, 1989, 1990, 1991

Larry McGrew, linebacker, senior
- Super Bowl Champion XXV

- New England Patriots, NFL

Mike McDonald, linebacker
- Cleveland Browns, NFL

Dennis Smith, cornerback, junior
- 1st Team All-Pro 1984 and 1986
- 2nd Team All-Pro 1989
- Pro-Bowl 1985, 1986, 1989, 1990, 1991, 1993

- Denver Broncos, NFL
- Denver Broncos Ring of Fame
- 1st Team All-American 1980.

Thirty-four of the players above went to the NFL. Four members of the NFL Football Hall of Fame were members of the 1979 team. Many were members of the USC Hall of Fame, though not mentioned above. The accolades and awards earned by the team members boggle one's mind. They are part of the argument that this exceptional group of players who went undefeated in 1979 deserve consideration as National Champions in 1979 and as one of the all-time great Trojan teams.

SYNOPSIS of the GOLDEN ERA of DOMINANT TROJAN COACHING ERAS:

National Championships: 5

    John McKay: 1962, 1967, 1972, 1974

    John Robinson: 1978

Conference Championships Total: 14

    Athletic Association of Western Universities (4): 1962, 1964, 1966, 1967

    Pac-8 Conference (6): 1968, 1969, 1972, 1973, 1974, 1976

    John Robinson: Pac-10 Conference (4): 1978, 1979

        (Conference championships between Robinson's two coaching periods at USC: 1984, 1987, 1988, 1989).

    John Robinson's second coaching period in Pac-10: 1993, 1995

Rose Bowl Victories: 9

    John McKay: 1963, 1968, 1970, 1973, 1975

    John Robinson: 1977, 1979, 1980, 1996

Rose Bowl Losses: 3

    John McKay: 1967, 1969, 1974

Heisman Trophy Winners: 4

    Mike Garrett, 1965

    O.J. Simpson, 1968

    Charles White, 1979

    Marcus Allen, 1981

Heisman Trophy Runners-Up: 2

    O.J. Simpson, 1967

    Ricky Bell, 1976

Record: 231-75-12 (.755) - ties are not counted.

    John McKay: 127-40-8 (.760)

    John Robinson: 104-35-4 (.748)

Jess Hill, Athletic Director during most of McKay's tenure as Trojan Coach (1960-1972).

ATHLETIC DIRECTOR JESS HILL:

Athletic Directors deserve recognition for helping create the Golden Era. Jess Hill was responsible for five national championships in 1972: in football, winning the College World Series that year in baseball, also a National Championship in Swimming and Diving, in Indoor Track and Field, and finally Men's Golf, a sport that the Trojans no longer field a team.

Hill established himself as the greatest in a long line of USC Athletic Directors. John McKay followed Hill at USC and held the dual job of both football coach and Athletic Director, from 1973-1975. Richard Perry finished McKay's year after he resigned to go to the Tampa Bay NFL team. Perry continued as Athletic Director through the 1984 athletic year.

Photo Gallery 2

Los Angeles Area Basketball, Volleyball, and Hockey Arenas

Greater Los Angeles, Sports Capital of the World

Crypto.com Arena, formerly Staples Center, home of the Los Angeles Lakers and Los Angeles Clippers basketball teams, plus the Los Angeles Kings hockey team. A new arena for the Clippers is being built in the Inglewood Sports Complex. *bithub.pl.photo*

Arena is located just south of downtown Los Angeles and just north of Exposition Park, the Los Angeles Memorial Coliseum, and the USC Campus. *la.urbanize.city photo*

Above: Honda Center, home of the Anaheim Ducks hockey team. *cyclenews.com photo*

Below: The Forum in the Inglewood Sports Complex, located next to SoFi Stadium. Former home of the Los Angeles Lakers and still able to host basketball events. *pinterest.com photo*

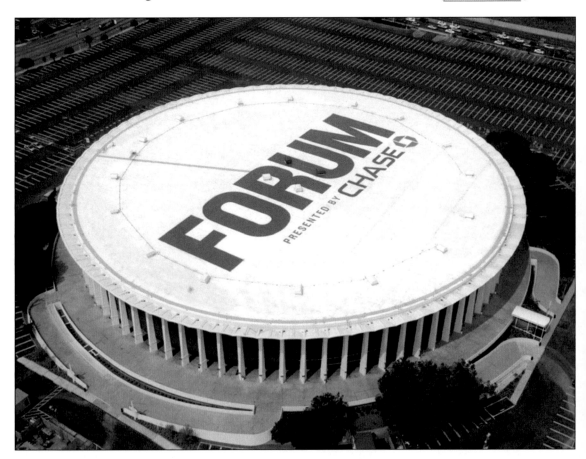

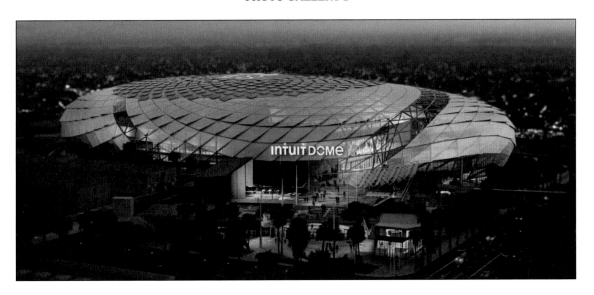

Above: Artist Rendering of the Intuit Dome, future home of the Los Angeles Clippers. The Dome, being built in the Inglewood Sports Complex next to the Forum and SoFi Stadium, will open in 2024.

Below: Construction of the Los Angeles Clipper's Intuit Dome arena in May, 2023.
msn.com photo

Pauley Pavilion, located on the UCLA Campus, is home to UCLA Bruins Basketball. The UCLA Campus will be home to the Olympic athletes and vwill be the Olympic Village during the 2028 Los Angeles Olympic Summer Games. *Kovach Building Construction, kovach.net*

Above: The massive Galen Center, home of USC Trojan Basketball and USC Trojan Volleyball. The Center is located adjacent to the USC Campus, in the foreground, with clear views of downtown Los Angeles in the near distance to the north. The 1962 National Champion USC Men's Gymnastics Team currently does not have a campus home and, instead, trains at Klub Gymnastics in downtown Los Angeles. *Kovach Building Construction, kovach.net*

Chapter Six
Trojan Coaching in the Rose Bowl
Measure of Success

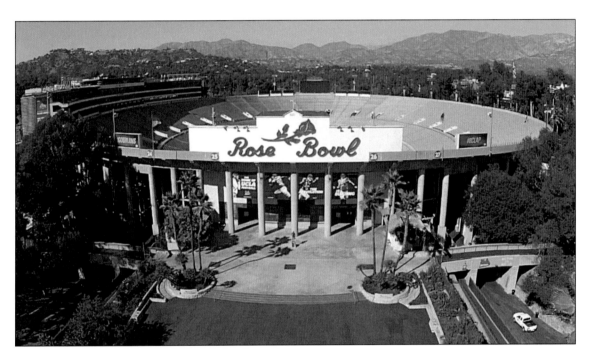

The Rose Bowl stadium in Pasadena, California, with San Gabriel Mountains backdrop.
youtube.com photo

The Rose Bowl game, initially called the Tournament East-West Football Game, is well known as the oldest of the American football bowl games. First played in 1902, it has been played annually since 1916. No other bowl games were played until 1935, when three other New Year's Day games were established.

USCs record in the Rose Bowl is unmatched by any team in any bowl in the country. It is not even close. As of this writing, the Trojan record is 25 wins against only nine losses. The 34 appearances are also significant. Big Ten teams from the American Midwest could often count on meeting USC on the traditional New Year's Day gridiron.

Other Pacific Coast teams have also had success in the Bowl. Washington and Stanford each have had seven wins. But Washington also has had six losses and Stanford has had seven, giving each a winning percentage of .538 and .500, hardly equating to the Trojan winning percentage of .735.

UCLA has had five wins, but also seven losses. Oregon has had success in the 21st century with

First game played in the Rose Bowl Stadium. In 1923, USC beat Penn State 14-3. The horseshoe shape was later enclosed to form the bowl. *espn.com photo*

three wins, but overall has a total of only four wins against three losses. California has two wins, but six losses. After that, only Arizona State, Oregon State, and Washington State each had single victories.

USC in the ROSE BOWL (25-9 as of 2022):

The year that the Rose Bowl is played is not the Trojan season year. For example: The 2023 season of football is played in the fall of 2023. The Rose Bowl, which includes successful teams from the 2023 season, is played in January of 2024 and is listed as being played in 2024. So fans wanting to see how conference champions did in one year of play, need to check the following year's entry for the Rose Bowl, or any other bowl played in January.

To Southern Californians who grew up with the Rose Bowl, it is more than just a game. It is part of the Tournament of Roses, which includes the colorful and famous New Year's Day Parade as well as the Rose Bowl football contest. The entire Tournament is an institution and part of SoCal culture, which includes thousands of volunteers who decorate the many floats that participate in the New Year's Day Parade. For fans, it is arriving early to grab a seat to watch the parade. Often early means the night before, which also means celebrating New Year's Eve on a cold bench along the route of the parade. It also means parties with friends and family to celebrate.

For players, the Rose Bowl is special. It means feasting at Lawry's "Beef Bowl" and enjoying the many venues throughout Pasadena and the rest of Greater Los Angeles. Visiting teams are guests and are feted as royally as the West Coast teams. It is an honor to play in the Rose Bowl and Southern California makes sure that players are aware of that honor.

Often overlooked, coaching staffs of the winning teams are also rewarded on New Year's Day by coaching their teams before national television audiences. While players have sacrificed their time and energy in practice and games, coaches have sacrificed as much or more. Coaching is their livelihood. It usually means that families do not see much of their coaching husbands and fathers during the evenings of football season. Coaching is a profession requiring continual planning and evaluation. It means endlessly watching game film and often grabbing fast food when better fare waits at home.

The following pages are devoted to the success that Trojan coaches have found at the Rose Bowl, which lies only 16 road miles to the north of the USC campus.

THE DOMINATING UNDEFEATED YEARS (From Henderson to the end of World War II):

Rose Bowls highlighted in yellow were played after national championship seasons. Those highlighted in green were games played after seasons in which USC came in second in polling for the national championship.

YEAR	COACH	SCORE	
1923	Gus Henderson	USC 14	Penn State 3
1930	Howard Jones	USC 47	Pittsburgh 14
1932	Howard Jones	USC 21	Tulane 12
1933	Howard Jones	USC 35	Pittsburgh 9
1939	Howard Jones	USC 7	Duke 3
1940	Howard Jones	USC 14	Tennessee 0
1944	Jeff Cravath	USC 29	Washington 0

The game was played between two Pacific coast teams due to World War II

YEAR	COACH	SCORE	
1945	Jeff Cravath	USC 25	Tennessee 0

Until the end of World War II, USC had never lost a Rose Bowl in eight games played. In the last three Rose Bowls, played between 1940 and 1945, the opponents did not score a point. Even more impressive were the score totals: **USC 192, Opponents 41**

THE FIRST INTERIM YEARS:

After WWII, the situation changed. College football across the country was constantly improving. USC was being challenged for supremacy in the West and regional powerhouses were improving in the East.

Alabama, with more National Championships than any other university, also has an outstanding record in the Rose Bowl. If not for the agreement, agreed to in 1946, between the Pacific Coast Conference and the Big Ten that relegated the Bowl exclusively between those two conferences, USC might have had historic matchups with the Crimson Tide that match those between USC and Ohio State.

YEAR	COACH	SCORE	
1946	Jeff Cravath	Alabama 34	USC 14
1948	Jeff Cravath	Michigan 49	USC 0
1953	Jess Hill	USC 7	Wisconsin 0
1955	Jess Hill	Ohio State 20	USC 7

Alabama had only one blemish on its Rose Bowl record, that being a 13-0 loss to the Cal Bears in 1938. Before that, they won in 1926, 1927, 1931, and 1935. Their last Rose Bowl meeting was against the Trojans, and they defeated USC 34-14 (see chart on previous page).

Jess Hill managed to salvage the honor of the West with the victory over Wisconsin. Hill was an outstanding coach, and his success was detailed in Chapter 4. If he had more time to devote to football, it is speculated that he might have established a record as one of the Trojan greats.

THE GOLDEN YEARS of TROJAN DOMINANCE:

As mentioned in the previous chapter, John McKay and John Robinson were both assistant coaches at Oregon. They came together to Southern Cal with McKay the head coach and Robinson the assistant. Robinson would later follow McKay as head coach in 1976 and had an outstanding record in the Rose Bowl. McKay, the greatest USC football coach in history, started their return to glory in 1963. Following his national championship year in 1962, he led the Trojans to a victory over Wisconsin that matched their victory ten years before. The victory was in doubt until the final seconds. Down to USC 42-14 in the 4th quarter, #2 ranked Wisconsin Quarterback Ron Vanderkellen guided his team on a historic comeback. Given a few more minutes, it was probable that Wisconsin would have won.

McKay and Robinson matched the eight Rose Bowl victories earned by Henderson, Jones, and Cravath up to the end of World War II. In their first seven Rose Bowls, they went 4-3 with Ohio State as their opponent on three occasions. However, for the six years from 1975 through 1980, they went 4-0 with Ohio State and Michigan each playing in two of the classic contests.

YEAR	COACH	SCORE	
1963	John McKay	USC 42	Wisconsin 37
1967	John McKay	Purdue 14	USC 13
1968	John McKay	USC 14	Indiana 3
1969	John McKay	Ohio State 27	USC 16
1970	John McKay	USC 10	Michigan 7
1973	John McKay	USC 42	Ohio State 17
1974	John McKay	Ohio State 27	USC 16
1975	John McKay	USC 18	Ohio State 17
1977	John Robinson	USC 14	Michigan 6
1979	John Robinson	USC 17	Michigan 10
1980	John Robinson	USC 17	Ohio State 16
1996	John Robinson	USC 41	Northwestern 32

From 1970 through 1980, McKay and Robinson coached seven Rose Bowls, winning six of them. Games highlighted in yellow (above) were after national championship seasons. Those highlighted in green were after seasons coming in second in national championship polling.

John Robinson left USC to coach the Los Angeles Rams in 1982. His 1979 team was second to Alabama, which was the overwhelming national champion that year. However, while Bama went 12-0, USC was also undefeated at 11-0-1. The 1979 Trojan team had more players that excelled in the NFL than any other Trojan team in history. In retrospect, it might have deserved greater recognition.

THE SECOND INTERIM YEARS:

Apart from the four years when Robinson returned from the Rams to again coach USC, the period leading up to Pete Carroll's ascendancy was highlighted by mediocre coaching. What is considered mediocre by Trojan standards might be something else for lesser-achieving teams. They might be called mediocre, but they managed to win three of five Rose Bowls played during those interim years.

The second coming of John Robinson saved the period from only achieving a break-even record. Robinson was one of only two Trojan coaches, the other being Howard Jones, who achieved a perfect coaching record in the Rose Bowl, other than the "one-and-done" single-season victories posted by Henderson, Tollner, and Helton.

YEAR	COACH	SCORE	
1985	Ted Tollner	**USC** 20	Ohio State 17
1988	Larry Smith	Michigan St. 20	**USC** 17
1989	Larry Smith	Michigan 22	**USC** 14
1990	Larry Smith	**USC** 17	Michigan 10

THE DOMINATING EXCELLENCE of the PETE CARROLL ERA:

The arrival of Coach Pete Carroll to USC amounted to a revival. Apart from 2006, from 2002 up through the 2007 season, USC came in either first or second in national championship polling in five of those six years. That success also showed in his Rose Bowl appearances. Who can forget the epic struggle in the 2006 Rose Bowl when Texas tied the Trojans in the final minutes to force an overtime and then won by three points in those last seconds. The Texas victory snapped a 34-game winning streak for the Trojans and deprived them of a three-peat for a third straight national championship.

During this century, the Orange Bowl and other New Year's bowls have attained equal status with the Rose Bowl. The BCS and national playoffs have changed the dynamic. The Rose Bowl now hosts games without any team from the West Coast. Pete Carroll ended two seasons by playing in the Orange Bowl, winning both games by substantial margins. It is those Orange Bowl appearances that denied the Rose Bowl from hosting Carroll-coached USC teams after national championship seasons.

The author and his wife attended one of those two Orange Bowl victories. It pitted the Trojans against the Oklahoma Sooners for the championship. USC completely dominated and won 55-19. It was the most dominating game against a ranked opponent that he had ever seen. It was one of a handful of Trojan games that have been epic.

Perhaps the most epic was in 1974 when the Trojans met the #1 nationally ranked Notre Dame defense. While the game is described in detail elsewhere in this book, it is worth mentioning again. The author sat in seats adjacent to the goalposts on the SE side. The Coliseum was packed. The crowd frenzy was the most intense ever seen. The crowd's emotional content was visceral, and the Trojan teammates seemed as affected as the crowd. USC destroyed Notre Dame 55-24, the best game the author has ever seen.

The Carroll record below is a visual recognition of the excellence of his Trojan teams. His one lone Rose Bowl loss was by three points in overtime that ended a Trojan 34-game win streak. His other victories were not close ones like those of the McKay-Robinson era. His point margins were: +14, -3, +14, +32, and +17.

As before, games highlighted in yellow mark those years when USC won national championships. Those highlighted in green are those years when they ended up second in national championship polling.

The Trojan record in Rose Bowls since the start of the century:

YEAR	COACH	SCORE	
2004	Pete Carroll	**USC** 28	Michigan 14
2006	Pete Carroll	Texas 41	**USC** 38
2007	Pete Carroll	**USC** 32	Michigan 18
2008	Pete Carroll	**USC** 49	Illinois 17
2009	Pete Carroll	**USC** 38	Penn State 21
2017	Clay Helton	**USC** 52	Penn State 49

Since the departure of Carroll to the NFL, USCs involvement in the Rose Bowl has suffered its longest period of inactivity since that first victory 100 years ago. One lonely victory in 13 years of playing in the greatest postseason classic.

The final USC appearance in the Rose Bowl was coached by Clay Helton. With USC moving to another conference, that game has become a bookend to that played in 1923.

USC and UCLA to the BIG TEN:

The importance and meaning of the movement of the Los Angeles teams to the Big Ten will be dealt with more completely in a later chapter.

With USC joining the Big Ten at the same time as the advent of a twelve-team national playoff, the spirit and importance of the Rose Bowl will diminish. How will Southern Californians react to the Trojans being a visiting team in the hometown Rose Bowl? Since the top twelve teams in the country will all be a part of a playoff system, the Rose Bowl will only regain importance as part of that playoff system. Things do change, but the passing of what the Rose Bowl meant to so many millions of football fans in the United States is still a matter of sadness.

Still, the memories of the many Rose Bowls and USC's participation in them is a cause of recalled pleasure. The site of the Rose Bowl Stadium still sends chills as does the site of the Memorial Coliseum. They are a part of Southern California. They are a part of UCLA and USC football. They are a part of the Olympics past and present. They have been a part of the Los Angeles Rams, the Los Angeles Chargers, the Los Angeles Raiders, and the Los Angeles Dodgers. They are a part of us.

The Rose Bowl has also been a part of those fans who wake up from the revelry of a New Year's celebration to then watch the beauty and pageantry of the Rose Parade followed by the annual football clash between the titans of the West against the titans of the Midwest.

TROJAN ROSE BOWL COACHING RECORDS:

Howard Jones	5-0
John Robinson	4-0
Pete Carroll	4-1
John McKay	5-3
Jeff Cravath	2-2
Gus Henderson	1-0

(Does not include the Christmas Festival victory)

Ted Tollner	1-0

(Served as USC head football coach from 1983 to 1986. He later was head football coach for San Diego State from 1994 to 2001. He served as an assistant coach in the National Football League (NFL) for 15 seasons (see story below).

Clay Helton	1-0
Jess Hill	1-1
Larry Smith	1-2

THE STORY of the 1960 CAL POLY "MUSTANG" FOOTBALL TEAM:

This story is not about the Rose Bowl, but it is about one who coached USC in the Rose Bowl. Cal Poly Public Affairs shared this story about Coach Ted Tollner:

In 1960, Tollner was quarterback of the Cal Poly football team. They were scheduled to play Bowling Green (Ohio) in the 1960 season. The year before, the Mustangs had gone 6-3 and hopes rested on their senior quarterback. With only eight seniors, their heavily-weighted sophomore and junior team had difficulty finding victories.

Mustang Coach Leroy Hughes had a stellar career with Cal Poly. Under Hughes, they had gone 73-37-1 from 1952 to 1959. Cal Poly "opened the 1960 season at Brigham Young University and lost by a score of 34-14. The Mustangs came home to defeat San Diego State

34-6 and then suffered three straight losses to Montana State, Fresno State, and Long Beach State. Their next game forced them to travel to Ohio with a matchup against Bowling Green. Bowling

Green was no pushover. In fact, Cal Poly was just crushed, losing 50-6. Anyone who has been on a team that was beaten that badly knows exactly how difficult the plane ride home can be.

They departed Toledo, Ohio on their trip back to Southern California on a foggy night. Liftoff was normal. Tollner was sitting over the left wing and at about one-hundred feet in the air, Tollner shared that "The engine sputtered and then it just stopped." The aircraft was a twin-engine military type, and it was later determined that the left engine quit. "The plane started shaking and vibrating uncontrollably." With low airspeed during takeoff, and a dual-propeller-powered aircraft losing its only left engine, there would have been a very strong nose-over tendency to the left.

"I knew we were going down," Tollner said. "You just kind of tucked up into a ball and covered your head. The next thing you know, there was a crash." The plane landed nose-down on the other airport runway. The impact split the aircraft in half. Some of the players were thrown out of the aircraft onto the ground. "It was chaos," offered Tollner.

Tollner was unconscious. When he awoke, Tollner shared that "the sounds of people scrambling and explosions were just some of the things I recollect." Through all the debris, smoke, and fire, Tollner's instinct was to get up and help his teammates. "But I couldn't figure out why I couldn't walk."

He had suffered a foot injury and he was one that had to be helped.

Sixteen players, one student manager, a member of the Mustang Booster Club, the two pilots, and two others died in the crash, which was the first involving a United States sports team. It left five women widows and nine children without fathers. Tollner stated that "Pretty much the players that did not make it were in front of me. That was where all the fire and stuff was."

Surviving such a traumatic event had to have left mental and emotional scars. To his credit, Tollner never made an issue of the accident, and his participation is largely unknown. But it must have registered in his mind every time an aircraft, loaded with a team that he has coached, lifted off the runway.

Head Coach Hughes survived the crash but retired the following year.

TITANIC ROSE BOWL BATTLES BETWEEN the TROJANS and OHIO STATE:

The most hard-fought battles ever witnessed in the Rose Bowl were those fought between the very physical USC and Ohio State football teams, especially those coached by Woody Hayes. Ohio State's first Rose Bowl was a 1921 28-0 drubbing by California, one of the strongest teams in the country in those early days. A matchup between Ohio State and Southern California had to wait until 1955. Just as with Michigan, the Ohio State Buckeyes started strong against the Trojans.

As evidence of how evenly matched were the Ohio State and USC teams, the last three Trojan Rose Bowl victories against the Buckeyes were decided by a total of only five points. It was a measure of the respect between the two teams. Ohio State has been a very worthy adversary.

HISTORY of MICHIGAN vs USC in the ROSE BOWL:

Michigan has a rich history in the Rose Bowl. The first game ever played was in 1902 and Michigan crushed Stanford 49-0. It did not play again in the Rose until 1948, when it again crushed

The 2004 Rose Bowl could have been called the Colorful Bowl. USC beat Michigan 28-14.

espn photo

a Pacific Coast team, USC, by an identical score of 49-0. It marked a low point for USC and a high point for Michigan in the Bowl. It was also the second in a string of humiliating defeats of the Pacific Coast Conference by the Big Ten. From an Illinois defeat of UCLA 45-14 in the 1947 Rose Bowl, until a final Iowa defeat of California in the 1959 Rose Bowl, the PCC only won one time, that being a 1953 face-saving 7-0 defeat of Wisconsin by USC.

While Michigan still had success in the Rose Bowl against other Pacific teams, after that 1948 domination of the Trojans, it has been a different story:

YEAR	ROSE BOWL FINAL SCORE	
1948	Michigan 49	**USC** 0
1970	**USC** 10	Michigan 3
1977	**USC** 17	Michigan 6
1979	**USC** 17	Michigan 10
1989	Michigan 22	**USC** 14
1990	**USC** 17	Michigan 10
2004	**USC** 28	Michigan 14
2007	**USC** 32	Michigan 18

The irony of any evaluation of USC against Big Ten teams is that, starting in 2024, USC will be conference-mates with Michigan, Ohio State, and the rest of the Big Ten, and it may be USC or UCLA playing Pacific teams in the Rose Bowl.

After a period of years, when Pacific teams played against the rest of the country, even though the teams playing will be those who do not make the playoffs, having USC and UCLA playing against the Pac-12 in the Rose Bowl will be very hard for fans in Los Angeles to digest. For many it will seem surreal.

The Rose Bowl will only appear relevant when it hosts playoff teams. When it is not scheduled to host in the playoffs, its options to pick top teams will be limited to those rated 13th in the nation or lower. With the inclusion of the Rose Bowl as one of the venues in a twelve-team playoff, it is questionable if the Rose Bowl will ever play a game independent of the national playoffs. As has recently happened, it may not even host West Coast teams. And if it does host West Coast teams, the likelihood of those teams being UCLA and USC from an "enemy" conference coming home to the Rose Bowl is real.

HISTORY of the ROSE BOWL STADIUM:

The Rose Bowl might have been the first bowl game ever scheduled, but the honor of naming a game facility as a bowl belongs to Yale University. The Rose Bowl, which belongs to the City of Pasadena, was designed, and named after the Yale Bowl. Both Yale, Princeton, and Harvard of the Ivy League traded mythical football national championships for quite a few years in the 1800s when football was just a club sport and was played by very few colleges. The three universities set the early precedent and were emulated by other, emerging schools.

The stadium, located ten miles to the north of downtown Los Angeles, has a modern, fully-seated, capacity reported by the Tournament of 92,532, while tenant UCLA reports a capacity of 91,136. The 2006 Rose Bowl reported a crowd of 93,986, while the 2011 Rose Bowl reported 94,118.

Construction was undergoing at the same time as that of the Los Angeles Memorial Coliseum and was completed in October 1922 in time for its first Rose Bowl game in January 1923 that pitted USC against Penn State.

That first Rose Bowl game in 1923 was not the first game played in the stadium. That was an October, 1922 contest between California and Southern California. Cal beat USC 12-0. It was the only blemish on the Trojan season in 1922 and allowed Cal an undefeated season. The surprising honor of USC being the first Rose Bowl host team only occurred due to Cal declining the Rose Bowl invitation.

The Rose Bowl is the "16th largest stadium in the world, the 11th largest stadium in the United States, and the 10th largest NCAA stadium. It still is the largest stadium for post-season bowl games in this country. It is "one of the most famous venues in sporting history." It was designated a U.S. National Historic Landmark in 1987.

The institution known as the Rose Bowl was initially housed in Tournament Park, which is adjacent to the Pasadena campus of the California Institute of Technology, more popularly known as Cal Tech. The Tournament Park stadium only seated 40,000 and by 1921 it became obvious that

View of a filled Rose Bowl Stadium (showing a soccer playing surface), home for UCLA football as well as the traditional Rose Bowl Games in January. *patch.com*

a larger stadium was needed for the burgeoning crowds of fans.

Seating has varied at the Bowl. Its record attendance was 106,869 for the 1973 Rose Bowl when top-ranked USC beat Ohio State. "For many years, the Rose Bowl had the largest stadium capacity in the United States until surpassed by the enormous Michigan Stadium at 107,601." Initially, seating was on wooden benches which later changed to concrete. Then it improved to aluminum benches. Even later, actual seats with backing were included. With the addition of seats, maximum capacity was lessened.

UCLA, a Rose Bowl tenant since 1982, is not the only team that has called the Bowl home: Caltech Beavers (NCAA) from 1923-1976. They claim to have played before more empty seats than any other football team. Loyola Lions (NCAA) 1951; Cal State University of Los Angeles Diablos 1957-1960 and 1963-1969; Los Angeles Wolves (NASL) 1968; Pasadena Bowl 1946-1966 and 1969-1971; Los Angeles Aztecs (NASL) 1978-1970; and Los Angeles Galaxy (MLS) 1996- 2002.

In addition to hosting UCLA and USC football, the Rose Bowl Stadium has hosted five Super Bowls, third most of any venue. As a noted soccer stadium, it has also hosted the 1994 FIFA World Cup Final and the 1999 FIFA Women's World Cup Final. During the Los Angeles 1984 Olympic

Left: Original horseshoe construction. **Right:** Aerial view of empty stadium from the south in 2018. *Wikipedia photos*

Games, the Rose Bowl was the site of the Olympic Soccer Gold Medal Match. Professional soccer now has a home at the new soccer stadium that is in Exposition Park, adjacent to the Coliseum.

An event that most have forgotten in SoCal, was the Junior Rose Bowl. "The stadium hosted the Junior Rose Bowl from 1946 to 1971 and 1976 to 1977." It was a very popular event that pitted the California Junior College football champions against the NJCAA (National Junior College Athletic Association) national champions. Still hosting the game for the best junior colleges, it was billed as the Pasadena Bowl from 1967 to 1971. Many remember the great battles between the juggernauts from California, often from Bakersfield or Compton, battling against the national JC champions who were often junior college teams from Texas. Texas teams such as West Texas State, Henderson County JC, Texas, Tyler JC, Texas, Arlington JC, Texas, and Kilgore College, Texas with its famous Kilgore Rangerettes.

It is a shame that the Junior Rose Bowl is history. Players deserve recognition such as that provided for the teams that play in the annual Rose Bowls. Junior College players also deserve that recognition. It is part of their rewards for their dedication and success.

It remains to be seen how the current major changes for football players will affect the game. NIL (name, image, and likeness) will change the game. Is it just a prelude to the direct payment of college players? Is seems so.

While change is in the wind, some institutions remain the same. USC and UCLA will still be the same, whether in the Pac-12 or the Big Ten. USC will still play its home games in the Coliseum. They will still reside on their respective campuses. UCLA will still call the Rose Bowl its home stadium. Over the hundred years that it has been a part of Greater Los Angeles, the Rose Bowl has become an institution, "our" institution, and a beloved part of our football world.

USC in OTHER BOWLS:

Bowls other than the major six January 1st bowls began to appear during the broken reign of McKay-Robinson (shown in red). Broken by Robinson's stint as Ram Coach. McKay's record was 1-0, compared to his 5-3 Rose Bowl record. John Robinson's record was 3-1, added to his unblemished 4-0 Rose Bowl record makes him the best bowl coach in Trojan history.

The Tollner and Smith-led bowl games were part of the lean years, as was Hackett's. Pete Carroll (shown in green) had a 3-1 record, only blemished by the Las Vegas defeat by 4 points that was at the start of his remarkable, yet too short, Trojan career.

BOWL	YEAR	COACH	SCORE (WINNER IN BOLD)	
Christmas Festival	1924	Gus Henderson	**USC 14**	Penn State 3
Liberty Bowl	1975	John McKay	**USC 20**	Texas A&M 0
Bluebonnet Bowl	1977	John Robinson	**USC 47**	Texas A&M 28
Fiesta Bowl	1982	John Robinson	USC 10	**Penn State 26**
Aloha Bowl	1985	Ted Tollner	USC 3	**Alabama 24**
Florida Citrus	1987	Ted Tollner	USC 7	**Auburn 16**
Sun Bowl	1990	Larry Smith	USC 16	**Michigan State 17**
Freedom Bowl	1992	Larry Smith	USC 7	**Fresno State 24**
Freedom Bowl	1993	John Robinson	**USC 28**	Utah 21
Cotton Bowl	1995	John Robinson	**USC 55**	Texas Tech 14
Sun Bowl	1998	Paul Hackett	USC 19	**TCU 28**
Las Vegas Bowl	2001	Pete Carroll	USC 6	Utah 10
Orange Bowl	2003	Pete Carroll	USC 38	Iowa 17
Orange Bowl	2005	Pete Carroll	USC 55	Oklahoma 19
Emerald Bowl	2009	Pete Carroll	USC 24	Boston College 13
Sun Bowl	2012	Lane Kiffin	USC 7	**Georgia Tech 21**
Las Vegas Bowl	2013	Clay Helton	**USC 45**	Fresno State 20
Holiday Bowl	2014	Steve Sarkisian	**USC 45**	Nebraska 42
Holiday Bowl	2015	Clay Helton	USC 21	**Wisconsin 23**
Cotton Bowl	2017	Clay Helton	USC 7	**Ohio State 24**
Holiday Bowl	2019	Clay Helton	USC 24	**Iowa 49**

The Trojan record in bowls other than the Rose is not stellar. It seemed a harder task to inspire players when not in the Rose at the end of the year. Part of the reason for the losing record is that the explosion of bowl games occurred during the "forgotten years" of mediocre coaching. Mediocre should also be measured by the effect of the unfair NCAA sanctions.

COACH RILEY'S REGULAR SEASON & BOWL RECORDS at OKLAHOMA and USC:

Lincoln Riley's trip to the bowls as a Trojan started out with a sputter. His last quarter collapse against Tulane in the Cotton Bowl was a heartbreaker. However, to turn a team around to an 11-3 season after going 4-8 the year before is extraordinary. Especially with two of the losses by only one point. It is hardly fair to judge a coach during his first year when he is coaching players recruited by others. Having said that, his regular seasons at both Oklahoma and Southern California have been extraordinary. His bowl record, less so.

Lincoln Riley has shown brilliance as a recruiter, has mastered the NCAA Transfer Portal, and has positively changed the Trojan culture. He has drastically changed personnel and reenergized the team and fan base.

It remains to be seen if his defense can meet the challenge of matching his unstoppable offense. It remains to be seen if Riley can emulate the great Trojan coaches of the past who have been so dominant. Time will tell, but the Trojan future does seem to hold great promise.

2017 Oklahoma Rose Bowl Big-12 Conference Champions	12-2 2018	Lincoln Riley	Oklahoma 48	**Georgia 54**
2018 Oklahoma Orange Bowl Big-12 Conference Champions Big-12 Coach of the Year	12-2 2019	Lincoln Riley	Oklahoma 34	**Alabama 45**
2019 Oklahoma Peach Bowl Big-12 Conference Champions	12-2 2020	Lincoln Riley	Oklahoma 28	**LSU 63**
2020 Oklahoma Cotton Bowl Big-12 Conference Champions	9-2 2021	Lincoln Riley	**Oklahoma 55**	Florida 20
2021 Oklahoma Alamo Bowl	10-2 2021	Lincoln Riley Bob Stoops	**Oklahoma 47**	Oregon 32
2022 USC Cotton Bowl	11-3 2023	Lincoln Riley	USC 45	**Tulane 46**
Riley's Regular Season Record: 66-13 Riley's Bowl Game Record: 1-4				

Chapter Seven

National Championships
in Football

USC has won eleven national championships in NCAA football. But have they? Up until recently, national championships have been mythical and certainly subjective. With first the BCS System and later the College Football Playoff (CFP) System, the national championship is not mythical, it is actual. It is not subjective but objective. Conference championships are also objective. With divisional playoffs, there is no doubt who is champion. Since football does not allow ties anymore, each participant in the conference championships got there on its won-loss record. The title game has a winner and a loser. The winner wins the conference title. Pretty simple.

Without a national playoff, how can a true national champ be selected? With a playoff, how can it be totally fair when the participants are chosen by polls or by committee? Polls should not be biased or political, but they are. Polls and committees are based on human preference. Decisions are not made based on records or quality of opposition but on the subjective analysis of individuals.

Heritage Hall, dedicated to the sports accomplishments and heritage of USC
wikipedia photo

Regional bias does exist. It has been apparent to many generations of Westerners, that many of those in the East hold a bias against the West. The time factor is also relevant. Television plays a huge role in selection. But who is in control of television? Not the NCAA.

Unless it is contractually provided for, those making the decisions on who gets televised and when they get televised are those working for the various television stations and their focus is on revenue. The determination on which teams will be televised locally and which nationally, what time they play, or if they are televised at all, are all decided by the television networks and that has a significant impact on the polling. Most of the headquarters for the various television networks are in New York and it is those living in the Eastern Time Zone who are making the decisions.

Notre Dame has a natural bias in its favor. Because it has a national following of mostly Catholics, NBC televises every Notre Dame game nationally. That gives Notre Dame an enormous advantage when it comes to national recruiting.

Often those who are tasked to vote in the various football polls and who live in the East are in bed by the time West Coast teams play. That is no way to evaluate. Money and the time of day should not be the defining factors, but they often are.

That is not to say that those associated with college football do not want change. Almost all seemingly do. But every time a system is put into place to try to fairly determine a national championship, they find flaws in the system inviting further changes. Perhaps the proposed 12-team national playoffs are approaching fairness? At least one of the chosen twelve must be deserving of being called the best. But there will be objections from those teams in conferences other than Division 1. With a 12-team playoff, at-large selections that can include other conference teams will be a part. But the selection of who is included in the twelve teams is decided, not on the playing field, but in committee.

Current Division 1, Power Five Conferences include: the Big 10, the Big 12, the Atlantic Coast Conference (ACC), the Southeast Conference (SEC), and the Pac-12.

Located outside Heritage Hall, this statuary was named by legendary Trojan assistant coach Marv Goux for the great 1969 defensive line.
insidesocal.com

It has been a long-term objective of the NCAA and most college and university football programs to create a true competition leading up to a national championship. There have been several unsatisfactory attempts and those will be shown later in this chapter.

Let us start at the beginning and see how national championships have been selected over the years. Howard Jones started off the string of Trojan national championships in 1928 and USC was also named in 1931, 1932, and 1939 under Jone's leadership. How were these teams selected?

A Sip of Sports (www.asipofsports.com) has written an article that explains the situation very well. It is titled The History of the College Football National Championship. Direct quotes from their articles will be included in blue (below).

Prior to 1998, there were six organizations that had widely recognized authority to name a legitimate "National Champion." The six organizations are as follows:

Associated Press (AP): The AP began releasing a weekly college football poll in 1936. The end-of-season polling was taken before the bowl games. Initially, in 1936 there were only four bowl games with which they had to contend. Using the AP poll was somewhat unfair in that it did not take into consideration the bowl games. Starting in 1967, the AP permanently changed (the polling) to after the bowl games. The AP was involved in the naming of a national championship in 1939, when USC was selected. However, did the AP select USC?

Prior to the AP, the only organizations from among the six that selected national champs, were the Helms Athletic Foundation (HAF) and the National Championship Foundation (NCF). The Helms Foundation (HAF) was founded by Paul Helms and Bill Schroeder in 1936, the same year as the AP poll was initiated and the number of bowls was expanded past just the Rose. Schroeder, a very knowledgeable football analyst, personally selected the National Champion in football from 1948-1982. He later retroactively named National Champions from 1947 back to 1883. These were well-researched selections. Mike Riter of the second organization, the National Championship Foundation (NCF), retroactively selected National Champions from 1869 to 2000. Thus, it was the highly regarded Schroeder of Helms and Mike Riter of NCF who selected USC as champions in 1928, 1931, and 1932. Or did they?

In 1936, when the Associated Press (AP) entered the picture, it became the most influential over the following years.

The fourth of the six recognized major selecting organizations was the National Football Foundation (NFF): Founded in 1947 by General Douglas MacArthur, of World War II fame, the highly regarded sports reporter Grantland Rice, and the highly regarded Coach of Army, Earl Blaik. The Foundation runs the College Football Hall of Fame in Atlanta. The current Chairman is Archie Manning.

The 5th is the Football Writers Association of America (FWAA): Founded in 1941, it consists of men and women across North America who cover college football for a living.

The 6th and final organization started as United Press International (UPI) or as earlier : designated, UP. UPI used a cross-section of coaches throughout the country and became known as the Coaches Poll. They released a college football poll weekly from 1950-1995. UPIs poll was taken at the end of the regular season until the 1973 season when it reverted to when the final poll was taken after the bowl games. In 1996, the *U.S.A. Today* Poll was created out of the Coaches Poll.

Prior to the AP Poll in 1936, there was no recognized (at the time) process to declare any school a "National Champion." The "National Champions" listed in the record books were retroactively selected by the Helms Athletic Foundation (HAF).

The article went on to say: Let us take 1930 as an example (of championship selection): Two schools have declared that they won the "National Championship," Alabama and Notre Dame. At that time, Notre Dame did not participate in bowl games so after their 27-0 rout of USC in their final game in Los Angeles, they stood at 10-0, thus claiming the "National Championship."

The only problem was that two other schools also finished the regular season unbeaten, Alabama (9-0) and Washington State (9-0), and they so happened to meet in the Rose Bowl. Alabama won easily, 24-0. When you look at the record books of both Notre Dame and Alabama, they both claim 1930 as one of their "National Championships." Both the Helms Foundation (HAF) and the National Championship Foundation (NCF) have retroactively declared Notre Dame the "National Champion." How legitimate is that?

Let us now look at 1926; Stanford (10-0) and Alabama (9-0) both finished the regular season undefeated. They met in the Rose Bowl on January 1, 1927, and played to a 7-7 tie. Both the Helms Foundation and the National Championship Foundation (NCP) have gone back and declared them Co-National Champions. Two "National Champions," how does that work? Both schools now show 1926 as a "National Championship" year. Again, two "National Champions?"

How about 1922? Cal ended the season 9-0, while Cornel and Princeton finished 8-0. The National Championship Foundation has named both Cal and Princeton "National Champions," while the Helms Athletic Foundation went with Cornell. Three National Champions?

The situation improved greatly in 1936 when the Associated Press (AP) came out with its first college football poll. From 1936 through 1949, the winner of the final AP Poll was the National Champion. However, they still had problems.

In 1946 Notre Dame, with a record of 8-0-1, was voted #1 in the final AP Poll, and if you look at the record, 1946 is one of Notre Dame's undisputed "National Championships". Here is the rub: Notre Dame's one blemish was a 0-0 tie against Army. Going into the November contest, Army was ranked #1 and Notre Dame #2. Notre Dame would remain #2 until the last game of the season when the Irish easily defeated USC 26-6 and Army struggled in a 21-18 win over Navy. This allowed Notre Dame to jump Army and vault to #1. Army finished the year 9-0-1, while Notre Dame was 8-0-1. Notre Dame was the undisputed "National Champion"?

Let us also look at Notre Dame's 1947 "National Championship". The Irish finished the regular season 9-0. At that time, Notre Dame did not accept bowl invitations, so that would be their final record. Michigan, their record was 10-0, culminating in a 49-0 thrashing of USC in the Rose Bowl. Yet the Irish won the National Championship. Why not Michigan? Well, the last AP Poll was conducted prior to the bowl games, so Michigan's impressive win over the Trojans had no impact.

Just about every year there is a similar situation showing that most of the time the "National Champion" was decided by consensus opinions. This problem still exists today.

The Coaches Poll (UPI) began in 1950 and lasted until 1995, *USA Today* then took over the

Coaches Poll, but like the AP, their final poll came out before the bowl games. In the first year of the Coaches Poll, Oklahoma cruised through the regular season with a 10-0 record, ranked #1 in both the AP and UPI final polls. A National Championship for the Sooners? Well, maybe not; Kentucky beat Oklahoma in the Sugar Bowl. This was not the only time a team finishing #1 in the final polls lost their bowl game: Tennessee in 1951, Maryland in 1953, and Minnesota in 1960. At the time, the AP and UPI polls were the most important of the polls and often decided the championship. It has never made sense to the author that they both did not wait until after the bowls to select.

In the mid-1960s, the AP changed to conducting their final poll after the bowl games. So, when #1 ranked (in both polls) Michigan State lost the Rose Bowl following the 1965 season, the AP replaced the Spartans with Orange Bowl winner Alabama, but Michigan State still won the UPI "National Championship." Teams should be rated on how they end a season. When Pete Carroll's Trojan team of 2002 (11-2) ended the season so strong, despite losing two games, some voted the Trojans national champions. It was prescient, as USC then went on to score 34 straight wins and won the Championship in 2003, 2004, and came so close to winning in 2005 when they lost to Texas in the last seconds of the national championship game played in the Rose Bowl.

The year that convinced the coaches to conduct a poll after the Bowls was 1973. Alabama finished the regular season ranked #1 in both polls but lost to #5 ranked Notre Dame in the Sugar Bowl. AP moved Notre Dame all the way to #1, but even after the loss Alabama still claimed the UPI "National Championship". Alabama still claims it as a championship.

Before 1965, the two polls did not always agree on the best team. In 1954, Ohio State won the AP poll, and UCLA the UPI. In 1957, Ohio State again shared the title, this time with Auburn. (Today), all four schools claim that they are "National Champions."

Heritage Hall contains the seven Heisman Trophies earned by Trojan footballers. Someday soon, the Reggie Bush trophy will rightfully be restored to this Hall of Champions commemorating the most Heisman trophies won by any university. *thetomagency.com*

View of the impressive display of Heritage Hall Heisman Trophies. *USC photo*

In back-to-back years in 1990 and 1991, the organizations selecting the "National Champion" had different winners. In 1990, 11-1-1 Colorado was selected by AP, FWAA, and NFF as the champion, but UPI chose the Georgia Tech Yellow Jackets. Then in 1991, both Washington and Miami finished the regular season 11-0, then crushed worthy opponents in their bowl games to go 12-0. Who is #1? The Huskies were honored by the UPI, FWAA and NFF, while Miami secured the top spot from AP. Again, two "National Champions."

Due to the chaos that 1990 and 1991 created, the conferences and the bowls worked out a system in 1992, where the two highest-rated teams at the end of the season would meet in one of the major bowls. **That was called the Bowl Coalition.** The only problem was that the Big 10, the Pac-10, and the Rose Bowl declined to participate. That allowed another split "National Championship."

In 1997, Michigan (11-0) was ranked #1 in both polls, but due to the Rose Bowl policy of selecting teams from the Pacific schools to play the Big 10, they were forced to play #8 ranked Washington State (10-1) in the Rose Bowl. The Orange Bowl then took the two highest-ranked teams available: Nebraska (12-0) and Tennessee (11-1). Nebraska routed Tennessee (42-17), while Michigan won a tight game with WSU (21-16). Nebraska replaced Michigan as #1 in the final Coaches Poll, while Michigan remained as #1 in the AP. **Again, two schools claiming to be champion.**

In 1998, the Big Ten, Pac-12, and Rose Bowl decided to join and the BCS was then inaugurated. The #1 and #2 teams would then meet in a "Championship Game" in an end-of-season bowl that would be rotated between the Rose Bowl, the Sugar Bowl, the Orange Bowl, and the Fiesta Bowl. The problem was, how do you determine who the best two teams are?

Computers are only as good as the data placed in them. The BCS at first used a complicated computer formula. The result was more confusion. That confusion is best represented by what happened in 2000 and 2001. Oklahoma was undefeated (11-0) and ranked #1 following the 2000 regular season. But who was #2? Five teams had only one loss (Miami, Washington, Florida State, Oregon State, and Virginia Tech) and by coincidence, all five teams had played at least one game against the other four. Miami beat Florida State and Virginia Tech but lost to Washington. Washington had also beaten Oregon State, so the Huskies were 2-0 while the Canes were 2-1. All the other one-loss teams were 0-1 against the others.

Logic tells you that either Miami or Washington should be ranked #2 and face Oklahoma, but no, the computers said that Florida State was the 2nd best team, and they went to the Orange Bowl, where they lost to the Sooners. Of course, just to complicate things further, both Miami and Washington soundly beat their opponents in the Sugar and Rose Bowls respectively.

The year 2001 would be even more strange. Miami finished the regular season undefeated and ranked #1. The Oregon Ducks won the PAC-12 and were ranked #2 in both polls, but the computer said that Nebraska was #2, even though they had just been crushed by the Colorado Buffaloes (62-36) in their last regular season. That allowed Nebraska to play for the "National Championship" even though they did not even win the North Division of the Big-12. Fortunately for the BCS, Miami easily beat Nebraska 38-14. What about Oregon? They beat 3rd ranked Colorado in the Fiesta Bowl, 38-10.

Two years later, 2003, was another fiasco. USC finished the regular season 11-1 and ranked #1 in both the AP Poll and the Coaches Poll. Again the computers did not agree. They rated Oklahoma (which lost the Big-12 Championship Game to Kansas State, 35-7) and LSU ahead of the Trojans. The Trojans beat #4 Michigan (28-14) in the Rose Bowl, but when LSU beat Oklahoma in the Sugar Bowl (21-14), the Coaches Poll *(USA Today)*, which was contractually obligated to rank the winner of the BCS Championship Game #1, moved LSU from #3 to #1, ahead of USC. **That was not only unfair, but it just does not make any sense.**

What the BCS avoided with Nebraska's loss to Miami in 2001 came back to bite them in 2011. Alabama, which lost to LSU during the regular season, did not win the West Division of the SEC (LSU did). Somehow, this 11-1 non-conference champion was chosen to participate over the Big-12 Champion Oklahoma State Cowboys (also 11-1) in the BCS Title Game, and when they beat LSU in the rematch, they became "National Champions" when they were not even SEC Champions. How does that work?

The College Football Playoffs (CFP) took over from the BCS in 2014, which now involved a 4-team playoff. A committee of 13 ranks the schools. The teams rated 1,2,3, and 4 are seeded accordingly and invited to participate in the College Football Playoff. One plays 4, and 2 plays 3. The winners meet for the Championship. Immediately in 2014 controversy reigned, when five teams with one loss were battling for three playoff spots. Two of those teams were from the Big 12 who ended up in a tie for the Big 12 Title (TCU and Baylor). Again, the two Big 12 teams were left out.

When college football became such a popular sport, big money started flowing into Athletic Departments and the motivation of schools seemingly changed. For organizations like the NFL, the NBA, and MLB, it was always a money game. For the NCAA, it became a huge money game. As Jerry McGuire pointed out in his movie, "Follow the money." If something does not make sense in

Rear view of Heritage Hall. *flickr.com photo*

sports, "follow the money."

In 2017, there was only one undefeated team in Division 1 football, the University of Central Florida (12-0), but the powers that be chose not to include them. Instead, they included a team that did not even win their division in their conference. Again, it was Alabama (do we see a pattern here). Of course, Alabama would go on to win the "National Championship." How can you be National Champ if you are not even Conference Champ? **Remember, if it does not make sense, follow the money.**

The examples listed are just examples. Every year, since college football polling began, somebody felt slighted. A final thought: In 1984, BYU finished the season 13-0 and won every major organization selecting the National Champions (AP, UPI, FWAA, and NFF). Brigham Young's strength of schedule was 82nd out of 110 Division 1 football teams. They closed the season with a 24-17 win over a 6-6 Michigan team in the Holiday Bowl. They beat every team on their schedule and one can make a good case that they were the best team in the country, **but they had a weaker schedule than almost every team vying for the mythical championship. That is just not right or is it fair.**

A factor that does not make sense to the author is that all too many of those decision-makers seem to value undefeated seasons. While important, they should not allow an undefeated team with a weak strength of schedule to be placed above a team with a much stronger strength-of-schedule with perhaps a single or even two losses. It is much easier for coaches to prepare a team for only a few strong teams on a schedule than to have to prepare for a full schedule of strong teams.

HOW THE PLAYOFFS WORK:

From 1869 through 1991, the National Champion was decided by national polls, with the earlier years decided retroactively. From 1992 through 1994, it was controlled by the Bowl Coalition. When that did not work, the Bowl Alliance took control from 1995 through 1997. When that did not work, the Bowl Championship Series (BCS) ruled from 1998 through 2013. Now, we have the College Football Playoff (CFP), which has been in control from 2014 until the present.

Four teams vie for the National Championship. While it is decided on the gridiron, the four teams are selected by committee. The selected teams must come from one of the "so-called" power five conferences consisting of: the Southeastern Conference (SEC), the Atlantic Coast Conference (ACC), the Big-10 Conference, the Big-12 Conference, and the Pacific PAC-12 Conference. Is it fair to exclude teams not belonging to those conferences?

All independents are also excluded, except for Notre Dame. The ranks of independents are dwindling. For football, the following teams are independent: Army, BYU, Liberty, New Mexico State, Notre Dame, UConn, and UMass. Air Force and Navy are committed to conferences and BYU has committed to a future conference relationship.

Currently, the CFP selects four teams for the national playoffs. They are selected by a 13-member committee consisting of Athletic Directors of all the Power Five Conferences, former head coaches, faculty members, school superintendents, NCAA executives, former players, former politicians, military personnel, conference commissioners, and former reporters. The . . . . members decide which teams go to the CFP and the New Year's Six bowl games.

Committee members have three-year terms and replacements are selected by the committee itself. They rank the best teams 1-4, with 1 playing 4 and 2 playing 3 in the semi-final games.

The CFP has decided to go to a 12-team playoff, with the first games on December 20 and 21 of the 2024 playoff season. The twelve selectees will be determined by the committee as it currently does for the final four.

By now, the reader must be either exhausted or confused, perhaps both. The situation is in obvious chaos and filled with a history of absurdities. But the process is finally, seemingly getting it right. If the criterion for selecting teams includes at-large berths that allow promising teams and those from non-Power Five Conferences to be included, then the playoffs will finally be as fair as the committee allows.

It remains to be seen how team schedules will work out and scheduling will rule out any further increase in playoff teams. What should be considered the maximum total schedule for student-athletes to play? With a usual nine-game conference schedule and a possible four-game playoff schedule, how many non-conference games will be allowed? Traditional rivalries across conference lines need to be considered. And what happens to the "other" bowls? Will all the playoff games be given to the bowls? How will that work? If the bowls, other than the New Year's Six, are not included, what happens to them?

Stay tuned.

TROJAN CLAIMS for NATIONAL CHAMPIONSHIPS:

Author's Note: *This section is not meant to criticize USC for claims regarding what has been considered football National Championships at USC. There is legitimacy for all the Trojan claims and the university is not about to make changes.*

What the author is attempting to do is describe the convoluted process of selection that has been changing throughout the century that USC has been in the National Championship picture. The author is also trying to portray what has been happening in the process and how the championships have been determined.

Throughout the history of the championships, there has been dissatisfaction in the fairness of the outcomes based on the selection criterion in-place at the time. The coming 12-team playoffs should dispel most of those criticisms. Twelve teams, however they are selected, should include the best team and that will be determined by play on the field and not by evaluation off the field.

USC NATIONAL CHAMPIONSHIPS (11) (highlighted in yellow) & SEASONS with TEN VICTORIES or MORE (29):

Ten-win seasons have often been a hallmark of coaching success. Over the years, the tendency has been for a slow increase in the total number of games played in a season, which makes achieving a ten-win season easier. Still, the accomplishment of Pete Carroll (below) is singular.

Jones and McKay each had 16-year careers at USC and each had only five 10-win seasons, while Carroll only had nine total seasons, with a last year (2009) nearly reaching the goal with a nine-win season. To win 11 games or more for seven consecutive seasons is a fete worthy of mention and acclaim. During those remarkable seven years, Carroll went 82-9 (.901).

YEAR	COACH		RECORD
1921	Gus Henderson	(2)	10-1
1922	Gus Henderson		10-1
1925	Howard Jones	(5)	11-2
1928	Howard Jones		9-0-1
1929	Howard Jones		10-2
1931	Howard Jones		10-1
1932	Howard Jones		10-0
1933	Howard Jones		10-1-1
1939	Howard Jones		8-0-2
1952	Jess Hill	(1)	10-1
1962	John McKay	(5)	11-0
1967	John McKay		10-1
1969	John McKay		10-0-1
1972	John McKay		12-0
1974	John McKay		10-1-1
1976	John Robinson	(3)	11-1
1978	John Robinson		12-1
1979	John Robinson		11-0-1

YEAR	COACH		RECORD
1988	Larry Smith	(1)	10-2
2002	Pete Carroll	(7)	11-2
2003	Pete Carroll		12-1
2004	Pete Carroll		13-0
2005	Pete Carroll		12-1
2006	Pete Carroll		11-2
2007	Pete Carroll		11-2
2008	Pete Carroll		12-1
2011	Lane Kiffin	(1)	10-2
2013	Lane Kiffin		3-2
	Ed Orgeron		6-2
	Clay Helton		1-0
	Total Season:		10-4
2016	Clay Helton	(2)	10-3
2017	Clay Helton		11-3
2022	Lincoln Riley	(1)	11-3

SIMILARITIES BETWEEN the USC CAREERS of NATIONAL CHAMPIONSHIP WINNING TROJAN COACHES HOWARD JONES and JOHN McKAY:

Howard Jones went 121-36-13 (.750) at SC. John McKay compiled a record of 127-40-8 (.749). Each coached the Trojans for 16 years and won four national titles. Each had five ten-win seasons. McKay won nine conference titles, while Jones won seven. Jones' teams played in five Rose Bowls and won all five, while McKay also won five Rose Bowls.

	HOWARD JONES	JOHN McKAY
Years Coached USC	16 (1925- 1940)	16 (1960- 1975)
Record	121-36-13	127-40-8
Percentage Victories	.750	.749
National Titles	4	4
Conference Titles	7	9
Rose Bowl Victories	5	5
Ten-Win Victories	5	5

HISTORY'S GREATEST TEAM — THE NATIONAL CHAMPION 1972 TROJANS:

John McKay coached what some consider the greatest team in college football history in 1972. They won each game by an incredible margin of victory of 27.75 points. They played six nationally ranked teams with three being in the top ten. They beat all six by an equally impressive margin of victory of 20.2 points.

They played much of each game with their reserves, led by sophomore quarterback Pat Haden, and their reserves scored at a clip almost as fast as the starters. The author was in the stands for many of those victories and can attest first-hand to the greatness of that team.

USC / SCORE		NATIONAL RANKING AT GAMETIME	OPPONENT / SCORE		MARGIN OF VICTORY
USC	31	#4	Arkansas	10	+21
USC	51		Oregon State	6	+45
USC	55		Illinois	20	+35
USC	51		Michigan State	6	+45
USC	30	#15	Stanford	21	+9
USC	42		California	14	+28
USC	34	#18	Washington	7	+27
USC	18		Oregon	0	+18
USC	44		Washington State	3	+41
USC	24	#14	UCLA	7	+17
USC	45	#10	Notre Dame	23	+22
USC	42	#3	Ohio State	17	(Rose Bowl) +25

BREAKDOWN of NATIONAL CHAMPIONSHIP DATA (full listing of national champions is included in the Support Section at the end of the book):

The full national championship figures can be hard to digest. There were 41 teams that were either undisputed national champs or co-champs from 1888-2022. Twelve of those 41 were single-season victors:

The 1st tier: Chicago, Syracuse, TCU, Texas A&M, Maryland, Colorado, BYU, and Washington. Others were single co-champs: Ole Miss, Arkansas, Stanford, and UCLA.

An additional 13 were in a **2nd tier**, gaining two or three championship seasons: Tennessee-2, Cornell-2, Georgia Tech-2, California-2, Illinois-2, Penn State-2, Florida State-3, Florida-3, Clemson-3, Georgia-3 (although two of them have been in the last two years), Army-3, Auburn with 2, 1 being as co-champ, and Michigan State-2 with one being as co-champ.

The **3rd tier** includes six of those with four or five championships: Penn-4, Pitt-4, Miami-4, LSU-4 with 1 being co-champ, Texas is also 4 with 1 being co-champ, Nebraska-5 with two being as co-champ.

The **4th tier** includes seven of those with six or seven championships: The Ivy League teams of the early years: Harvard-7, Yale-7, and Princeton-6. Later champions include Miami-6 with one being as co-champs, Michigan-6 with one being as co-champ, Ohio State-6 with two being as co-champ, Oklahoma-7 with one being as co-champ,

UNIVERSITY	OUTRIGHT TITLES	CO-TITLES	TOTAL TITLES
Yale	7		7
Harvard	7		7
Oklahoma	6	1	7
Princeton	6		6
Miami	5	1	6
Michigan	5	1	6
Ohio State	4	2	6

The **5th and final tier** includes the three greatest championship teams in the United States: Alabama, Notre Dame, and USC.

The author's apology to USC fans: There may be some legitimacy for claiming 11 national championships, but an honest evaluation of the data and criterion includes only nine.

There can be an issue with the 1928 season. The selectors, however fairly acting, evaluated retroactively and that could be a problem for those teams newly arrived at the championship level of play. Reputation and past performance have often influenced selectors. The selection of Alabama, when they did not even win their conference championship yet won the national title, is a strong example.

Other universities also have claimed more than are credited here. The second greatest national champion is Notre Dame, with 10 championships, all of which left no doubt without any co-championship. The all-time leader is, of course, Alabama. From its first national championship in an undefeated 1925 to another undefeated championship in 2020, Alabama can claim 14 national championships, four of which are as co-champions.

The listing of the top modern-day football championship schools is as follows:

UNIVERSITY	OUTRIGHT TITLES	CO-TITLES	TOTAL TITLES
Alabama	10	4	14
Notre Dame	10		10
USC	6	3	9
Oklahoma	6	1	7
Michigan	5	1	6
Miami	5	1	6
Ohio State	4	2	6

Another consideration is the second-place finishing in the selection of National Championships. If both first and second place finishing were listed, USC would have 18 such finishes. In the listing of championships between 1888 and today, **the Trojans have come in second in 1928, 1929, 1933, 1939, 1976, 1979, 2002, 2005, and 2007.** That is a listing where USC has a strong probability of being first.

Other universities have also claimed championships in years where they were clearly selected second. Notre Dame archives list 11 national championships, which is only one above what is listed above. However, the Alabama archives list 18 championship years in football, four more than they deserve.

A final consideration regards those years in which USC claimed to win a National Championship and was clearly, in the author's opinion, not the winner. Below is included those contested years and those selectors who chose the Trojans and those who selected others.

YEAR	TEAMS CONSIDERED	RECORD	IDENTIFYING LETTERS FOR SELECTORS WHO CHOSE
	Detroit	9-0	PD
1928	**Georgia Tech**	10-0	BR, BS, CFRA, **HAF**, HS, **NCF,** PD, PS, SR, B(QPRS)
	USC	9-0-1	DiS, SR

In 1928, Georgia Tech was chosen by ten selectors, including both majors: Helms (**HAF**) and **NCF**. USC received two selections, both by minor selectors. Georgia Tech was crowned champion by most fans and selectors, yet USC claims to be champions that year.

YEAR	TEAMS CONSIDERED	RECORD	IDENTIFYING LETTERS FOR SELECTORS WHO CHOSE
	Cornell	8-0	L, SR
1939	**Texas A&M**	11-0	AP, BR, BS, CFRA, DeS, DiS, HAF HS, NCF, PS, SR, WS, B(QPRS)
	USC	8-0-2	DiS

In 1939, Texas A&M received 11 selections, including all three major selectors, which that year included the Associated Press (**AP**) in addition to Helms and the National Championship Foundation. Texas A&M was recognized as the true champion. USC was only chosen by one minor selector.

In 2004, USC petitioned the UCAA to give recognition that the Trojans were National Champions in 1939. The petition, sponsored by Athletic Director Mike Garrett, was granted that year, which was 56 years after the season was completed.

The author is a lifetime USC fan and would have strongly desired that USC had earned 11 National Championships. With consideration of the data on the previous page, readers are asked to judge for themselves.

While the author is questioning the legitimacy of championships in 1928 and 1939, he does feel that the 1979 team deserves recognition as co-champions. A detailed discussion of the 1979 team is included later in this book.

In 1979, Alabama won the championship with a 12-0 record and the support of AP, FWAA, NFF, UPI, Helms, and NCF. Undefeated USC was voted second with a 11-0-1 record. Too much emphasis was placed by the selectors on a team's record and not enough on the quality of opponents.

As is often seen, Alabama and the SEC were both accorded preferential treatment by the selectors. For fairness, undefeated USC should be reconsidered as co-champions based on its harder schedule than Alabama and the incomparable talent gathered for the team, which might have qualified as the greatest talent of any team in the long, glorious history of the Trojans.

USC NCAA NATIONAL CHAMPIONSHIPS in ALL SPORTS (*Pac-12.com/champions*):

Men's football was added to the Pac-12 listing, as it has not been a recognized NCAA championship until recently.

YEAR	SPORT
2023	Women's Beach Volleyball
2022	Women's Beach Volleyball
2021	Women's Beach Volleyball, Women's Water Polo, Women's Outdoor Track & Field
2018	Men's Water Polo, Women's Water Polo, Women's Outdoor Track & Field
2017	Women's Beach Volleyball
2016	Women's Soccer, Women's Beach Volleyball, Women's Water Polo
2014	Men's Tennis
2013	Men's Water Polo, Women's Water Polo, Women's Golf
2012	Men's Water Polo, Men's Tennis
2011	Men's Water Polo, Men's Tennis
2010	Men's Water Polo, Men's Tennis, Women's Water Polo
2009	Men's Water Polo, Men's Tennis
2008	Men's Water Polo, Women's Golf
2007	Women's Soccer
2005	Men's Water Polo
2004	Women's Water Polo, Men's Football
2003	Men's Water Polo, Women's Volleyball, Women's Golf, Men's Football
2002	Women's Volleyball, Men's Tennis
2001	Women's Outdoor Track & Field
1998	Men's Water Polo, Men's Baseball
1997	Women's Swimming & Diving
1994	Men's Tennis
1991	Men's Tennis

YEAR	SPORT
1993	Men's Tennis
1990	Men's Volleyball
1988	Men's Volleyball
1985	Women's Tennis
1984	Women's Basketball
1983	Women's Basketball, Women's Tennis
1981	Women's Volleyball First Trojan women's championship. From 1981 forward, women have won 26 NCAA championships up through 2022. During the same time period, men have won 24 NCAA championships.
1980	Men's Volleyball
1978	Men's Football, Men's Baseball
1977	Men's Volleyball, Men's Swimming & Diving
1976	Men's Tennis, Men's Outdoor Track & Field, Men's Swimming & Diving
1975	Men's Swimming & Diving
1974	Men's Football, Men's Baseball, Men's Swimming & Diving
1973	Men's Baseball
1972	Men's Football, Men's Baseball, Men's Golf, Men's Indoor Track & Field
1971	Men's Baseball
1970	Men's Baseball
1969	Men's Tennis
1968	Men's Tennis, Men's Baseball, Men's Outdoor Track & Field
1967	Men's Football, Men's Tennis, Men's Outdoor Track & Field, Men's Indoor Track & Field
1966	Men's Tennis, Men's Swimming & Diving, Men's Outdoor Track & Field
1965	Men's Swimming & Diving
1964	Men's Swimming & Diving, Men's Tennis
1963	Men's Tennis, Men's Baseball, Men's Outdoor Track & Field, Men's Swimming & Diving
1962	Men's Football, Men's Tennis, Men's Gymnastics
1961	Men's Baseball, Men's Outdoor Track & Field
1960	Men's Swimming & Diving
1958	Men's Tennis, Men's Baseball, Men's Outdoor Track & Field.
1955	Men's Tennis, Men's Outdoor Track & Field
1954	Men's Outdoor Track & Field
1953	Men's Outdoor Track & Field

YEAR	SPORT
1952	Men's Outdoor Track & Field
1951	Men's Outdoor Track & Field, Men's Tennis
1949	Men's Outdoor Track & Field
1948	Men's Baseball
1946	Men's Tennis
1943	Men's Outdoor Track & Field
1942	Men's Outdoor Track & Field
1941	Men's Outdoor Track & Field
1940	Men's Outdoor Track & Field
1939	Men's Outdoor Track & Field, Men's Football
1938	Men's Outdoor Track & Field
1937	Men's Outdoor Track & Field
1936	Men's Outdoor Track & Field
1935	Men's Outdoor Track & Field
1932	Men's Football
1931	Men's Football, Men's Outdoor Track & Field
1930	Men's Outdoor Track & Field
1928	Men's Football
1926	Men's Outdoor Track & Field

Chapter Eight

Trojans and the Heisman

The Heisman Trophy is, by far, the most prestigious individual post-season trophy currently given in college football. It is not only a mark of individual success, but also for the receiving team and its coaches, both head coach and position coach. Four teams are at the top of the Heisman listing. USC is one of those four, with the others being the traditional powers Oklahoma, Ohio State, and Notre Dame, which all have garnered seven trophies. USC has been given eight, but one is not recognized by the NCAA.

Reggie Bush had his trophy rescinded for alleged violations of NCAA rules.

The penalties exacted on USC at the same time as Bush lost his Heisman, are included in the 2010 "University of Southern California Public Infractions Report." A more thorough discussion of that report in included in another chapter. There is a strong push to have the Bush trophy reinstated and the likelihood of that happening is good.

COLLEGES WITH THE MOST HEISMAN TROPHY WINNERS:

USC	8 (Includes disputed Reggie Bush trophy)
Ohio State, Oklahoma, Notre Dame	7
Alabama	4
Auburn, Army, Florida, Michigan, Nebraska, Florida State	3

GOLDEN ERAS of TROJAN PREDOMINANCE in the HEISMAN TROPHY VOTING

ERA of the TROJAN TAILBACKS (17 Years, 1965 to 1981):

YEAR	FIRST PLACE	SECOND PLACE	THIRD PLACE
1965	**Mike Garrett, USC Tailback**	Howard Twilley, Tulsa End	Jim Grabowski, Illinois Fullback
1967	Gary Beban, UCLA Quarterback	**O.J. Simpson, USC Tailback**	Leroy Keyes, Purdue Halfback
1968	**O.J. Simpson, USC Tailback**	Leroy Keyes, Purdue Halfback	Terry Hanratty, Notre Dame QB
1974	Archie Griffin, Ohio State Tailback	**Anthony Davis, USC Tailback**	Joe Washington, Oklahoma TB
1975	Archie Griffin, Ohio State Tailback	Chuck Muncie, California Tailback	**Ricky Bell, USC Tailback**
1976	Tony Dorsett, Pittsburgh Tailback	**Ricky Bell, USC Tailback**	Rob Lytle, Michigan Tailback
1979	**Charles White, USC Tailback**	Billy Sims, Oklahoma QB	Marc Wilson, BYU Quarterback
1981	**Marcus Allen, USC Tailback**	Herschel Walker, Georgia Tailback	Jim McMahon, BYU Quarterback

USC Heisman Tailbacks: 8 (two tailbacks are listed twice); **USC Heisman Quarterbacks: 0**

ERA of the TROJAN QUARTERBACKS (36 Years, 1988 to 2023):

YEAR	FIRST PLACE	SECOND PLACE	THIRD PLACE
1988	Barry Sanders, Oklahoma State TB	Rodney Peete, USC Quarterback	Troy Aikman, UCLA QB
2002	Carson Palmer, USC Quarterback	Brad Banks, Iowa Quarterback	Larry Johnson, Penn State TB
2004	Matt Leinart, USC Quarterback	Adrian Peterson, Oklahoma Tailback	Jason White, Oklahoma QB
2005	Reggie Bush, USC Tailback	Vince Young, Texas Quarterback	Matt Leinart, USC Quarterback
2022	Caleb Williams, USC Quarterback	Max Duggan, TCU Quarterback	C.J. Stroud, Ohio State QB

USC Heisman Quarterbacks: 5 (two quarterbacks are listed twice); **USC Heisman Tailbacks: 1**

TROJAN COACHES and the HEISMAN:

Five USC coaches have helped train and coach Trojans to places in the Heisman voting. Each is worthy of commendation:

COACH	FIRST PLACE	SECOND PLACE	THIRD PLACE
John McKay	**Mike Garrett**, 1965 **O.J. Simpson**, 1968	O.J. Simpson, 1967 Anthony Davis, 1974	Ricky Bell, 1975
John Robinson	**Charles White**, 1979 **Marcus Allen**, 1981	Ricky Bell, 1976	
Larry Smith		Rodney Peete, 1988	
Pete Carroll	**Carson Palmer**, 2002 **Matt Leinart**, 2004 **Reggie Bush**, 2005	Matt Leinart, 2005	
Lincoln Riley	**Caleb Williams**, 2022		

Caleb Williams was the third Heisman winner that Lincoln Riley has coached in only six years of head coaching, an unprecedented run. When including Jalen Hurts, who was runner-up in 2019, it means that during Riley's six head coaching years, he has coached four Heisman winners or runners-up. Nothing like that has ever happened in Heisman history. Not even close.

LINCOLN RILEY	
at USC	1st Place - **Caleb Williams**, Quarterback - 2022
at Oklahoma	1st Place - **Baker Mayfield**, Quarterback - 2017 1st Place - **Kyler Murray**, Quarterback - 2018 2nd Place - Jalen Hurts, Quarterback - 2019

TROJAN COACHES HAVE COACHED the FOLLOWING HEISMAN TROPHY 1st, 2nd and 3rd PLACE WINNERS:

Tailbacks (7)	Mike Garrett	Charles White	Reggie Bush
	O.J. Simpson	Ricky Bell	
	Anthony Davis	Marcus Allen	
Quarterbacks (7)	Rodney Peete	Baker Mayfield, Oklahoma	Caleb Williams
	Carson Palmer	Kyler Murray, Oklahoma	
	Matt Leinart	Jalen Hurts, Oklahoma	

USC Heisman Trophy Winners:

Reggie Bush, Tailback, 2005. *nydailynews.com photo*

Carson Palmer, Quarterback, 2002. *heisman.com photo*

After the celebration. Orenthal James (O.J.) Simpson, Tailback, 1968. *heisman.com photo*.

In addition to Riley's success training quarterbacks, USCs record of producing three quarterback winners or runners-up before the arrival of Riley is worth considering. The Trojans just produce winners.

An aspiring high school running back should also look to USC. Its record of producing seven tailback winners or runners-up is also unprecedented in Heisman history.

Charlie White, Tailback, 1979. *ABC7 photo*

The Heisman Trophy. *pinterest.com* photo

Matt Leinart, Quarterback, 2004.
heisman.com photo

Caleb Williams, Quarterback,
2022. *heisman.com* photo

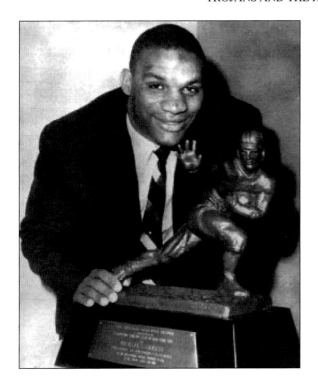

Mike Garrett, Tailback, 1965.
pinterest.com photo

Marcus Allen, Tailback, 1981.
heisman.com photo

Caleb Williams, Quarterback, 2022. *people.com photo*

Matt Leinart, Heisman Winner, 2004. *pinterest.com photo*

Reggie Bush, Heisman Winner, 2005.
bigmouthsports.com photo

Marcus Allen, Heisman Winner, 1981.
ebay.com photo

Carson Palmer, Heisman Winner, 2002. *pasadenastarnews.com photo*

Mike Garrett, Heisman Winner, 1965.
pinterest.com photo

Unstoppable O.J. Simpson, Heisman Winner, 1968.
youtube.com photo

Charlie White, Heisman Winner, 1979. *trojanswire.usatoday.com photo*

The versatile Caleb Williams can run as well as pass. *WTWO photo*

HONORS and ACCOMPLISHMENTS of the TROJAN HEISMAN WINNERS:

MIKE GARRETT, 1965 Heisman Winner:

Two-time All-American Mike Garrett was the man who began the great legacy of USC "I"-formation tailbacks. He was the Trojan's first, and only the West Coast's second, winner when he topped an outstanding list of candidates.

Mike set 14 NCAA, conference, and USC records in his three-year career, including an NCAA career rushing record of 3,221 yards in the days when 1,000-yard rushers were almost non-existent. He later starred for the Kansas City Chiefs and the San Diego Chargers.

O.J. SIMPSON, 1968 Heisman Winner:

Simpson became the second Trojan Heisman winner when he captured the award by the most one-sided margin in history. During the season, O.J. established an NCAA record for yards rushing, 1,709 in a single season (it has since been bettered). A two-time unanimous All-American, he equaled or bettered 19 NCAA, conference, and USC records.

CHARLES WHITE, 1979 Heisman Winner:

Charles White, USCs third Heisman Trophy winner, finished his four-year career as the NCAAs second leading rusher ever, with 5,598 regular season yards. If bowl games are included, he finished with a Pac 10 record of 6,245 yards.

A two-year unanimous All-American, White set or equaled 22 NCAA, Pac-10, USC, or Rose Bowl records. He gained more than 100 yards 31 times in his career, including 10 times in his final year, 1979. In that senior season, White averaged 186.4 yards a game, 6.2 yards a carry and led the nation in rushing, and for the second straight season, led the nation in all-purpose running.

MARCUS ALLEN, 1981 Heisman Winner:

Marcus Allen, USCs fourth Heisman Trophy winner, was college football's first 2,000-yard rusher. When he captured the award, Marcus set 14 new NCAA records and tied two others, including most yards rushing in a single season (2,342), highest per-game average (212.9), most 200-yard games in a single season (8), and most 200-yard games in a row (5). Allen also led the Trojans in receiving with 30 and 34 catches in each of his last two seasons.

CARSON PALMER, 2002 Heisman Winner:

Carson Palmer, USCs fifth Heisman Trophy winner, became the first Trojan quarterback chosen, and the first winner from the West Coast since 1981. Palmer, a 4-year starter, set or tied 33 Pac-10 and USC total offense and passing records, including becoming the league's career leader in total offense and passing yards.

In 2002, he completed 309 of 489 passes (63.2%) for 3,942 yards and 33 TDs, all USC records. He threw for 300-plus yards in a USC record seven games that season, including 3 in a row.

MATT LEINART, 2004 Heisman Winner:

Matt Leinart was the sixth USC winner and only the second quarterback winner, at a university previously known as "Tailback U." Matt threw for an unbelievable 108 touchdowns in only three years. During that time he had a career passing yardage total of 10,623 yards. He was a two-time All-American and the first Trojan junior to win the award.

REGGIE BUSH, 2005 Heisman Winner:

Tailback Reggie Bush, the seventh USC winner, was an electrifying runner. His rushing totals would have been much higher had he not been in a backfield with such a prolific passer as Leinart and another great runner, LenDale White. Having two Heisman winners in one backfield was a Heisman first. A career comparison is helpful:

TAILBACK:	YARDS:	YEARS:	TOUCHDOWNS:
Charles White	6,245	1976, 1977, 1978, 1979	49
Marcus Allen	4,810	1978, 1979, 1980, 1981	45
Anthony Davis	3,724	1972, 1973, 1974	44
Ricky Bell	3,689	1974, 1975, 1976, 1977	28
Ronald Jones II	3,619	2015, 2016, 2017	39
O.J. Simpson	3,423	1967, 1968	36
Mike Garrett	3,221	1963, 1964, 1965	25
Reggie Bush	3,169	2003, 2004, 2005	25
LenDale White	3,159	2003, 2004, 2005	52

Charles White garnered his yards in four years, three as a starter. Marcus Allen was a blocking fullback for Charles White in his first two years. Anthony Davis scored 44 times in only three years. Reggie Bush and LenDale White shared the football for three straight years. Combined, they totaled 6,388 yards for Pete Carroll.

Of note, LenDale White scored 52 times in only three years and, more importantly, O.J. Simpson ran for 36 touchdowns and almost 3,500 yards in only two seasons. Simpson's career marks are the best among Trojan tailbacks and Marcus Allen easily had the best single year of any in 1981. It might have been the greatest single year of running in NCAA history.

CALEB WILLIAMS, 2022 Heisman Winner:

Caleb followed Coach Lincoln Riley from Oklahoma. He became the eighth Trojan winner and the first to win it as a sophomore. He was also the third in the last four USC Heismans who were quarterbacks.

Caleb set a single-season passing record at USC of 4,537 yards while passing for 42 touchdowns and running for 10 more. Both the passing touchdowns and the combined passing and rushing touchdowns are USC records. Leinart clearly is the best quarterback in USC history, but Williams could eclipse that, depending on how he performs in 2023, undoubtedly his last year before going to the NFL.

USC FOOTBALL RECORDS:

TOTALS		
Total touchdowns	Matt Barkley	116
Total touchdowns single-season	Caleb Williams & LenDale White	52
Total touchdowns single-game	Cody Kessler	7
Total offense yards	Matt Barkley	12,214
Total offense single-season yards	Caleb Williams	4,919
Total offense single-game yards	Caleb Williams	503

SINGLE GAME		
Single-game passing touchdowns	Cody Kessler	7
Single-game rushing touchdowns	Charles Dean, Howard Elliot, Orv Mohler, Ambrose Schindler, Clark Holden, O.J. Simpson, Anthony Davis (twice), Sam Cunningham, Ricky Bell (twice), Charles White (twice), Marcus Allen, Ryan Knight, LenDale White, Ronald Jones II	4
Single-game passing yardage	Kedon Slovis	515
Single-game rushing yardage	Ricky Bell	347
Single-game receptions	Robert Woods	17
Single-game reception yardage	Marquise Lee	345
Single-game receiving touchdowns	Robert Woods & Amon-Ra St. Brown	4
Interceptions single-game	Adrian Young	4
Tackles single-game	Sam Anno	23
Sacks single-games	Marcus Cotton, Junior Seau, Tim Ryan, Lawrence Jackson	4
Field goals made single-game	Ryan Killeen	5
Field goal percentage single-game	Mario Danelo	93.8%

SINGLE SEASON		
Single-season passing yardage	Caleb Williams	4,537
Single-season passing touchdowns	Caleb Williams	42
Single-season rushing yardage	Marcus Allen	2,427
Single-season rushing touchdowns	LenDale White	24
Single-season receptions	Marquise Lee	118
Single-season reception yardage	Marquise Lee	1,721
Single-season receiving touchdowns	Mike Williams & Dwayne Jarrett	16
Interceptions single-season	Jim Psaltis	9
Tackles single-season	Rex Moore	206
Field goals made single-season	Quin Rodriguez	19
Sacks single-season	Tim Ryan	20

CAREER		
Career passing yardage	Matt Barkley	12,327
Career passing touchdowns	Matt Barkley	116
Career rushing yardage	Charles White	6,245
Career rushing touchdowns	LenDale White	52
Career receptions	Robert Woods	252
Career receiving yards	Marquise Lee	3,655
Career receiving touchdowns	Dwayne Jarrett	41
Career interceptions	Ronnie Lott	20
Career tackles	Keith Davis	481
Career sacks	Marcus Cotton	38
Career field goals made	Quin Rodriguez	57
Career field goal percentage	Mario Danelo	92.9%

Chapter Nine
Perfection and Unfulfillment
2001 - 2009

The third and last Trojan Dominant Coaching Era is that of Coach Pete Carroll. His legacy is lasting, but it was unfortunately too short. After the greatest period of Trojan dominance, from 2002 to 2008, Carroll moved back to the NFL, which seemed to be his intent all along.

The siren call of the NFL is undoubtedly a challenge to coaches. Three of the greatest Trojan coaches succumbed to the call and left USC for the NFL: John McKay, John Robinson, and Pete Carroll. McKay voiced his regret at leaving and Robinson physically returned to USC for another five years. It is unknown if Carroll harbors any regret for leaving, and one may wonder at the reason for his leaving, but if he had stayed, he might have become the all-time greatest Trojan coach and have established a legacy that far surpassed that of any NFL coach.

Trojan Coach Pete Carroll. *myhero.com photo*

CARROLL'S OUTSTANDING TROJAN RECORD:

National Championships: 2 — 2003 and 2004

Second in Coaches Poll — 2005 & 2008

Conference Championships: 7 — Pac-12: 2002 (co-champs), 2003, 2004, 2005,
2006 (co-champs), 2007 (co-champs), and 2008.

Rose Bowl Victories: 4 — 2003, 2006, 2007, and 2008

Rose Bowl Losses: 1 — 2005 in the BCS Championship against Texas

Orange Bowl Victories: 2 — 2002 and 2004 (no losses)

Heisman Trophy Winners: Carson Palmer in 2002, Matt Leinart in 2004, Reggie Bush in 2005. Matt Leinart was third in 2005.

Record: 97-19 (.836); Second best to Gus Henderson in USC history.

From 2002 through 2008, Carroll posted a record of 82-9 (.901) and an even better record from 2003 to 2005 of (.949), which is the greatest 3-year stretch in Trojan history.

PERCENTAGE STRETCHES of the GREATEST TROJAN COACHES:

Coach Gus Henderson (1920-1922) . . . . 3 years . . . . (.929)

Coach Howard Jones (1925-1933). . . . . 9 years . . . . . . (.884)

Coach Howard Jones (1931-1933). . . . . 3 years . . . . . . (.938)

Coach John McKay (1967-1969) . . . . 3 years . . . . . . (.935)

Coach John McKay (1972-1974) . . . . 3 Years . . . . . . (.912)

Coach John Robinson (1976-1979) . . . . . . 4 years . . . . . (.875)

Coach Pete Carroll (2002-2008) . . . . 7 years . . . . . (.901)

Coach Pete Carroll (2003-2005) . . . . 3 years . . . . . . (.949)

ANNUAL CARROLL RECORD:

2001 6-6		2006 11-2	
2002 11-2		2007 11-2	
2003 12-1		2008 12-1	
2004 13-0		2009 9-4	
2005 12-1			

The author has made this chapter short to match the shortness of Carroll's career coaching at USC. However, the shortness does not diminish the brilliance of Carroll's tenure with the Trojans. The record really does speak for itself. John Robinson's second coming did not match his first and the slide into mediocrity after Robinson left was not properly resurrected until Carroll made his appearance.

After Hackett's disastrous three years, it was refreshingly needed to have another flash of greatness and dominance that matched those of the first two dominant Trojan coaching eras. While the author has selected John McKay as the greatest of Trojan football coaches, the tenure of Carroll is unmatched at any period in USC history. If he had stayed, Carroll undoubtedly would have been considered the greatest of a long line of great Trojan coaches.

Trojan fans worldwide are waiting to see if Coach Lincoln Riley can join the elite members of legacy Trojan coaches. From all accounts, that wait will be fruitful.

Photo Gallery 3

USC Athletic and Health Facilities
The Tools that Create Greatness in Trojan Sports

Recent $270 million upgrades to the L.A. Memorial Coliseum. USC has more football players in the NFL Hall of Fame than any other university. *neontommy.com photo*

On-campus Uytengsu Aquatics Center. *news.usc.edu photo*

Above: Galen Basketball Center. *pinterest.com photo*

Below: Uytengsu Aquatics Center. *pinterest.com photo*

Above: Loker (on-campus) Track and Field Stadium, used for other sports, including football, practice. *usc.edu photo*

Below: Lyon (on-campus) Center for student fitness. *recsports.usc.edu photo*

Team Training Center. *recsports.usc.edu photo*

Trojan Warrior in Heritage Hall of
Champions. *pinterest.com photo*

USC Football renovated football practice facility.
USC has won 11 National Championships in NCAA
Football. *youtube.com photo*

USC Football Practice Facility. *foxsports.com*

Above: Heritage Hall of Champions. USC has won more Heisman Trophies than any other university (8). *news.usc.com*

Below: USC Football Practice Facility. *chatsports.com*

Above: John McKay Center for Trojan Football. USC has won 39 Conference Championships in NCAA Division 1 Football. *news.usc.com*

Below: John McKay Center. *diehardsport.com*

John McKay Center. *diehardsport.com*

USC has won 107 National Championships in 17 different sports. The official NCAA top-four listing: Stanford (123), University of California at Los Angeles (UCLA) (118), USC (107), and Oklahoma State (52). The three California schools indicate superior: climate, coaching, training, organization, university leadership, athletic departments, motivation, facilities, and fitness.
diehardsport.com

Above: Traveler, USC famed "Trojan Horse. *dailytrojan.com*

Below: The USC "Wild Bunch" of defensive football fame. USC Campus honors its football heroes. *pinterest.com*

Above: Trojans are Warriors…Tommy Trojan in campus center. *si.com*

Below: Neil Armstrong at the USC Viterbi School of Engineering. First man to land on Earth's Moon. Trojans are warriors, whether on the field or off. *usc.edu*

USC GRADUATES WHO FLEW IN SPACE:

Neil A. Armstrong	USC Master of Science in Aerospace Engineering Flew in Gemini 8 and Apollo 11 (Moon landing in 1969)
Karol J. Bobko	USC Master of Science in Aerospace Engineering Flew in *Challenger*, *Discovery*, and *Atlantis*
Charles F. Bolden	USC Master of Systems Management Flew in *Challenger*, *Discovery*, and *Atlantis*
Gerald P. Carr	USC Bachelor of Science in Mechanical Engineering Flew in Skylab
Nancy J. Currie	USC Master of Science in Safety Engineering Flew in *Endeavour*, *Discovery*, and *Columbia*
Brian Duffy	USC Master of Science in Systems Management Flew in *Atlantis* and *Endeavour*
J.M. Linenger	USC Master of Science in Systems Management Flew in *Discovery*, *Mir* Space Station (4 months), and *Atlantis*
James A. Lovell	Graduate of USC Aviation Safety School (non-degree) Flew in Gemini 7 & 12, Apollo 8 and commanded the crippled Apollo 13
Carlos I. Noriega	USC Bachelor of Science in Computer Science Flew in *Endeavour*
Kenneth S. Reightier Jr.	USC Master of Science in Systems Engineering Flew in *Discovery*
Pierre J. Thuot	USC Master of Science in Systems Engineering Flew in *Atlantis*, *Endeavour*, and *Columbia*

Hecuba, Queen of Troy, located in USC Village. Hecuba defended the City of Troy with fierce passion & loyalty, a symbol for female Trojan athletes. *pressroom.usc*

City of Troy Trojan warriors are also honored on campus. *playbuzz.com*

Coach John McKay Center. *diehardsport.com*

John McKay, the greatest of Trojan coaches.

Winner of 4 National Championships (1962, 1967, 1972, 1974); 9 Conference Championships (1962, 1964, 1966, 1967, 1968, 1969, 1972, 1973, 1974); and the coach of two Heisman Trophy winning tailbacks and two Heisman Trophy winning tailback runners-up. While Bell won the award under Robinson, McKay was largely responsible for his training and development.

1965 Winner Mike Garrett
1967 Runner-Up O.J. Simpson
1968 Winner O.J. Simpson;
1974 Runner-Up Anthony Davis

Galen Center Men's Volleyball. *galencenter.org*

USC's Beach Volleyball Stadium, Home of the NCAA Women's Champions.
USC has won NCAA Championships in: Baseball (12); Women's Basketball (2);
Beach Volleyball (6); Football (11); Women's Golf (3); Gymnastics (1); Women's Soccer (2)
Men's Swim & Dive (9); Women's Swim & Dive (1); Men's Tennis (21), Women's Tennis (7),
Men's Track & Field (28). USC has won more Olympic Gold Medals than any other American
University: Women's Track & Field (3); **Men's Volleyball (6)**; Women's Volleyball (6);
Water Polo: Men's (10) and Women's (7). In April, 2023, Women's beach volleyball
won their 3rd straight NCAA title.

Top & Bottom: USC David X. Marks Tennis Stadium. *morleybuilders.com*, *vantagetcg.com*

John McKay Center. *hntb.com*

Trojan Swim Club. *swimswam.com*

USC provides nutrition "fueling stops" for its over 650 student-athletes. The Athletic Department spends over a million dollars annually on nutrition. *USC News photo*

Galen Center dining facilities. Trojan nutritrionists monitor caloric intake and concentrate on nutricinal betterment for each individual athlete. *USC Athletics photo*

John McKay Center facility for academic support of student athletes.
USC Athletics photo

John McKay Center with all-weather football facility and a portion of the football weight room. *HNTB photo*

University of Southern California Student-Athlete Academic Services.

Student nutrition at the University Village Dining Hall. *Architect Magazine photo*

CLUB SPORTS AVAILABLE at USC:

Archery	Fencing	Softball
Badminton	Field Hockey	Soul Cal Breaking
Barbell	Figure Skating	Squash
Baseball	Golf	Swim
Basketball	Gymnastics	Taekwondo
Dance	Ice Hockey	Tennis
Volleyball	Kendo	Track
Boxing	Kung Fu	Triathlon
Jiu Jitsu	Lacrosse	Ultimate
Cheer	Mixed Martial Arts	Underwater Torpedo
Chaotic	Ping Pong Posse	Volleyball
Climbing	Roundnet	Water Polo
Crew	Polo	Wrestling
Cycling	Rugby	Dragonboat
Cricket	Shinkendo	
Equestrian	Soccer	

Soni McCallister Field for USC Soccer & Lacrosse. *uscannenbergmedia.com*

USC Trojan footballers waiting to run onto the Coliseum. *pinterest.com*

USC Baseball, winners of 12 National Championships, call home the on-campus Dedeaux Stadium. Notable USC players: Mark Prior, Barry Zito, Aaron Boone, Bret Boone, Randy Johnson, Mark McGwire, Steve Kemp, Fred Lynn, Dave Kingman, Marcel Lachemann, Tom Seaver, Don Buford, Ron Fairly, Bob Lillis, Rod Dedeaux, and Jesse Hill.

Close friends Tommy Lasorda of the Los Angeles Dodgers and Rod Dedeaux of the USC Baseball Trojans. *dartentitles.com*

Coach Rod Dedeaux Field on the USC Campus. *dedeauxfoundation.org*

Honoring "Raoul" Rod Dedeaux. *offbeat.group.shef.ac.uk*

USC Engemann Student Health Center. *pinterest.com*

Leading the USC Marching Band at a Coliseum game. *ncaa.com*

The Famous Trojan Cheerleaders. *si.com*

Traveler the Trojan Horse. *mysantonio.com*

Quarterback Matt Leinart led the Trojans to two National Championships and just missed a third, losing in the playoff against Texas in the final seconds. He also led them to 34 straight victories, won the Heisman and was inducted into the College Football Hall of Fame. He graduated from Mater Dei High School in the Los Angeles Area, which has one of the finest football programs in the country.

Mater Dei can boast the following: **Three Heisman Trophy Winners, Four USA Today National Championships, 28 League Championships, 11 CIF Southern Section Championships and six undefeated seasons.**

Mater Dei is in the Trinity League, judged the toughest league in the country in 2021. The following is the final national ranking of Trinity teams in 2021. Mater Dei #1, Servite #6, St. John Bosco #8, Orange Lutheran #91, and Santa Margarita #144. In other words, three of the league teams were in the top ten national rankings. In 2022, Mater Dei ended up ranked 4th in the country. While at Mater Dei, Leinart was named the California Gatorade High School Football Player of the Year in 2001 and Led the Monarchs to the California Interscholastic Federation (CIF) Division 1 State Co-Championship. *theheismanwinners.com photo*

Howard Jones Field for football practice. *wikipedia.com photo*

Renovated Howard Jones Football (on-campus) Practice Facility. *Saturday Blitz photo*

Peristyle End of the USC-controlled Memorial Coliseum. USC Athletics photo

Coach Lincoln Riley in the Coliseum. *Wall Street Journal photo*

Honoring Trojan Athletes. *247 Sports photo*

Caleb Williams admiring the $270 million Coliseum renovation. *CBS Sports photo*

Parker Hughes Atrium, McKay Center. *SB Nation photo*

Heritage Hall. *DLR Group photo*

Brian Kennedy Field with Howard Jones Field on top, Loker Track & Field Stadium to the lower right, John McKay Center on upper right and Dedeaux Field on upper left. *Image of Sport photo*

Brian Kennedy (on-campus) Field. The USC football practice facilities include two named fields. Howard Jones Field lies next to Brian Kennedy Field, which is on the south side.
D.A. Hogan & Associates photo

USC football tackle Marion Morrison, also known as John Wayne. *Outsider photo*

Western Movie Star and USC football lineman John Wayne. His counterpart at tackle was another Western Star, Ward Bond. *MeTV photo*

The 50 Greatest Trojan Football Players of All Time

This listing is not definitive. It was compiled by Rick McMahan and published on March 31, 2010. It is one person's opinion. It is impossible to fairly-rank USC football players who played under different conditions, with different teammates, and played in different times. Every one of the following was an All-American, either in fact or in opinion. Many of those listed below could be considered as the greatest Trojan of all time. The author's reasons for including it is not necessarily to rank, but just to show and remind us all just how many great athletes that USC has been privileged to claim as its own.

A lot of other worthy players are not included, yet deserve recognition. The author apologizes if any former player or former player's family or friends are offended. Any listing is bound to offend someone and no listing should be defined as accurate. There have just been too many great players at USC and many could lay claim to being number one. An example is Shaun Cody, listed below as #45. Yet Coach Pete Carroll urged Shaun to come to USC and judged that the historical Carroll Era of excellence could not have been possible without Cody. How does one judge that? For faithful USC fans, USC families, and USC faculty, all of those listed below are number one and deserving of our historical recognition.

1 Marcus Allen	**2** O.J. Simpson	**3** Mike Garrett	**4** Charles White	**5** Morley Drury
6 Matt Leinart	**7** Reggie Bush	**8** Anthony Davis	**9** Lynn Swann	**10** Sam Cunningham
11 Ricky Bell	**12** Jon Arnett	**13** Richard Wood	**14** Ronnie Lott	**15** Anthony Munoz
16 Hal Bedsole	**17** Ron Yary	**18** Dennis Smith	**19** Bruce Mathews	**20** Frank Gifford
21 Pat Haden	**22** Ron Mix	**23** Dennis Thurman	**24** Charles Young	**25** Tony Boselli
26 Troy Polamalu	**27** Mosi & Lofa Tatupu	**28** Mike & Marlin McKeever	**29** Keith Van Horne	**30** Willis Wood
31 Mark Carrier	**32** Don Mosebar	**33** Junior Seau	**34** Brad Budde	**35** Joey Browner
36 Willie McGinest	**37** Clay Mathews Jr. & Clay Mathews III	**38** Chris Claiborne	**39** Carson Palmer	**40** Rodney Peete
41 Tay Brown	**42** Tim McDonald	**43** Tim Rossovich	**44** Paul McDonald	**45** Shaun Cody
46 Jim Sears	**47** Marvin Powell	**48** Lynn Cain	**49** Mike Williams	**50** Keyshawn Johnson

The "heart" of the Coliseum renovation. *Sports Business Journal photo*

Chapter Ten
The Forgotten Years
1983 - 2021
(with breaks during the years of Carroll and Robinson)

COACHES from 1983 to and including 1992:

Ted Tollner . . . . 1983-1986 . . . . . . 26-20-1 (.564)

Larry Smith . . . . 1987-1992 . . . . . . 44-25-3 (.632)

The Author has elected to expand information on just the more important coaches during these disappointing periods. The "forgotten years" include 1983-1992, 1997-2000, and 2010 to 2021.

The break between the forgotten years, from 1993 to 1997, belongs to one of the genuinely great historical USC coaches. It was the second coming of Coach John Robinson. Robinson, along with John McKay, created the Golden Era from 1960 to 1982. Robinson left to coach the Los Angeles Rams where in nine coaching years he went 75-68.

Robinson was a much better college coach than a professional, as he was great with young, raw, talent. He was a developer of tailbacks. As assistant to John McKay and later as head coach, he proved a master running backs coach. Under his tutelage, tailback Anthony Davis, tailback Ricky Bell, tailback Charlie White, and fullback/tailback Marcus Allen all developed into world-class stars. Bell was picked #1 in the 1977 NFL draft, selected ahead of Heisman winner Tony Dorsett.

The ten years of the Tollner/Smith period began with a very nice guy guiding a very poorly led USC to a miserable .564 winning percentage. That was under Tollner. Larry Smith turned out to be a good coach, going to three straight Rose Bowls. Surprisingly, his record was almost identical to that of Clay Helton. His teams were "good, but not great" and his bowl record was anything but great.

COACH LARRY SMITH:

Larry Smith coached USC for six years (1987-1992). If he had quit after the first three years, he would have been considered a success. However, how the Trojans do in contests with Notre Dame and UCLA and in bowl games matters a great deal to fans and the USC administration. His record during those first three years was 27-8-1. However, he lost 17-20 to Michigan State in the Rose Bowl after the 1987 season and lost to Michigan 14-22 in the Rose Bowl after 1988. He did manage to beat Michigan 17-10 in the 1989 Rose Bowl.

It was Smith's last three years that caused his firing at the end of the 1992 season. During those last three years, his record was 15-17-2, which is horrible at any respected football university like USC. In 1990, he lost to Michigan State in the John Hancock Bowl by one point: 16-17. In 1991, he lost his last six games. In 1992, he was destroyed by an underdog Fresno State in the Freedom Bowl by 17 points, 7-24. Fans were up-in-arms. That was his undoing.

Against Notre Dame, he lost every game (0-6): 15-26, 10-27, 24-28, 6-10, 20-24, 23-31.

Against UCLA he managed to do better, but not by much (2-3-1): 17-18, **31-22**, 10-10, **45-42**, 21-24, 37-38. However, they were close, exciting games. Two of the losses were by only one point and the other by three points. With one tie and a 3-point victory, Smithed coached five of the six games with only a total eight-point differential. In other words, he lost all three games by a total of five points. His two victories were by three and nine points.

One could attribute some of the losses to bad luck. But great coaches have good luck. Great coaches win those close games.

Coach Larry Smith's record at USC was a respectable 44-25-3. However, at USC, that is not considered respectable or acceptable. Like another good but not great coach, Clay Helton. Helton went 46-24-0 at USC, similar to Smith's record. By the time Helton coached, there were no more ties allowed.

COACH from 1993 to and including 1997:

John Robinson . . . . 1993-1997 . . . . . . 37-21-2 (.638)

A comparison of Robinson's two coaching periods shows the drop-off in the percentage of victories:

1976 . . . . . 11-1 . . . . . . Won Rose Bowl- #2 in Coaches and AP Poll

1977 . . . . . 8-4 . . . . . . Won Astro-Bluebonnet Bowl

1978 . . . . . 12-1 . . . . . Won Rose Bowl; #1 in Coaches Poll

1979 . . . . . 11-0-1 . . . . . Won Rose Bowl; #2 in Coaches and AP Poll

1980 8-2-1

1981 . . . . . 9-3 . . . . . . Lost Fiesta Bowl

1982 8-3

1993 . . . . . 8-5 . . . . . . Won Freedom Bowl

1994 . . . . . 8-3-1 . . . . . Won Cotton Bowl

1995 . . . . . 9-2-1 . . . . . Won Rose Bowl

The last two years of Robinson's second tenure proved his undoing.

1996 6-6

1997 6-5

In Robinson's second coming, his main tailback talent was Deion Washington, who was good but not in the same league as the historically great Trojan tailbacks. However, Robinson's record with his tailbacks at USC is comparable to that of Lincoln Riley with his quarterbacks at Oklahoma and later at USC.

COACHES from 1998 to and including 2000:

Paul Hackett . . . . 1998-2000 . . . . . . 19-18 (.514)

It was only a three-year break between Robinson and Pete Carroll, but it was an awfully bad three years for the Trojans. Paul Hackett was just not a good coach for a program like that at USC. His .514 winning percentage over three years is almost a losing one.

Thankfully, the reign of Pete Carroll intervened. His record was dealt with earlier in this book and it was extraordinary. It left many Trojan fans longing for his return during what could justifiably be called the "Turmoil Years."

COACHES from 2010 to 2021:

COACH LANE KIFFIN (2010-2013):

Lane Kiffin took over after Carroll left for what he thought were greener pastures in the NFL and Pacific Northwest. Fans were not sure if Carroll was venturing to or escaping from. The NCAA Sanctions that were the second to most severe ever levied against an NCAA team were surely part of the reason for his departure. They were draconian and will be dealt with in a later chapter.

Kiffin is an anomaly. Obviously brilliant, he was a rising star at an early age. He was also very immature and created problems that should not have existed. His first attempt at coaching in the "Big Leagues" was as Offensive Coordinator for Pete Carroll at USC. He did that between 2005 to 2006, when he was selected to jump to the pros as head coach of the NFL Oakland Raiders. It did not go well. He ended up fired after just a short stay (2007-2008). From the NFL, he jumped back to college as head coach of Tennessee in the Southeast Conference. He only lasted a year when he left them in a lurch and signed on as the Trojan Head Coach.

His USC record was:

```
2010 . . . . . . . 8-5
2011 . . . . . . . 10-2
2012 . . . . . . . 7-6
2013 . . . . . . . 3-2
2010-2013 . . . . 28-15 (.651)
```

He was the first of the three USC coaches fired during the "Turmoil Years." The Trojan Athletic Director fired Kiffin on the airport tarmac as he arrived back from a thorough whipping that USC leaders felt was not in the "Trojan Way."

Kiffin was always resilient. From that tarmac, he next landed at Florida Atlantic for three years, going:

```
2017 . . . . . 11-3
2018 . . . . . 5-7
2019 . . . . . 11-3, which was a roller-coaster ride.
```

Next, he was back in the SEC, this time with Ole Miss:

2020 5-5

2021 10-3

2022 . . . . . 8-5, which was a respectable record in the toughest conference in the country. His overall bowl record was a mediocre 3-4, but he has shown that the immature actions seem to be far behind him.

After the airport firing at USC, Ed Orgeron was hired to take over as interim coach after five games. He went 6-2, which would have been enough to have him permanently hired. Orgeron is a fine coach. He served as Defensive Coordinator for Hackett and then Carroll, eventually ending up leading a terrific LSU team to the National Championship. He always loved USC and was sorry when he was forced to leave after such a promising start. SC players and fans loved Orgeron in return. John Robinson agreed to act as Orgeron's eyes and ears as an analyst for LSU. With Orgeron and Robinson working together again, they worked magic.

Ed Orgeron (interim) . . . . . 2013 . . . . 6-2 (.750)

Steve Sarkisian. . . . . 2014-2015 . . . . . 12-6 (.667)

Clay Helton 2015-2021   . . . . 46-24 (.657)

Donte Williams (interim) . . . 2021 . . . . 3-7 (.300)

Of interest, is that the records of Kiffin (.651), Helton (.657), and Sarkisian (.667) are so coincidentally similar.

COACH STEVE SARKISIAN (2014-2015):

Coaching at a major university like USC, Notre Dame, Michigan, Ohio State, Texas, Oklahoma, Alabama, Georgia, or Clemson, is a pressure-cooker environment. Steve lasted only a year and a half in the pressure cooker until it was revealed that he had an addiction to alcohol. After a series of embarrassing incidents, the USC administration acted and Sarkisian became the second casualty of the Turmoil Years.

Sarkisian has managed to get back on his feet. He is now head coach of a very good Texas Longhorn football program.

COACH CLAY HELTON (2013-2021):

Helton was interim coach in 2013 for one game, which he won. That victory was in the Las Vegas Bowl. He was finally confirmed as head coach in 2015, when he went 5-4, losing in the Holiday Bowl. In 2016, he had a 10-3 record and won the end-of-season Rose Bowl in a spectacular game against Penn State. The next year he went 11-3 and lost in the Cotton Bowl.

From then on, it was all downhill. His record:

2013 1-0   Won the Las Vegas Bowl as interim coach

2015 5-4   Lost the Holiday Bowl

2016 10-3   Won the Rose Bowl

2017 11-3   Lost the Cotton Bowl

2018 5-7	Did not qualify for a bowl game
2019 8-5	Lost the Holiday Bowl
2020 5-1	Short season due to the COVID pandemic
2021 1-1	After two games, he was fired

The last coach on the list acted as secondary coach under Helton. Donte Williams deserved better. Inheriting a team that loved their father-figure fired coach so much was difficult, and he was unable to plug the hole in the dike.

Williams also landed on his feet. He is an excellent recruiter and stayed on under Coach Riley as a coach of safeties and cornerbacks. Read more about him in the chapter on the current Trojan coaching staff.

In 2022, Clay Helton continued his losing ways as coach of Georgia Southern. His record was 6-7, losing another bowl game, this time the Camelia Bowl. Helton is well-liked by his players. He is more of a father figure than a coach. His character is above reproach. But a coach with a good character does not necessarily mean a good coach.

Helton was an adequate game planner. His scripted plays to start a Trojan game often worked well. It was the lack of effective in-game adjustments that caused his downfall. He just could not adjust properly as the game progressed. He was blessed with exceptional talent, but he squandered it. He was not a good developer of players. Often the television camera panning the Trojan sideline caught Helton with that questioning look in his eyes. It was like a light shining in a deer's eyes. He just did not know what to do in too many critical situations. Those eyes sometimes showed confusion and more often a muted panic. He was out of his element.

For several years under Helton, USC was able to recruit good talent based on prior success, but that level of talent started a steady decline. Athletic Director Bohn was patient in handling Helton. "What do you need to make this a winning program?" He listened to Helton's spoken needs. He adjusted and made investments in the football program to meet those needs. After all the increased staffing and increased monetary investment, when Helton still had a shaky program, Bohn had to make a move before the decline in recruitment became critical. It was the right move. Those of us who were fans of USC during Helton's coaching days, like the man. He is hard not to like. We wish him well in his coaching future and hope for his success. Meanwhile, excitement is back in the Trojan program and ardent fans await what the future might offer.

Chapter Seven

Trojan Horses — All-Americans and "The League"

THE MATHEWS, FIRST FAMILY of the TROJANS and the NFL:

Long-time Trojan fans are very familiar with the name Mathews. The exploits of the family are part of Trojan lore, and it seems to be an incomplete tale. It all started with the family patriarch H.L. Mathews who was born in 1889 in Jefferson, Ohio. After serving in World War I, "he held tenures as a boxing, baseball, and track coach for The Citadel," a military school, from 1926 to 1953.

H.L's son, Clay Mathews Sr., "began the family's legacy in football. After playing for the Georgia Tech Yellow Jackets, he played offensive tackle, defensive tackle, and defensive end for the San Francisco 49ers. His career was interrupted by service in the Korean War as a paratrooper," after which he played three more seasons for San Francisco.

Clay's sons, Bruce and Clay Jr., each played football for the USC Trojans, and each was selected in the first rounds of their respective drafts to the NFL.

BRUCE MATHEWS at USC and the NFL:

Bruce Mathews is in the USC Hall of Fame, the Tennessee Sports Hall of Fame, and the NFL Pro Football Hall of Fame. For USC, he was the principal blocker for the famed "Student Body Right" play. He was named to the First Team All-Pac-10 in both his junior and senior seasons. As a senior, he earned consensus All-American honors and won the Morris Trophy, which is awarded to the best lineman in the conference.

"Mathews is one of the most versatile offensive linemen ever to play in the NFL. He stared at all five offensive line positions in addition to being a snapper on field goals, PATs, and punts. Bruce was selected to 14 Pro Bowls, which at the time tied a record. He was also named to the first-team All-Pro nine times and an All-American Football Conference selection 12 times. Mathews retired after having played more games (296) than any (other) NFL player, other than kickers and punters." He never missed a game due to injury and started 229 consecutive games, an NFL record.

CLAY MATHEWS Jr. at USC and the NFL:

Clay Mathews Jr., brother of Bruce, owns the third-most tackles in NFL history, with just under 1,600. He played 278 games, proving to be one of the most durable defensive players in NFL history. He registered a sack 103 days before his 41st birthday, making him the oldest player to ever record one in NFL history. He played in four Pro Bowls and in 1984, was a first-team All-Pro selection.

In 2005, he was inducted into the Trojan Hall of Fame. In 2010, Mathews was selected by the

Bleacher Report as the 37th best player in Trojan history. While at USC, he was a consensus All-American and played on "some of the best USC defenses" during the McKay-Robinson Era.

KYLE MATHEWS at USC:

Kyle, one of three sons of Clay Mathews Jr., played safety for the USC Trojans.

CLAY MATHEWS III at USC and the NFL:

Clay the Third, also a son of Clay Jr., was a late bloomer and was only a walk-on at USC. He played linebacker for the Trojans and "was drafted by the Green Bay Packers, earning six Pro Bowl selections, a victory in Super Bowl XLV, appeared in three NFC Championship Games, and is the Packers all-time sacks leader."

CASEY MATHEWS:

The third son, Casey, was an outstanding linebacker for the Oregon Ducks, after which he played in the NFL from 2011-2015.

KEVIN MATHEWS:

Kevin, the first son of Bruce, played football for Texas A&M, and as a center for the Tennessee Titans of the NFL as well as two other NFL teams from 2010-2014.

JAKE MATHEWS:

Jake, the second son of Bruce, also played for Texas A&M, and as an offensive tackle for the Atlanta Falcons of the NFL, he helped defeat his cousin Clay III and the Packers to advance to Super Bowl LI.

MIKE MATHEWS:

Mike, the third son of Bruce, also played for Texas A&M and spent time on off-season rosters for the Cleveland Browns and Pittsburgh Steelers of the NFL.

LUKE MATHEWS:

Luke, fourth son of Bruce, continued the A&M tradition. Perhaps the best of the four brothers, he played interior offensive lineman, but suffered a severe shoulder injury that kept him out almost the entire 2021 season. That followed missing all of 2020 with another injury. In 2022, he participated in the Aggies opener against Kent State, but then was on the injured list for the rest of the season. Coach Jimbo Fisher of the Aggies said that Mathews is done playing football. It was a greatly disappointing end of a very promising career.

TROY NIKLAS:

The nephew of Bruce was a two-way standout on both the offensive and defensive lines for Servite High School, a Trinity League member (see chapter on recruiting), "He helped Servite to a 14-1 record in 2010 and a second straight CIF Southern Section Division Title and runner-up to the state playoffs. He was named the *Los Angeles Times* California Lineman of the Year in 2010." He played college football at Notre Dame and for the Arizona Cardinals of the NFL.

ASHLEY NICK:

Ashley, a granddaughter of Clay Sr., played soccer at USC from 2005-2008. She was co-captain of the USC 2007 NCAA Women's Soccer National Champions. She was named to the All-Pac 10 First Team in both 2007 and 2008. Currently, she plays midfielder for Kansas City of the National Women's Soccer League.

Five members of the famed Mathews are USC graduates and four of them have had outstanding professional careers. Clay Mathews Jr. was a member of the 1974 USC National Championship team. Clay Mathews III was a member of the USC 2004 BCS National Champions. Bruce Mathews was the primary blocker who led USC Heisman Trophy winner Marcus Allen through opposing defensive lines in 1981, and, as mentioned, Ashley Nick was co-captain on the 2007 USC National Champion Soccer Team.

While many sets of brothers have played for the Trojans, there is no doubt that the amazing Mathews family is the "First Family of USC Athletics" as well as the already bestowed "First Family of the NFL." It proves that genes do count.

The name All-American does not mean as much today as it did when the author was much younger. To be named an All-American was the greatest honor, besides the individual trophies like the Heisman, Outland, and Lombardi, that the system could bestow upon an athlete.

TROJANS in the NFL:

The number of All-Americans also bestows honors on the coaches and universities. The more All-Americans, the greater the recognition of the successful molding of talent.

The following chart lists the number of Consensus All-Americans by era:

COACH(ES)	YEARS		ALL-AMERICANS	RATIO
Henderson - Jones	1926-1940	15 years	10	.667
Cravath - Hill	1942-1955	14 years	5	.357
McKay - Robinson	**1960-1982**	**23 years**	**34**	**1.478**
Robinson II	1993-1997	4 years	3	.750
Tollner - Smith - Hackett	1983-2000	12 years	9	.750
Pete Carroll	2001-2009	9 years	9	1.000

TROJANS in the NFL HALL of FAME:

USC Athletes	Marcus Allen	1978- 1981
	Tony Boselli	1992-1994
	Red Badgro	1924-1926
	Frank Gifford	1949-1951
	Ronnie Lott	1977-1980
	Bruce Mathews	1980-1982
	Ron Mix	1957-1959
	Anthony Munoz	1976-1979
	Troy Polamalu	1999-2002
	Junior Seau	1988-1989
	O.J. Simpson	1967-1968
	Lynn Swann	1972-1973
	Willie Wood	1957-1959
	Ron Yary	1965-1967
SC Assistant Coaches	Al Davis	1957-1959
	Joe Gibbs	1969-1970
	Mel Hein	1951-1965

UNIVERSITIES with the MOST NFL ATHLETE HALL of FAMERS:

USC	**14**
Notre Dame	13
Alabama	8
Michigan	8
Pittsburgh	8
Syracuse	8
Miami (Florida)	7
Minnesota	7
Illinois	6

UNIVERSITIES with the MOST ATHLETES SENT TO THE NFL SINCE 1970:

The following list was compiled by 24/7 Wall Street.

RANK	UNIVERSITY	PLAYERS SENT TO THE NFL
1	USC	325
2	Ohio State	318
3	Notre Dame	279
4	Penn State	278
5	Miami (Florida)	278
6	Nebraska	275
7	Oklahoma	267
8	Michigan	265
9	Florida	264
10	Alabama	254

TRAVELER, the REAL TROJAN HORSE:

The Tournament of Roses has had a place in Trojan lore since that first Rose Bowl game and victory played in the Rose Bowl stadium in 1923. Thirty-eight years later, in 1961, the USC Director of Special Events, Bob Jani, spotted a magnificent white horse prancing in the Rose Parade in advance of the traditional Rose Bowl game.

Traveler IX, part of the USC Trojan Family and a Trojan tradition. *USC Archive photo*

Traveler makes his appearance after each Trojan touchdown at home games when he races past the north-side Coliseum students to the strains of the uplifting "Conquest."

Traveler's name changed when he was retired. He then became Traveler I and the first in a long line of Trojan mascots that now include Traveler IX. Traveler was not the first Trojan mascot, but certainly the fastest. Indeed, he is probably the fastest mascot on Earth.

THE FIRST TROJAN MASCOT:

The honor of being the first official Trojan mascot belongs to a dog. "It's been more than 70 years since a feisty dog named George Tirebiter was first spotted on campus, but his statue near Zumberge Hall keeps a steady eye toward the Coliseum."

One of the original buildings on the USC campus, Zumberge Hall was originally known as "Science Hall" and was renamed in 2003 in honor of the passing of former USC President and professor of geology, James Zumberge. Currently, Zumberge Hall is home to USC's Department of Earth Sciences as well as the Southern California Earthquake Center.

In 1940, George "Tirebiter" was a campus fixture often seen chasing cars down Trousdale Parkway (then called University Avenue and open to traffic). "He eventually chased his way into the hearts of students and faculty, and on October 23, 1947, the student body voted to make him

George "Tirebiter," USC's first official mascot, wondering why he had to wear a Trojan sweater.
USC Archive photo

the first official mascot of USC." Students standing today at the corner of University Avenue and Hoover Street might wonder at the paw prints embedded in the cement. "Tirebiter" has left us his mark.

UCLA helped make "Tirebiter" an accidental celebrity when Bruin students kidnapped him and shaved UCLA on his back. It made headlines across the country. It made even more headlines when the dog bit Joe Bruin during a USC-UCLA football game.

The dog's celebrity created lots of tales, and some seemed "larger than life." One true tale tells of him chasing Oski, the University of California, Berkeley bear mascot, up a goalpost. He also rode in triumph sitting beside the then-President of USC in a convertible at a Coliseum football game.

"George was retired to a farm near the Mexican border, where he would chase his last tire. "After his passing, the Daily Trojan wrote: "Gone to Heaven, where he will have cushion rides for breakfast, white sidewalls for lunch, and cold rubber recaps for dinner." Today's students may not realize, but once white-sidewall tires were the rage.

"Tirebiter" may have been replaced by a horse, but his legacy lives on. It is rumored that the loyal pooch is responsible for the Trojan motto of "BITE ON." Rest in Peace.

Chapter Twelve
Trojan Recruiting

FERTILE SOUTHERN CALIFORNIA HUNTING GROUNDS:

In the introduction to this book, a discussion was included about the fertile grounds in the Los Angeles Area for Trojan recruiting. The Greater Los Angeles area is now the best "hunting grounds" for high school football talent.

The great Trojan Coach John McKay said it best when he was quoted, "I can find enough great football players within 60 miles of the USC campus to provide for a championship team." He then went out and proved it. Below are listings that will help verify that claim.

In 2022, High School Football America 100 compiled its final rankings of the best teams in the nation. The rankings for the top 100 are as follows as well as the final composite rankings from *MaxPreps* and the final ranking from *USA Today*, which sponsors the Coaches Poll.

FINAL HIGH SCHOOL FOOTBALL AMERICA TOP 100 (2022):

RANK	SCHOOL / LEAGUE		RECORD
1	**St. John Bosco (Southern California)**	**Trinity League**	13-1
2	Miami Central (Florida)		14-0
3	St. Thomas Aquinas (Florida)		14-0
4	**Mater Dei (Southern California)** **Trinity League,** *judged by High School Football America (HSFA) in 2021 and 2022 as the toughest league in America, includes parochial schools: Mater Dei, St. John Bosco, J-Serra Catholic, Orange Lutheran, Santa Margarita, and Servite*	**Trinity League**	12-1
5	**Bishop Gorman (Las Vegas, Nevada)** *Bishop Gorman has become a recruiting "provider" for USC. It is part of the USC area of influence in Southern California*		14-1
6	Duncanville (Texas)		15-0
7	St. Francis Academy (Maryland)		8-1
8	IMG Academy (Florida)		8-1
9	Chaminade-Madonna (Florida)		13-1
10	North Shore (Texas)		15-0
21	Basha (Arizona)		12-1
29	**Mission Viejo (Southern California)**		10-2

RANK	SCHOOL / LEAGUE	RECORD
30	**Corona Centennial (Southern California)** *One of the powerhouse SoCal teams.*	9-2
41	Kahuku (Hawaii) *Polynesian players have been prominent for USC. Southern California has the largest Samoan/Tongan community in the United States. Hawaii is also a hotbed of Trojan recruiting.*	12-2
43	**Lincoln (Southern California)** *Reggie Bush played for Helix High in San Diego. Lincoln is also part of the San Diego teams that provide talent to the Trojan Program.*	13-1
44	Saguaro (Arizona) *Saguaro has provided quality USC players. Arizona and Utah are both "rising stars" for Trojan recruitment*	9-4
49	**Serra (Southern California)**	13-1
57	Liberty (Arizona)	11-1
67	**Los Alamitos (Southern California)** *Provided two five-star players who will be Trojan freshmen in 2023.*	9-3
68	Chandler (Arizona)	9-3
69	Skyridge (Utah)	15-0
76	Folsom (California)	12-1
85	Corner Canyon (Utah)	10-2
87	Concord De La Salle (California)	10-4
91	Hamilton (California)	8-3
92	Lehi (Utah)	14-0

FINAL COMPOSITE 2022 RANKINGS as COMPILED by MAX PREPS:

RANK	SCHOOL	CITY / STATE
1	**St. John Bosco**	Bellflower, California
2	**Mater Dei**	Santa Ana, California
3	Central	Miami, Florida
4	**Bishop Gorman**	Las Vegas, Nevada

FINAL *USA TODAY* 2022 SUPER 25 HIGH SCHOOL FOOTBALL RANKINGS:

RANK	SCHOOL	CITY / STATE
1	St. John Bosco	Bellflower, California
2	Bishop Gorman	Las Vegas, Nevada
3	Mater Dei	Santa Ana, California

All three high schools are "providers" of the prodigious talent at USC. "Since 2000, five teams have received consensus 100% of selectors" for the High School Football National Championship:

Bishop Gorman	2016
Mater Dei	2017
St. John Bosco	2019
Mater Dei	2021
St. John Bosco	2022

In other words, the three teams have won 100% of the selectors in 2016, 2017, 2019, 2021, and 2022 for the mythical High School National Championship. Bosco and Bishop Gorman are more recent hotbeds of Trojan recruiting. Mater Dei has more of a history. At the end of this chapter are listed the ten best footballers in Mater Dei and St. John Bosco history. Six of the top eight from Mater Dei attended USC.

PAROCHIAL vs PUBLIC SCHOOLS:

From the above lists, it is apparent that there seems to be a preponderance of parochial schools versus public schools at the top of the lists. That is not by coincidence. Public schools are required to only include students within their geographical districts. Parochial schools are not restricted to that requirement and can "recruit" students who happen to be good football players from other public-school districts. Thus, high school sports have long entered another phase where they can recruit just like the colleges. Public schools can do it as well, but they must have the family of the recruit move within their district. Parochial schools are not bound by that restriction making their recruitment that much easier.

Examples of parochial schools are St. John Bosco in Bellflower, Bishop Gorman in Las Vegas, Mater Dei in Santa Ana, Servite in Anaheim, Orange Lutheran in Orange, Oaks Christian in Westlake Village, JSerra Catholic in San Juan Capistrano, Cathedral Catholic in San Diego, De La Salle in Concord, and Central Catholic in Modesto. Except for Bishop Gorman, each of the teams listed are in the top 20 of successful California high school football programs. De La Salle, in Northern California, has been the most successful during the last three decades.

De La Salle is the school with the longest win streak in American high school history. From 1992 through 2003, they won 151 straight games. The next closest high school was Independence from North Carolina which won 109 games from 2000-2007.

OTHER FERTILE AREAS for TROJAN RECRUITING:

The process of rebuilding Southern California recruiting by Lincoln Riley is already underway. He has a long way to go to get back to the level of recruitment under Coaches McKay or Carroll.

In addition to SoCal, the following regions have been recently productive for the Trojans: Texas, Washington, Nevada, Arizona, Utah, and Northern California. The Oregon program, funded by Nike, has been tough to match in the State of Oregon.

INTERNATIONAL RECRUITING:

Professional sports are leading the way in international recruiting. In 1987, the Dodgers opened Campo Las Palmas in the Dominican Republic. It has been used to identify and develop Latin American talent as well as those from the Dominican. The cost of the campo was $750,000. Not to be outdone, today "all 30 big league teams have academies" in the Dominican. "In the past 10 years, 15 academies have been built" there at an average cost of $4 million. "The more modern and luxurious have cost" upwards of $8.5 million. "The impact of the academies has been huge. In the Dominican Republic, 450-500 players are being signed a year."

The *Los Angeles Times* revealed on May 4, 2023, that the Dodgers now have a "secret" baseball academy in Uganda, in Africa. It is only a matter of time before the other teams follow the Dodger's lead, as they did in the Dominican.

A growing area of football recruitment is also in Africa. In June of 2022, the NFL conducted its "first official event in Africa, staging a prospect camp, a 'fan zone,' and a flag football clinic in Accra, Ghana. It appears that is just a start for the NFL in evaluating African talent.

High schools seem also to be capitalizing on African talent. This is mainly coming from Africa to America and not from America to Africa. African parents are often well-aware of the money being made in American sports. It has become an avenue for them to provide a bright future for their talented sons.

Nigeria, the most populous black nation on earth and one predicted to become as populous as the United States by 2050, is providing many of the recruits. The Republic of Cameroon has a common border with Nigeria and is also providing talent to the United States.

Through a process of identifying areas in the United States that might be willing to accept gifted African athletes, families in American localities play host to the athlete and provide a home. Those families are often fans of local high school football powerhouses.

The introduction of black African athletes to American sports is not just for football. Basketball has capitalized on many talented players who were either born in Africa or had parents born in Africa. The high school programs are then a "proving ground" for college recruitment. It is a process in its infancy, but is also a process that is spreading.

NFL games played in London, England have created an interest in the United Kingdom and America is now hosting recruits from England and Scotland. Mainland Europe is also contributing, with notable football recruits from Sweden and Germany.

The Pacific islands have also played their part. Polynesians have long been recruited by American college teams. USC has had many, mostly from the large Samoan/Tongan communities in Hawaii,

Southern California, and American Samoa itself. Those coming from American Samoa include a large contingent from the pure Polynesian areas of Tonga and Samoa (formerly Western Samoa).

AREAS of CONCERN:

While the Trojans have realized a great deal of recruiting success, there are areas of concern. Florida vies with Texas and California as producers of successful high school football talent. USC has not developed Florida sufficiently as a recruiting base.

California is not the best recruiting base for defensive linemen, which has been a weakness on Trojan teams. The SEC territory is perhaps the best in the country for the development of those needed defensive linemen. The Trojans have made recent inroads in that area, but need to develop a lot more to succeed in joining the truly elite programs that participate and win the College Football Playoffs (CFP). Two recruits in the 2024 class are from Georgia, so the process of developing the SEC areas seems to be working.

A BREWING SCANDAL:

In line with the admonition to "follow the money," there is a situation that has received no attention in the media. With the increased incidence of money going to college athletes, especially with the advent of NIL and the more lucrative NFL contracts, it is very tempting for high school athletes and their families to consider using growth hormones and/or performance-enhancing drugs.

The size of high school athletes today have greatly increased over high school football athletes of several generations ago. The increase does not seem to equate to greater human sizes evident today due to better nutrition and protein. Human growth hormones (HGH) seem a possible reason for the evident increase.

With so much money involved, the temptation is to use whatever means are available to create an advantage over athletes. Parents sometimes use whatever means, legal or illegal, to give their children advantages. It is something that colleges might be willing to ignore.

This is just speculation and not based on any actual observation of use. But, based on logic, it seems likely to be the subject of a future scandal.

TEN GREATEST MATER DEI PLAYERS in its HISTORY:

1. **Matt Leinart**, Quarterback. Graduated in 2001
   College: USC

"Leinart is best known for his time at USC, where he won the Heisman Trophy in 2003 and back-to-back National Championships" in 2003 and 2004. Before he became one of the greatest college quarterbacks of all time, he was named the 2000 California Gatorade Player of the Year as a senior at Mater Dei and led the Monarchs to the California Interscholastic Federation (CIF) Division 1 co-championship as a junior.

2. **Bryce Young**, Quarterback, Graduated in 2020
   College: Alabama

Bryce Young transferred to Mater Dei from Cathedral High in Los Angeles. He threw for 4,528 yards and 58 touchdowns as a senior, when he was named California Gatorade Player for the Year and named *USA Today* Offensive Player of the Year.

Young was a backup on the University of Alabama College Football Playoff National Champions in 2020. The next year he won the Heisman Trophy, the year prior to Caleb Williams, after he threw for 4,872 yards, 47 touchdowns, with only seven interceptions.

3. **Matt Grootegoed**, Running Back, Defensive Back, and Linebacker. Graduated in 2000.
   College: USC

USC head coach Pete Carroll said it best about Grootegoed: "Things just happen when he's on the field." Grootegoed was a four-year starter at linebacker for USC and was a significant defensive player on the two Carroll National Championships in 2003 and 2004 alongside fellow Monarch and Trojan, Matt Leinart. He was an AP All-American his senior year.

4. **J.T. Daniels**, Quarterback, Graduated in 2019, but was reclassified to 2018.
   College: USC, followed by Georgia and West Virginia.

"Daniels was a two-time California Gatorade Player of the Year and the Gatorade National Player of the Year as a junior at Mater Dei in 2017, when he led his team to a 15-0 record along with a CIF Championship and a National Championship.

In 2018, when he should have been a senior at Mater Dei, he was starting quarterback for USC. In 2019, he lost his spot due to a very severe injury. He transferred to Georgia and was backup quarterback on their 2021 CFP National Championship team."

5. **John Huarte**, Quarterback, Graduated in 1961.
   College: Notre Dame

Huarte is in the amazing position of being only 5th on this listing and having won the Heisman Trophy for Notre Dame in 1964. He starred for Mater Dei in the 1950s and after graduation for Notre Dame played 11 seasons of professional football for the AFL, the NFL, and the WFL. He was a backup with the Kansas City Chiefs when they won the Super Bowl in 1969.

6. **Matt Barkley**, Quarterback, Graduated in 2009.
   College: USC

Barkley was a four-year starter at quarterback for Mater Dei, named as Gatorade National Player of the Year and Gatorade National Male Athlete of the Year as a junior in 2007.

He was widely considered one of the best prep quarterbacks of all time. His time at USC included being a four-year starter like at Mater Dei, but otherwise, his collegiate career fell flat. However, he dd set several Trojan records, including throwing for more yardage than any other quarterback at USC. Starting all four seasons will allow that. In the NFL, he has had a career as backup but never as a starter. In his last ten seasons, Barkley served on nine different teams.

For Pete Carroll at USC, Matt Barkley, and Matt Leinart, both Mater Dei graduates, served as his starting quarterbacks, Leinart in 2003, 2004, and 2005, and Barkley in 2009, 2010, and 2011. In his senior year, 2012, Barkley started for Lane Kiffin.

7. **Amon-Ra St. Brown,** Wide Receiver, Graduated in 2018
   College: USC

Amon-Ra St. Brown was a *USA Today* All-American as a Mater Dei senior in 2017 when he had 72 receptions for 1,320 yards and 20 touchdowns playing with JT Daniels, the National Gatorade Player of the Year. They both joined the Trojans and figured on continuing their unmatched high school record of continual passing completions. That ended abruptly on the field in USCs second game of the season when Daniels went down in a heap due to a severe injury that effectively ended his career at USC

Brown was All Pac-12 his senior year at USC. Joining the Detroit Lions of the NFL, Brown set the Lions franchise rookie record with 912 receiving yards in 2021.

8. **Domani Jackson**, Cornerback, Graduated in 2022
   College: USC

Jackson has seemed NFL-bound since he first stepped onto a football field at Mater Dei. In just his freshman year, he earned MaxPreps All-American honors. He again was named on the same All-American list during his sophomore year. He lost his junior year due to the pandemic and his senior year due to a knee injury.

Jackson was the #1 recruit in California in 2022 and already picked to be a first-round NFL pick when eligible. He will be a sophomore for the Trojans in 2023. His upside is almost unlimited as he has the speed and leaping ability to stay with anyone. As a senior at Mater Dei, he tied the California state record in the 100-meter dash in a "blazing 10.25 seconds." The national high school record is 10.00 seconds.

9. **Larry Williams**, Offensive Lineman, Graduated in 1981.
   College: Notre Dame

Williams, standing 6 foot 5 inches tall and weighing 295 pounds, was a two-time All-American at Notre Dame. He played 9 seasons in the NFL before going into athletic administration where he was an athletic director for the Universities of Portland, Marquette, and Akron.

10. **Thomas Duarte**, Tight End, Wide Receiver, Graduated in 2013
    College: UCLA

Duarte was named *USA Today* All-American in 2012 when he had 58 receptions for 1,025 yards and 15 touchdowns. He was named *Los Angeles Times* Player of the Year and Orange County Register Offensive Player of the Year.

In his junior year, 2015, he had a breakout season at UCLA and was named All-Pac-12, where he excelled as the "go-to" guy on the Bruin offense. He made the common mistake and opted to go to the NFL his senior year before he had a chance to jell his considerable pass-catching talents. He played only two seasons for the Miami Dolphins.

As a prime example of the Trojan recruiting in the Los Angeles area, USC had six of the top eight Mater Dei players in their history, three of which were quarterbacks. The quality of the Mater Dei players is evident with three Heisman Trophy winners, 6 college All-American elections, 4 high school All-American selections,4 National Gatorade Player of the Year selections, and seven who played in the NFL.

That is significant in the listing because two of the ten are still in college (Daniels at West Virginia and Jackson at USC) plus Young has not entered the NFL yet (as of this writing) but was selected the #1 overall pick in the 2023 NFL draft. With the other honors bestowed on Mater Dei, it is incredible that one school could develop so much talent.

Yhe three Heisman winners were all quarterbacks. Three of the six Monarch players that committed to USC were also quarterbacks. Five of the top six on the above list were quarterbacks. The Trinity League, which includes Bosco and Mater Dei, also includes Santa Margarita. Santa Margarita produced 2002 USC Heisman Trophy-winning quarterback Carson Palmer.

TEN GREATEST ST. JOHN BOSCO PLAYERS in its HISTORY:

1. **Wyatt Davis**, Offensive Line, Graduated in 2016
   College: Ohio State

Davis is probably the best offensive lineman to come out of SoCal in a generation. USC let him get away and lived to regret it.

Davis "is the only offensive lineman to win the *Los Angeles Times* Glenn Davis Award as the top high school player in California. He was named a *USA Today* All-American in high school and was a two-time All-American at Ohio State." He was named the Big Ten Offensive Lineman of the Year in 2020 and currently plays for the Saints in the NFL.

2. **D.J. Uiagalelei**, Quarterback, Graduated in 2020
   College: Clemson

"Uiagalelei led the Braves to a 15-0 record and a CIF Open Division State Championship on the way to being named California Gatorade Player of the Year and *USA Today* (National) Offensive Player of the Year, all in his junior year. He was again named *USA Today* All-American as a senior.

3. **Josh Rosen**, Quarterback, Graduated in 2015
    College: UCLA

Rosen led the Braves to their first National Championship and the CIF Open Division State Championship as a junior in 2013. He was named the *Los Angeles Times* Glenn Davis winner and a *USA Today* All-American as a senior in 2014.

At UCLA, he "was the #1 quarterback recruit in 2015 and won Pac-12 Freshman Offensive Player of the Year in 2015 and an All-Pac-12 selection in 2017."

4. **Matayo Uiagalelei**, Defensive End, Tight End, Graduated in 2023
    College: Oregon

Perhaps the best of all the Bosco footballers, he is larger at 6'-5" and 265 pounds than his older brother (#2). One of the key targets of the Trojans, he was another Bosco baller who got away.

5. **Sean McGrew**, Running Back, Graduated in 2016
    College: Washington

McGrew was a key part of the Bosco 1st National Championship in 2013, when the Braves beat Concord De La Salle for the CIF Open Division State Championship. He came within one win of another national title as a senior when Bosco lost to Corona Centennial for the State Championship. He was named Gatorade California Player of the Year after scoring 30 touchdowns.

Named All-Pac-12 as a senior in 2021.

6. **Todd Husak**, Quarterback, Graduated in 1996
    College: Stanford

Husak led Stanford to the Rose Bowl as a senior when he was named All-Pac-10 and the MVP of the 2000 Hula Bowl. He led the NFL Europe Berlin Thunder to a victory in the World Bowl in 2002, in addition to playing for the Washington Redskins.

7. **Trent McDuffie**, Cornerback, Graduated in 2019
    College: Washington

"A U.S. Army All-American in high school, he became a two-time All-Pac-12 selection at Washington. He was named AP All-American as a junior in 2021 and left school early to enter the NFL draft."

8. **Jaleel Wadood**, Defensive back, Wide Receiver, Graduated in 2014
    College: UCLA

The best player on the 2013 National Champions, he had 78 receptions for 1,293 yards and 21 touchdowns on offense. On defense, he had 115 tackles and four interceptions. In high school, he was CIF Defensive Player of the Year and the *Los Angeles Times* Glenn Davis Award winner as well as a MaxPreps All-American and U.S. Army All-American.

At UCLA he was named All-Pac-12 three times.

9. **Jacob Tuioti-Mariner**, Defensive Tackle, Graduated in 2014
    College: UCLA

After starring on the National Champion 2013 Bosco team, he was a three-year starter at UCLA and an All-Pac-12 selection as a senior. He played for the Falcons and Panthers in the NFL.

10. **Leon McFadden**, Cornerback, Graduated in 2009
    College: San Diego State

McFadden was a football and track star at Bosco and at San Diego State. He ended his career as "one of San Diego State's greatest defensive backs ever. He was a four-year starter and just the 5th player in school history to be named All-Mountain West Conference for three seasons in a row." He played for five seasons in the NFL.

Three Bruins but not one Trojan. Bosco presents a challenge for Lincoln Riley. If he meets and beats that challenge, it will go a long way to resurrect USC as one of the best, if not the best, college teams in the nation.

VENTURA COUNTY HIGH SCHOOLS THAT PRODUCE FOOTBALL PLAYERS:

OAKS CHRISTIAN:

Oaks Christian is not a Ventura County school, but it was originally scheduled to be built in Thousand Oaks until its 20-acre property was purchased by the City of Thousand Oaks to build a Transportation Center. It is currently located within yards from the Ventura County line, which is the town limit for Thousand Oaks.

Oaks Christian produces footballers. USC needs to cultivate this school because UCLA is currently in the drivers-seat for its talent. The private school was started in 2000 and boasts the following accomplishments of its football program: Six consecutive section titles in football, five CIF State titles, two Gatorade State Players of the Year, and one National Gatorade Player of the Year.

The following NFL players are graduates: Alex Bachman (2020-2021), Cassius Marsh (2014-2021), Alani Fua (2015-2016), Jordan Payton (2016), Jimmy Clauson (2010-2015), Chris Owusu (2012-2015), Francis Owusu, Marc Tyler, Malcolm Jones, Cameron Judge, and Casey Mathews (2011-2014) of the famous Trojan Mathews family. Current NFL graduates include Colby Parkinson (2020-2022), Michael Pittman, Jr. (2020-2022), and Kayvon Thibodeaux (2020-2022).

College players include UCLA standouts Bo Calvert and Zach Charbonnet, and Nick Montana (son of Joe Montana) of Tulane. Calvert committed to USC as a sophomore but flipped to UCLA. His two brothers also graduated from Oaks. Josh played for Washington and Ethan was the third highest rated football recruit in University of Utah history.

SIMI VALLEY HIGH:

Simi Valley High is included based on its coach, Jim Benkert. Benkert built the Moorpark High program into a local powerhouse and then helped do the same for Oaks Christian.

MOORPARK HIGH:

Graduates include Brian Blechen at Utah and Darrell Scott at South Florida. NFL players: Dennis Pitta, Ravens; Greg Estrada, Jacksonville; Chad Hansen, Jets; Chastin West, Lions; Drake London (USC standout WR), Falcons.

Current Trojan offensive tackle Jonah Monheim.

ST. BONAVENTURE (VENTURA):

One of the greatest, Trojan linebacker Rey Maualuga, graduated from St. Bonnies. He played in the NFL from 2009-2017. Tailback Lorenzo Booker (NFL 2007-2011) and Troy Hill (NFL 2015-2022).

St. Bonnies has a rich football history: State Champions in 2000, 2001, 2005, 2007, and 2008. They were league champions 20 times and CIF-SS (Southern Section) Champions in 1968, 1996, 1999, 2000, 2001, 2002, 2004, 2005, 2007, and 2008.

THE SECOND GREATEST PRODUCER of NFL PLAYERS in the UNITED STATES:

LONG BEACH "POLY" POLYTECHNIC:

Long Beach Poly has produced more NFL players (58) than any other high school in America, other than Virginia's Fork Union Military Academy. As of 2021, the following list includes the top 10 high schools in California in producing NFL players. Due to ties, the list includes 13:

LARGEST PRODUCERS of NFL PLAYERS in CALIFORNIA:

RANK	HIGH SCHOOL	PLAYERS	CITY
1	Long Beach Poly	58	Long Beach
2	Dorsey	33	Los Angeles
3	Abraham Lincoln	25	San Diego
4	Crenshaw	25	Los Angeles
5	Compton	23	Compton
6	Junipero Serra	22	Gardena
7	Santa Monica	20	Santa Monica
8	Bakersfield	20	Bakersfield
9	Pasadena	19	Pasadena
10	Manual Arts	19	Los Angeles
11	John Muir	19	Pasadena
12	John C. Fremont	19	Los Angeles
13	Carson	19	Carson

All 13 high schools are Southern California schools, with Lincoln and Bakersfield the only two outside Los Angeles County.

For comparison, the following listing represents the top high school in each of the Pac-12 States. Admittedly, with a population of 25 million in Southern California, most other states are at a disadvantage. However, when considering that all but two of the above list are in Los Angeles County, with a population of 10 million, then the quality of SoCal football programs, in comparison with the rest of the Pac-12 states, really stands out.

LARGEST PRODUCERS of NFL TALENT in EACH PAC-12 STATE (Other than California):

SCHOOL	PLAYERS	CITY
Gonzaga Prep (Washington)	11	Spokane
Chandler (Arizona)	13	Chandler
South Mountain (Arizona)	13	Phoenix
Denver South (Colorado)	9	Denver
Jefferson (Oregon)	11	Portland
Logan (Utah)	9	Logan

THIRD MOST SUCCESSFUL CURRENT SOCAL HIGH SCHOOL:

CORONA CENTENNIAL:

NFL players from Centennial include Jared Norris (2016-2021), Vontaze Burfict (2012-2019), Will Sutton (2014-2016), Kevin Smith (2015), Brandon Magee (2013-2014), and Lonie Paxton (2000-2011). Current players in the NFL include Drake Jackson (2022), who starred at USC, and Segun Olubi (2022).

Every year, Corona Centennial is one of the top prep football programs in Southern California. Currently, the top SoCal programs are Mater Dei, St. John Bosco, and Corona Centennial.

WHAT RECRUITS MUST ASK THEMSELVES:

Recruits considering an institution should evaluate many things before reaching a decision as to which university should be their home. Of course, academics are the most important. USC is one of the more highly rated academic institutions in the country.

"Does the football program contain enough for me to reach my goals." Lincoln Riley brings a lot to the table. So does USC.

Some considerations that are important are sometimes overlooked by those recruits so focused on their football goals that they do not consider other things. Consider why Notre Dame schedules all its late-season games with USC in Los Angeles. The weather gets awfully cold in South Bend.

What is there to do in Georgia, in Alabama, in Ohio State, or Notre Dame when a recruit is not doing football? Do any of them have the mountains and deserts of Southern California to explore? Do any have an ocean that provides lots of activities? Do any provide nearby skiing as is available in SoCal? Water skiing and snow skiing are all within a short distance away.

Southern California is the entertainment capital of the world, providing unlimited varieties from which to choose. Cultural venues and museums abound. The number, quality, and variety of restaurants in the Greater Los Angeles area is astounding.

College social life is equally important. What about the college girls? Songwriters have been extolling California girls for generations and the Trojan cheer and song leaders, as well as the entire student body, are beautiful examples. When selecting a college, recruits should ensure that they research all aspects of college life, not just the football program.

Chapter Thirteen

A Case Against the Unfair and Unjust NCAA Sanctions

The records of several of the USC football coaches, who served after Pete Carroll left for the NFL, would have been better had they not had to deal with the draconian penalties imposed on the Trojans for violations of NCAA rules regarding student-athletes. The affected coaches were mainly Lane Kiffin and Steve Sarkisian, both of whom had served as offensive coordinators for Carroll and both who would later serve in the same capacity for Nick Saban and the Alabama Crimson Tide.

Kiffin and Sarkisian are both very good coaches. "Prior to his first head coaching job, Kiffin spent six years as an assistant coach for Pete Carroll, including two years as the offensive coordinator (2005-2006). During his first tenure with the Trojans, USC captured two national championships and compiled a 65-12 record."

Sarkisian was hired by Carroll in January 2001, as an offensive assistant before USC had even played a down for Carroll. Sarkisian, after later serving as Trojan head coach, was fired by then-Athletic Director Pat Haden, who also fired Kiffin, for an alcohol issue. Sarkisian had spoken at a USC preseason event using slurred speech and profanity while addressing those attending. Sarkisian checked himself into a "residential treatment facility" to get back on his feet.

USC assistant coach Steve Sarkisian discusses offensive plan with quarterback Matt Leinart and Head Coach Pete Carroll. *Photo by Kevork Djansezian AP file, 2005, appeared in The News Tribune, a McClatchy Media Network newspaper.*

Kiffin followed Carroll as USC head coach. His coaching career did not immediately transfer from Trojan assistant to head coach. First, he was hired by the NFL Oakland Raiders as its head coach but then was fired by former USC assistant coach Al Davis, owner of the Raiders. His first head coaching job with Oakland (2007-2008) did not go well, as he had a record of 5-15 in less than two full NFL seasons.

Kiffin was then hired by SEC powerhouse Tennessee as its head coach (2009), but he quit that job after going 7-6 to become head coach at USC. He coached the Trojans from 2010-2013, amassing a record of 28-15, which was respectable considering the penalties imposed by the NCAA. Those penalties will be discussed later in this chapter. After being fired by Haden, Kiffin was hired by Alabama as offensive coordinator. While there (2014-2016), his tutelage helped create both a Biletnikoff Award winner and a Heisman Trophy winner. His dynamic offense "helped the Crimson Tide to a national championship in 2015."

Kiffin next was head coach at Florida Atlantic (FAU) from 2017 to 2019, where he compiled a 26-13 record. His current coaching gig is back at the SEC as head coach at Ole Miss. "In 11 years at the NCAA level, Kiffin has posted an all-time record of 84-47, including a 23-13 mark at Ole Miss." With the vaunted recruiting history of USC, Kiffin undoubtedly would have done better had he not had to contend with the NCAA penalties, which cut his allowable scholarship players from 85 to 75 and denied the Trojans the much-needed bowl exposure by imposing a ban on any post-season games for two years. Based on statements made by recruits who did not join USC, it made a significant difference to the Trojan win-loss record under Kiffin.

Sarkisian had a similar coaching timeline as Kiffin. He served as an analyst and quarterbacks

USC Head Coach Lane Kiffin was troubled with the on-field problems created by the overly severe NCAA sanctions. *CBS Sports photo*

coach (2001-2003) under former BYU coach Norm Chow, who was offensive coordinator for Carroll. Chow had been his head coach at Brigham Young when Sarkisian was their star quarterback.

Next, Sarkisian spent one year (2004) as quarterbacks coach for the Oakland Raiders, beating his co-assistant-coach Kiffin to the Raiders by three years. He then returned to the Trojans as quarterbacks coach, associate head coach, and then as offensive coordinator for Pete Carroll (2005-2008).

Coach Sark left the Trojan program in 2009 when presented with the opportunity to be head coach at Washington (2009-2013). He went 34-29 during those five years. Nothing remarkable but his teams got steadily better. His final Husky team went 8-4 before Sarkisian again returned to USC, this time as head coach. His 2014 season at USC was moderately successful, going 9-4 with a Holiday Bowl win. Then he hit bottom in 2015 with his alcohol-influenced season, going 3-2 before being fired for multiple alcohol-related offenses.

Kiffin headed the USC program from 2010 to 2013, while Sarkisian followed him from 2014 to midway through the 2015 season. Both suffered from the scholarship penalty and the post-season ban. Both assuredly would have posted better records without the 2010 penalties.

BIAS AGAINST USC in the NCAA INVESTIGATION:

During and immediately after the NCAA investigation, speculation was rampant among USC followers that the NCAA had a bias against the Trojans. Several different possibilities were mentioned as causes for the alleged bias, from Trojan recruiting advantages due to area and climate, as well as a reported arrogance shown by the USC Athletic Department.

Mike Garrett was the USC Athletic Director at the time. Several statements attributed to Garrett, which might have been called arrogance, could also have been called pride. Over the years, all of us who have been fans, former players, administrators, families, and staff, plus untold others, have had pride in Trojan accomplishments in all sports. Pride in Trojan success can often be seen, by those in other regions of America, as arrogance.

Statements made by the NCAA Infractions Committee members spoke of "setting an example." The infractions committee was comprised of Chairman Paul T. Dee, and members: Britton Banowsky, John S. Black, Melissa Conboy, Brian Halloran, Eleanor W. Myers, Josephine (Jo) Potuto, and Dennis E. Thomas.

A principal target of the investigation was USC football's running back coach Todd McNair. The penalties imposed on USC and on McNair, which will be explained in full later in this chapter, proved devastating to his career. He was unemployable anywhere in American football for almost ten years, until the lawsuit was settled through mediation.

As a result, McNair filed a defamation lawsuit against the NCAA. A result of the lawsuit is that USC finally had access to documents relating to the investigation. The *Los Angeles Times* stated in 2015 that "The unsealing of nearly 500 pages of documents in Todd McNair's defamation lawsuit against the NCAA provided a window into the way the governing body for college sports conducted its investigation and punished McNair and USC."

The documents "included emails and memos by members of the NCAA infractions committee that (incredibly) compared the evidence in the scandal to the Oklahoma City bombing, mocked USC's response to the matter, and derided the hiring of Lane Kiffin as Trojans football coach."

After reading over the unsealed documents, USC stated that it was evident that there was a "bias against McNair and USC by and on behalf of the NCAA and its Committee on Infractions." The USC statement went on to say, "We are extremely disappointed and dismayed at the way the NCAA investigated, judged, and penalized our university throughout this process."

Athletic Director Pat Haden agreed saying that "These recent documents confirm what we've believed all along, that we were treated unfairly in this investigation and its penalties."

Eleanor Myers, mentioned above as one of the members of the infractions committee, said in a March 2010 email to the NCAA, that the organizations enforcement staff "botched" a key interview with McNair, stating that McNair "did not have a good opportunity" to explain a phone call with sports marketer Lloyd Lake that the NCAA used as evidence in the case. More on Lake and the phone call later.

The California Second District Court of Appeal reviewed the evidence in the defamation lawsuit and made the following statement: "This evidence clearly indicated that the ensuing NCAA infractions committee report was worded in disregard of the truth to enable the (NCAA committee) to arrive at a predetermined conclusion that USC employee McNair was aware of the NCAA violations."

The above quote from the California Court of Appeal comes from judges who understand law and the need for proof in any "legitimate" investigation leading to penalties. Actual proof, and not supposition, is required in any court of law. "Hunches" do not count.

The conclusions of the Dee committee were evaluated by the Court and determined to be "in disregard of the truth." Four years of investigation led to such weak conclusions that the Court deemed that the purpose of the investigation was to "arrive at a predetermined conclusion" about McNair. It also seems that Dee and his fellow conspirators had a predetermined conclusion about the university which was so unfairly maligned.

This author has read through and thoroughly studied the 67-page "University of Southern California Public Infractions Report" dated June 10, 2010. Repeatedly, throughout the NCAA document, are statements about loose and out-of-control areas of concern at USC. Specifically, it mentioned uncontrolled football practice "sidelines" and facilities, including locker rooms.

The author can refute one reported aspect, that of the football practice sidelines. They were not out of control. When Pete Carroll became football coach, he opened up different areas of the football program to give fans, friends, and family members of the players better access to football. He stated that he wanted to make it a fun experience for everyone and proceeded to make practices fun for the players. He also invited fans, friends, and family members to attend practices with the team.

At the time, the author was a member of the Trojan Club. With another Club member, they would occasionally attend practices together. The other member was an accountant and he would change from his working attire to more casual clothing at an on-campus facility. Then he and the author would both go to the sideline to watch practice. USC provided all Trojan Club members, and presumably all other similar Trojan support organizations, with a brochure detailing dos and don'ts for Club members regarding any semblance of recruiting. It was made very clear to all members what was permissible and what was not regarding athlete recruitment. Those rules seemed never to be violated by support institutions like the Trojan Clubs throughout the Southland, and other Trojan support groups such as Cardinal and Gold. It all was very much "in control."

The sidelines were great. It was a very congenial atmosphere. A large part of the group consisted of family members of those practicing. Those of us who were friends and fans, were relegated to a certain area of the stands. It was a very relaxed, easy-going, friendly atmosphere. Fans, friends, and families walked around and chatted. It was a chance to get to know the families. The sidelines were a rewarding and fun experience. There was never any" incident" of any kind and certainly it was not "out-of-control" as the NCAA alleged.

What is the purpose of having fans? Fans support institutions, such as USC. Without fans, there would be no revenue from sports merchandise, no stadium ticket and food revenue, no stadium parking money, and no television revenue. Fans must turn on those televisions to get the response needed by the networks. Why is it then the NCAAs seeming-desire to take some of the fun out of the fan experience? The Infractions Committee was made up of members who had full-time jobs, many in athletics, which paid them salaries. Fans are the ones that created the salaries for which the committee members were paid.

Item (20) in the committee's listing of penalties states: "The Committee is troubled by the institution's (USC) failure to regulate access to practices and facilities, including locker rooms. Therefore, for the period of probation (four years), USC shall prohibit all non-institutional personnel (fans), including representatives of the institutions' athletic interests (except media, family members, and others approved by the compliance office on a case-by-case basis) from doing the following:

A. Traveling on football and men's basketball team charters;

B. Attending football and men's basketball team practices.

C. Attending or participating in any way with institutional football and men's basketball camps, including the donation of funds to the camps; and

D. Having access to sidelines and locker rooms before, during, and after football and men's basketball games. Exceptions may be granted by the compliance office to prospective student-athletes, and their families on official, paid visits or unofficial visits. The exceptions must be stated in writing and issued by the compliance personnel.

What is the served purpose of penalizing fans who had nothing to do with the supposed actions that caused the committee to act? Isn't the purpose of the NCAA to create interest in their sports? Why then penalize fans and football players for the actions of one man? (More on that later).

The criticisms of the sanctions imposed were widespread, even those of some NCAA football writers, including ESPN's Ted Miller, who wrote, "It's become an accepted fact among informed college football observers that the NCAA sanctions against USC were a travesty of justice, and the NCAA's refusal to revisit that travesty is a massive act of cowardice on the part of the organization."

Miller also expanded by adding: "During a flight delay last year, I was cornered at an airport by an administrator from a major program outside the Pac-12. He made fun of me as a 'USC fanboy' because of my rants against the NCAA ruling against the Trojans. But we started talking and it turned out he agreed with just about all my points. He just did not like USC.

He told me, after some small talk and off-the-record, that "everybody" thought USC got screwed. He said that he thought the NCAA was trying to scare everyone with the ruling, but subsequent major violation cases put it in a pickle (the specific case involved the University of Miami while the Infractions Committee Chair Dee was its athletic director).

Then he told me that USC was punished for its "USC-ness" that while many teams had closed-down access, to media, and to fans, etc. USC under Pete Carroll was completely open, and that was widely resented. There was widespread belief that the national media fawned over USC because of this. Further, more than a few schools thought that the presence of big-time celebrities, such as Snoop Dogg and Will Ferrell, at practices and at games constituted an unfair recruiting advantage for the Trojans. When the same schools do the same thing, such as Mathew McConaughey at Texas football games, they laud it. Farrell is a USC graduate just like McConaughey at Texas (1993). The evident hypocrisy is apparent throughout this chapter.

It (the actor fans) was not against the rules, but everyone hated it. This, as he assessed his own smell test, was a subtext of the so-called atmosphere of noncompliance that the NCAA referred to. An atmosphere that oddly yielded very few instances of noncompliance around the football program, even after a four-year NCAA investigation.

The NCAA punishment was the second most severe in the history of the NCAA. The most severe was that meted out to SMU which caused that university to temporarily shut down its football program. Afterward, it was referred to as the "death penalty."

The penalty was not only against the football program, but also against USCs basketball and women's tennis. Reggie Bush and O.J. Mayo, of the basketball team, were charged with forfeiting their amateur status by accepting gifts from agents. The Tennis team was "charged" with "unauthorized phone calls made by a former player." The Trojan tennis team was barred from post-season activity for four years, based on one ex-player making unauthorized telephone calls. Just phone calls involving one former player. Keep that in mind when you read of the University of Miami scandal of 2011, only one year after the publication of the USC investigation findings.

The draconian penalties were exacted against the university, but also against Bush, Mayo, and the Trojan football and basketball teams. Does it make any sense at all to penalize 84 of the 85 scholarship football players for the guilty actions of only one player? The other players were innocent of any wrongdoing, yet had the records of their accomplishments erased from the record books. One of the stated purposes of the hypocritical NCAA was to protect student-athletes. In the USC decision, they effectively threw the Trojan players "under the bus." Was that an example of protecting student-athletes?

The author feels that the accusations against Reggie Bush, will someday soon be overturned. Overturned because of bias and penalties that did not match the severity of the "crime." It will also be overturned based on the NIL. It will be overturned due to the statements of the California

Appeals Court that reviewed the documents purportedly against USC that were referenced in the final report. It will be overturned and the Bush Heisman Trophy will be returned based on a very questionable investigation.

NIL stands for Name, Image, and Likeness. In June 2021, the Supreme Court of the United States unanimously ruled against the NCAA stating that the NCAA could not limit education-related payments to student-athletes. Trojan players are now signing NIL contracts with providers that will pay them significant amounts, depending on each athlete, of money for their NIL as created on the football field.

Part of the many penalties imposed on USC by the NCAA is their insistence that all information about the USC 2005 football season must include the forfeited games in the form of continued punishment. Is it fair to continue punishing USC for Bush's illegal actions that are now considered legal by a unanimous Supreme Court a mere 11 years after the action? Doesn't the Supreme Court action imply that payments should have always been legal? The feelings expressed by many were that the universities were enriching themselves with their "exploitation" of their athletes. The author does not agree with those considerations.

LLOYD LAKE:

Much of the investigation rested on the testimony of a man named Lloyd Lake. He was one of two sports agents mentioned repeatedly throughout the NCAA charging document. He was variously described as "Agency Partner A," "Sports Agent A," and "Sports Marketer A." The importance of his testimony can be seen by the number of references made of him in the document.

From page 4 through page 36 of the Infractions Report, Lake, and occasionally his mother, are referenced a total of 168 times. His testimony formed the basis for most of the charges against USC. His girlfriend was quoted an additional eight times, She was later described as his "ex-girlfriend." His "sister" was quoted seven times. Who is Lloyd Lake and is he credible? As stated on Report pages seven and 15 "The Committee finds Agency Partner A (Lloyd Lake), credible."

On Report page 6, item (11), the document states, "In June 2005, during the investigation that while Agency Partner A was incarcerated…" Incarcerated, why and for what?

That information was clarified on report page 30. The USC General Counsel reported "that, in 1995, sports marketer A (Lloyd Lake) 'pleaded guilty to mail fraud for defrauding the NFL.'"

In other words, the NCAA did not believe Coach McNair, who had never been charged with a felony offense, while it did believe the voluminous testimonies of a convicted felon who was "incarcerated" during the time of the investigation.

The convicted felon was quoted 168 times in the report. It boggles the mind. Having said that, it is also the author's opinion that most of the comments and testimony referenced in the report and attributed to Lake are probably valid. It is reported by the NCAA that there are backup tapes to verify, but those tapes were not provided by the NCAA to the committee.

What does negatively impress the author was the lack of professionalism in the report. When it repeatedly referenced dollar figures that were reported as "about" $5,000 or "about" $3,500. What is "about" about? One might conclude that, in a report of this magnitude, specific bank figures would be included. The inexactness of "about" followed by a number followed by three zeros indicates that it was extracted from memory and not from bank records to verify.

The telephone call from Todd McNair to Lake is a very important part of the "proof" included in the document. Proof that was supposedly verified by Lake's girlfriend, who stated that she remembered the call, but then stated, "So, I'm assuming that it's him (Assistant Coach McNair), but I am not sure" (page 26). According to testimony by both Bush and McNair, it is questionable that the verified call was between McNair and Lake at all. McNair was trying to get in touch with Bush and reportedly talked with Bush at 1:34 in the morning. Bush testified he used Lake's phone number as a call number to reach him in San Diego for McNair on the weekend in question.

In other words, the committee believed the girlfriend of a convicted felon who still stated that she was not sure if it was McNair. Is this "proof" that Lake and McNair had a 2 minute and 23 second conversation? The phone records are proof that a conversation did take place, but not proof of who the parties were that were talking. While it may be partially correct, the proof presented is not convincing.

What is convincing is the sheer volume of reported money transfers from either Lake or his mother to Bush or his father. While Reggie Bush clearly committed a violation of NCAA rules and should receive some form of penalty, it does not mean that the school or the USC football team should be penalized There is nothing in the document that unequivocally states that USC knew what Bush and his family had been doing. There was no proof, just "gut-feeling" speculation on the part of the committee. Remember, the committee had four years to find proof of USC's actual knowledge and involvement, yet never did.

McNair reported to the committee that "I don't ever recall talking to Lloyd Lake in my life" (page 24). Yet the committee did not believe him. McNair offered a very plausible explanation: On the night in question, Reggie Bush was supposed to host a five-star recruit at USC. It was later verified by others that Bush forgot and remained in San Diego instead of going to the USC campus to host the recruit.

Prior to the weekend, the author recalls reading of the recruits to be entertained on the weekend in question and that Bush had the "honor" of hosting a five-star. That was all before the NCAA got involved. The charging document stated that the recruit had been left without escort past midnight as though it was another cause to claim the Trojan's "loose" control. Instead, it was further proof that McNair's version was correct.

McNair said that, when it became known the recruit did not have anyone to escort him, McNair tried to reach Bush in San Diego to find out why the recruit was left stranded. The contact number Bush had given to McNair, his position coach at USC, was the phone number for Lake. The committee felt that McNair had committed an offense by talking to a possible agent for Bush. McNair stated he, instead, talked to Bush who was with Lake, and that Lake had given Bush his phone when McNair had called. The discussion was all of two minutes and 23 seconds. Enough to establish that Bush was unable to come and perhaps to decide on an alternate plan. The call was made at 1:34 in the morning. Did the committee really think that McNair discussed Bush's agency connection in less than three minutes and at that time in the morning? Why would anyone make a phone call of that magnitude at 1:34 in the morning? It does not make sense.

The document also includes information that Lloyd Lake filed suit against Bush and his family to try to recover monies spent. This is not to imply that those comments by Lake reported in the document as proof are untrue. It does imply that Lake had ample reason to lie and to smear Bush in his attempt to try to recover monies given by Lake to Bush and his father and mother. If true, USC would also have had to be included in the smear to make it seem valid.

Bush clearly was at fault. But, the first instance of the Bush family asking for money from Lake came from Bush's father and not from Bush himself. Both of Bush's parents were from law enforcement. Could that family background have influenced Bush? One's father can be a strong influence on a son. It may not have had any influence, because it is also clear that Bush knew he was violating NCAA rules. But, it may have had an influence.

When the report came out, Reggie Bush was long-gone to the NFL and was playing for the New Orleans Saints. The punishment did not affect his income. Clearly, his pride was hurt and he voluntarily returned his Heisman Trophy. That was an admission of guilt. But he really suffered no other penalty. The other 84 scholarship members of the 2005 team, whose record was wiped off the map, were penalized even though they were innocent.

It takes a lot of money, personnel, and effort to stage a football season for USC or any other major football program. At the end of that year, they were voted second by all the National Championship selecting agencies. It was a great year. Bush did not win it by himself. Most of his 2005 teammates did not have the advantage of going to the NFL. Their reward for their participation was the joy of playing the game and the memory of their success on the field. Bush's actions denied them, with the NCAA sanctions, the recordation of that success in any form. He should be ashamed for putting his teammates in such a position because of his own selfishness.

While Bush did not receive a monetary penalty, USC surely did. The punishments listed below will show that USC suffered for years of lost revenue because of Bush's selfish acts. Why should an innocent university have to bear the brunt of penalties while the perpetrator goes free from any dollar penalty? The entire process needs to be reevaluated.

The report has seven pages that include the punishments given to USC. The author apologizes at their length but that is the fault of the committee. The length itself tells a story.

It seems the sports world would agree that the Jerry Sandusky child-molestation scandal at Penn State far exceeds in importance to that of Bush and McNair, but Penn State petitioned the NCAA and had 112 wins it had lost in its investigation reinstated. USC petitioned the NCAA and got nothing.

Carroll said years after the NCAA decision came down that he thought it was a "terrible" decision. That " he had sat in on many meetings during the investigation and that the NCAA seemed very biased in their selection of questions and how they asked them."

THE PUNISHMENTS:

The following is a verbatim printing of the 25 penalties imposed against USC by the NCAA. Reggie Bush is included where the NCAA has listed "Student Athlete 1". O.J. Mayo is referred to as "Student-Athlete 2" while USC is referred to as the "institution". All Report wording is included in purple.

(1) Public reprimand and censure.

(2) Four years of probation from June 10, 2010, to June 9, 2014.

(3) The institution's (USC) men's basketball team ended its 2009-10 season with the playing of its last regularly scheduled, in-season contest and was not eligible to participate in any postseason competition, including a foreign tour, following the season.

(4) The institution's football team shall end its 2010 and 2011 seasons with the playing of its last regularly scheduled, in-season contest and shall not be eligible to participate in any postseason competition, including a bowl game, following the season. Moreover, during the two years of this postseason ban, the football team may not take advantage of the exceptions to the limit in the number of football contests that are provided in Bylaw 17.9.5.2, with-the-exception-of a spring game as set forth in Bylaw 17.9.5.2 (a).

(5) Pursuant to NCAA Bylaws 19.5.2.2 e-(2) and 31.2.2.3-(b), the institution will vacate all wins in which Reggie Bush competed, while ineligible, beginning in December 2004.

(6) Pursuant to NCAA Bylaws 19.5.2.2- e-(2) and 31.2.2.3-(b), the institution will vacate all wins in which O.J. Mayo competed during the 2007-08 regular season.

(7) Pursuant to NCAA Bylaws 19.5.2.2-e-(2) and 31.2.2.3-(b), the institution will vacate all wins in which the women's tennis student-athlete competed, while ineligible, between November 2006 and 2009.

(8) Regarding penalties C-5, C-6, and C-7, the vacations shall be effected pursuant to NCAA Bylaws 19.5.2.2-e-(2) and 31.2.2.3-(b) and shall include participation in any postseason competition, including football bowl games, conference tournaments, and NCAA championships. The individual records of Bush and Mayo and the former women's tennis student-athlete shall also be vacated for all contests to which they competed, while eligible. Further, the records of the head coaches of the affected sports shall be reconfigured to reflect the vacated results. Finally, USC's records regarding football, men's basketball, and women's tennis shall be reconfigured to reflect the affected USC coaches, and student-athlete records in all publications in which records for football, men's basketball and women's tennis are recorded, including, but not limited to institutional media guides, recruiting materials, electronic and digital media, and institutional and NCAA archives. Any reference to the vacated results, including championships, shall be removed from athletic department stationary, banners displayed in public areas, and any other forum in which they appear.

To ensure that all institutional and student-athlete vacations are accurately reflected in official NCAA publications and archives, the sports information director (or other designee as assigned by the director of athletics) must contact the NCAA Director of Statistics to identify the specific student-athletes and contests impacted by the order of vacation. In addition, the institution must provide the NCAA statistics department a written report, detailing the discussions with the director of statistics. This document will be maintained in the permanent files of the statistics department. The written report must be delivered to the NCAA statistics department no later than 45 days following the initial Committee on Infractions Report release or, if the vacation is appealed, the final adjudication of the appeal.

(9) Limit of 15 initial grants-in-aid and 75 initial grants in football for each of the 2011-2012, 2012-2013 and 2013-2014 academic years.

(10) Limit of 12 grants-in-aid in men's basketball for the 2009-2010 and 2010-2011 academic years.

(11) Reduce by one the number of men's basketball coaches permitted to engage in off-campus recruiting activity in summer 2010. USC will never have more than two coaches on (the) road at any time (three is permitted).

(12) Reduce the total number of recruiting days in men's basketball by 20 days (from 130 to 110) for the 2010-2011 academic year.

(13) A fine of $5,000 for Bush's amateurism violations.

(14) Return to the NCAA the $206,020 that the institution received through the Pac-10 Conference for its participation in the 2008 men's basketball championship. Additionally, due to the ineligible participation of Mayo, and consistent with the NCAA Division 1 Infractions Appeals Committee's January 24, 2000, decision in the Purdue University appeal, this institution shall return to the NCAA all of the moneys it has received to date through Pacific-10 Conference revenue-sharing for its appearances in the 2008 NCAA Division 1 Men's Basketball Championship Tournament. Further, all future conference distributions to the institution resulting from its appearance in the 2008 Men's Basketball Tournament that are scheduled to be provided to the institution shall be withheld by the conference and forfeited to the NCAA. A complete accounting of this financial penalty shall be included in the institutions annual compliance reports and, after the conclusion of the probationary period, in correspondence from the conference to the office of the Committee on Infractions.

(15) Disassociation of student-athlete 1.

(16) Disassociation of student-athlete 2.

(17) Disassociation of representative B.

(18) Further, regarding the disassociations of student-athlete 1, student-athlete 2, and representative B, pursuant to NCAA Bylaws 19.5.2.2-(1) and 19.5.2.b, the institution shall show cause why it should not be penalized further if it fails to permanently disassociate student-athlete 1 and 2, and representative B, from the institution's athletics program based on their involvement in the violations set forth in this report. These disassociations shall include.

    a. Refraining from accepting any assistance from the individuals that would aid in the recruitment of prospective student-athletes or the support of enrolled student-athletes;

    b. Refusing financial assistance or contributions to the institution's athletic program from the individuals;

    c. Ensuring that no athletics benefit or privilege is provided to the individuals, either directly or indirectly, that is not available to the public-at-large, and

    d. Implementing other actions that the institution determines to be within its authority to eliminate the involvement of the individuals in the institution's athletics program.

The disparity between the required treatment of athletes in the USC penalties and the University of Miami penalties is profound. When reading about the Miami penalties (later in this chapter) against involved student-athletes, please compare them to the penalties you have just read.

(19) Release three men's basketball prospective student-athletes from their letters of intent.

(20) The committee is troubled by the institution's failure to regulate access to practices and facilities, including locker rooms. Therefore, for the period of probation (four years), USC shall prohibit all non-institutional personnel, including representatives of the institution's athletic interests (except media, family members, and others approved by the compliance office on a case-by-case basis), from doing the following:

   a. Traveling on football and men's basketball team charters;

   b. Attending football and men's basketball team practices.

The author cannot understand why the NCAA has imposed a penalty against innocent fans. Is it not a purpose of the NCAA to create a friendly environment for fans so that member institutions can profit accordingly. Without the fans, there is no NCAA.

   c. Attending or participating in any way with institutional football and men's basketball camps, including the donation of funds to the camps, and

   d. Having access to sidelines and locker rooms before, during and after football and men's basketball games. Exceptions may be granted by the compliance office to prospective student-athletes and their families on official paid visits or unofficial visits. The exceptions must be stated in writing and issued by compliance personnel.

While sidelines during games and locker rooms should be tightly controlled, sidelines during practice are very different and fans should be allowed. Locker rooms should be reserved just for the athletes and even media should not have access, as that is a private time for the athletes. The media have protected rights within, however, and that was a mistake.

Media rights seem based upon the fact that the media should be allowed inside   because players are newsworthy and will have later access to hefty NFL contracts. That ignores the fact that most players will not move on to the NFL. Player privacy rights should supersede media access rights. There is plenty of access time once players are dressed and depart the locker rooms.

(21) In reference to reporting and publicizing its infractions, the institution shall:

   a. Inform prospective student-athletes in football, men's basketball, and women's tennis, that the institution is on probation until June 9, 2014, of the violations committed in the prospect's sport, and the penalties imposed on that sport program. If a prospective student-athlete takes an official paid visit, then information regarding violations, penalties, and terms of probation must be included with information provided in advance of the visit (five-visit-rule, 48-hour rule, etc.). Otherwise, the information must be provided before a prospective student-athlete signs a national letter of intent and no later than when the institution provides a prospective student-athlete with the academic data report and information regarding team APR.

b. Publicize the information annually in the media guide (or web posting), if any, in football, men's basketball, and women's tennis, as well as in a general institution alumni publication to be chosen by the institution with the assent of the assistant director of the committee on infractions. A copy of the media guide, alumni publication, and information included in recruiting material shall be included in the compliance reports to be submitted annually to the committee on infractions.

(22) In maintaining institutional control and a rules-compliant athletics program, institutions must rely on the efforts of coaches and staff to abide by the rules and share any information they have regarding potential rules violations. The assistant football coach had knowledge that Bush and Agency Partners A & B "likely" were engaged in NCAA violations.

"Likely" is not a word connoting a truism. "Likely" means that the committee had no definite proof. If there is no proof, then how can the committee create penalties? Apparently, they have their own standards and the NCAA is plaintiff attorney, judge, and jury, all conveniently rolled into one.

He was not credible in his denials of knowing agency partner A (Lake) or in his claimed failure to remember a telephone call between him and Lake. The assistant football coach failed to report information to the compliance staff regarding potential NCAA violations related to the activities of Lake and agency partner B. He also attested falsely, that he had no knowledge of NCAA violations. His conduct impeded the institution from fulfilling its responsibilities under NCAA Bylaws. His conduct also resulted in findings that he violated NCAA ethical conduct legislation by providing false and misleading information to the enforcement staff as described in Finding B-1-b, and that he violated NCAA Bylaws 30.3.5 by signing a document attesting, falsely, that he had no knowledge of NCAA violations involving the institution.

For these reasons, the committee imposes on him a one-year show-cause period beginning on June 10, 2010, and running through June 9, 2011, during which he is restricted as follows in his athletically-related duties at the institution or any subsequent employing institution

a. The assistant football coach (McNair) is prohibited from engaging in any on or off-campus recruiting activities or interactions with prospective student-athletes (or their parents or legal guardians) prior to their first full-time enrollment at any institution at which he is employed and whether or not they have signed a National Letter of Intent, accepted an offer of financial aid, or are recruited by the institution as these are or may be defined in NCAA Bylaws.

a. Prohibited activities include, but are not limited to phone calls and phone conversations; contacts and evaluations as they are or may be defined in NCAA Bylaws: electronic transmissions, general correspondence, and other recruiting material as they are or may be defined in NCAA Bylaws; official and unofficial visit activities; and activities or interactions with prospective student-athletes that are prohibited to a representative of the employing institution's athletics interests.

b. If the assistant football coach is employed at the institution or another member institution at the time of the 2011 NCAA Regional Rules seminars, then he must attend a rules seminar at his own expense and, within one month, provide to the Director-Committees on Infractions, a list of the sessions he attended, together with his certificate of attendance.

c. Should an institution other than USC employ the assistant football coach while these penalties are in effect, it shall submit a report to the Director-Committees on Infractions no later than 30 days after its first employment of him. The report shall set forth the employing institution's understanding of the above-listed penalties that are in effect at the time of employment and its responsibilities to monitor compliance.

c. Pursuant to NCAA Bylaws 19.5.2.2-(1), it may challenge the continued imposition of the above-listed penalties restricting the athletically-related duties of the assistant football coach by scheduling an appearance before the Committee on Infractions to show cause why it should not be penalized for failure to comply with the penalties.

d. At the end of the show-cause period imposed on the assistant football coach or upon termination of employment while the show-cause order is in effect, the President of USC or any subsequent employing institution shall provide a letter to the committee affirming that the penalties were complied with during the time of employment. If the President is unable to so affirm, he shall so inform the committee.

(23) During this period of probation, the institutions shall:

a. Continue to develop and implement a comprehensive educational program on NCAA legislation, including seminars and testing, to instruct the coaches, the faculty athletics representatives, all athletics department personnel, and all institution staff members with responsibility for the certification of student-athletes for admission, retention, financial aid, or competition;

b. Submit a preliminary report to the office of the Committees on Infractions by July 31, 2010, setting forth a schedule for establishing this compliance and educational program; and

c. File with the office of the Committees on Infractions annual compliance reports indicating the progress made with this program by February 15 of each year during the probationary period. Particular emphasis should be placed on the monitoring of agents and their associates in their interaction with prospective student-athletes and student-athletes, monitoring student-athlete employment, monitoring access to facilities used by student-athletes for practice and competition, monitoring student-athlete activities involving prospective student-athletes on official visits, student-athlete automobile information, and student-athlete housing.

c. The institution shall include in each annual compliance report copies of any secondary violation self-reports in football, men's basketball, and women's tennis, together with information s to who committed the violation if such information is not provided in the self-report.

d. The reports must also include documentation of the institution's compliance with the penalties adopted and imposed by the committee.

(24) The above-listed penalties are independent of and supplemental to any action that has been or may be taken by the Committee on Academic Performance through its assessment of contemporaneous, historical, or other penalties.

(25) At the conclusion of the probationary period, the institution's president shall provide a letter to the committee affirming that the institution's current athletics policies and practices conform to all requirements of the NCAA regulations.

NCAA USC INFRACTIONS COMMITTEE CHAIRMAN PAUL DEE:

The most flagrant abuse of the system involved the very chair of the Infractions Committee that levied huge penalties against USC. Paul Dee was the Athletic Director of Miami during the 1990s (1993-2008) when the NCAA investigated Miami. He passed away in 2012, two years after the USC Infractions Report was published.

In 1994, one year after Dee took over at Miami, the *Miami Herald* claimed that Miami boosters were involved in a "pay for play" scheme from 1986 to 1992, "giving cash rewards to Miami University players for acts such as scoring touchdowns. The allegation was verified in a subsequent NCAA investigation, which also found that the University of Miami head football coach and the associate director of athletics for compliance and internal operations were both aware of the illicit payments.

Also in 1994, former University of Miami academic advisor Tony Russell pleaded guilty for helping 57 football players and more than 23 other scholarship-athletes falsify applications for Pell Grants. *Sports Illustrated* wrote a cover story suggesting Miami should temporarily shutter its football program and that athletic director Paul Dee should be fired. It was also the greatest abuse of the Pell Grant program in its history. This is the same autocratic and pedantic Dee who pushed through the USC sanctions without any proof that USC knew what was going on with Bush. It gets worse.

In 1995, the NCAA announced that the University of Miami had provided or allowed more than $412,000 of excessive aid to student-athletes between 1990 and 1994, failed to implement its drug-testing program, and lost institutional control over the football program. Sound familiar? What came of it? That December, the NCAA announced that the University of Miami's multiple infractions would result in severe sanctions, including a one-year ban from postseason play and a 31-scholarship reduction from 1996 to 1999.

This NCAA action was considerably less than for USC and it involved actual knowledge and support of the illegal actions by the Miami administration and coaches.

Admittedly, Dee was only on the job for one year when it all came down. He might not have known? One of the things that USC wants to avoid is athletic boosters who go to extremes and cross the lines of what is right and wrong. The Trojans go to excessive lengths to ensure that boosters comply.

A very rich and influential booster for Miami named Nevin Shapiro reportedly spent two million dollars from 2002-2010 in support of the football and men's basketball program. Now that kind of money cannot help but be noticed, and Dee had, by then, been at Miami for a long time.

In 2010, Shapiro was charged in New Jersey with securities fraud and money laundering and he pleaded guilty. In June 2011, he was sentenced to 20 years in prison and ordered to pay over 82 million dollars in restitution. He told the *Miami Herald* that he promised to tell how Miami had violated NCAA rules involving more than 100 Miami players. He was angry that once he helped the Miami players and after they then turned pro, they turned their backs on him. "It made me feel like a used friend."

Yahoo Sports published an article based on over 100 hours of jailhouse testimony by Shapiro where he stated that he gave an estimated two million dollars in prohibited benefits to at least 72 current and former Miami football and basketball players and coaches from 2002 to 2010. His reference to coaches indicates that Dee and the athletic administration had to know about it. Perhaps they were recipients? Shapiro detailed the allegations regarding his illegal and unethical behaviors and lack of oversight in the Miami athletic department.

Yahoo Sports declared that Shapiro, through his actions and donations, violated at least four major NCAA bylaws. They included extra benefits to athletes, lack of amateurism among the athletes, improper recruiting activity, and impermissible compensation to coaches.

The penalties against the players: Those who knowingly received impermissible benefits in the form of money were suspended. However, the suspensions were revoked upon paying restitution. The total restitution payments made were $4,000 with the largest individual payment only $1,200. How does that work?

Bush was never allowed to replay his "gifts." Instead of having to erase an entire year's worth of achievement, such as the 2005 Trojan team suffered, the NCAA had a one-game suspension for five athletes, a four-game suspension for two athletes, and a six-game suspension for one. The Miami basketball coach, who was in the know about illegal payments, was only suspended for five games. They sound more like benefits than penalties.

On October 22, 2013, the NCAA announced its sanctions against the University and four former coaches, alleging a "lack of institutional control" in the poorly monitored activities of a major booster.

The NCAA sanctions include three years of probation for the entire athletic program, the loss of nine football scholarships over three years, prohibiting players on unofficial visits from receiving more than one complimentary ticket to Miami home football games in 2014, and 2015, the loss of one basketball scholarship for the three seasons starting in 2014-2015 and suspension of the men's basketball coach for five games of the 2013-2014 season plus at two-year show-cause penalty for three assistant coaches.

Coaches and players received money with the full knowledge of Miami University and those are the penalties given? That is the very definition of a travesty. Is that what Dee meant when he said "high profile compliance."

Sports Illustrated's Stewart Mandel described Dee's involvement as follows:

Quote is in blue: "Dee, you may recall was the Committee on Infractions chairman for USC's much-publicized case last summer involving former stars Reggie Bush and O.J. Mayo, It was Dee who, in announcing some of the stiffest penalties of the last 20 years closed with the preachy reminder that "high-profile athletes demand high-profile compliance." Dee, Miami's AD for most of the period covering Shapiro's allegations, is retired and no longer under NCAA jurisdiction. Still, it seems only fair that he should spend a day at USC's Heritage Hall wearing a sandwich board with the word "Hypocrite."

NCAA president Mark Emmert, formerly from Oregon State, discussed the NCAA allegations: "If they are found to be true, it appears we have had a third-party individual that has a really pernicious impact on a huge cross-section of student-athletes. The breadth of that would be pretty shocking."

Sports Illustrated's Mandel went on to say, "It seems that the NCAA is big on words but inadequate when it comes to fairness in the impositions of sanctions. Perhaps, due to the obvious malpractice by Dee, USC can one day be cleared of the unfair penalties and the blatant hypocritical acts that unfairly imposed sanctions way beyond what others received for more serious violations."

The differences between the Miami case and that of USC are staggering. The USC infractions report itself is poorly written. The committee had four years to write the report, yet it describes a telephone call as being either two minutes and 23 seconds or two minutes and 32 seconds. The difference is insignificant, but the fact that the report lists two different times for the same event gives a reader cause to wonder about the report itself.

In the Miami case, over 100 athletes were involved, while at USC two athletes (Bush and Mayo) were involved. At Miami, at least four coaches were proven to be directly involved, and that they received money. The $2,000,000.00 given by Shapiro was to 72 individuals, including the coaches, which indicates that the University and Paul Dee were aware of the violations and thus must have implicitly approved. If the two million dollars were evenly spread, they would come to almost $28,000 per person. In his jailhouse confession, Shapiro said that he had paid over 100 Miami athletes. Admittedly, Shapiro was a convicted felon, just like Lake.

The Miami case was proved while the USC case was not. The report itself stated that McNair "knew, or should have known" about the agency relationship that existed between Lloyd Lake and Reggie Bush. "Should have known"? That statement is an admission that they had no definite proof against McNair and based their allegations against Assistant Coach McNair on suppositions and assumptions, not facts. And the suppositions were based on statements of a convicted felon.

Even with the alleged and unproven information given in the USC report, the Infractions Committee did not indicate that any employee of USC, including any coach, was the recipient of any money given by "Sports Agent A" (Lake), or any other.

That USC enforcement was lax, there is no doubt. It was in keeping with the atmosphere of trust between the USC staff and players that Carroll created. USC corrected the lax enforcement with a comprehensive program involving more than one individual whose sole duty was to ensure compliance with NCAA rules.

None of the players that were implicated in the Shapiro money scheme were kicked off the Miami football team. They received over two million dollars in illicit payments and were just given a few paltry games in which they could not play. That was their only punishment. And the travesty was compounded by the NCAA allowing the football players to play the games they were denied if they paid restitution. The player penalties were revoked by the NCAA after the players repaid only $4,000 of the $2,000,000 they had been illegally paid.

Did the NCAA regard the $4,000 as restitution? Did the fact that Paul Dee was the ramrod chairman of the USC investigation while he was Athletic Director of the same University of Miami that was committing the gross violations of NCAA rules, have anything to do with the huge differential between the penalties? The Shapiro money scheme happened under Dee's watch at Miami. Dee thus condoned far more flagrant violations at Miami while condemning USC with far worse sanctions for much lesser violations.

The author has seen too many situations where individuals claim others are guilty of the same crimes as they are committing. It is seen time and time again that an individual who habitually lies will be the first to accuse others of lying. They seem to feel that lying is the natural state of things. The fact that Dee was aware of gross violations of the NCAA rules at his own Miami seemed to have been a basis for his accusations of wrongdoing at USC. Miami did it so others must be doing it. Right?

One final concern regarding most of the NCAA penalties imposed on the various universities is the self-serving part that feels very much a conflict of interest. By the NCAA penalties imposed, the NCAA makes the case that it is doing it to protect amateurism for the student-athlete.

It acts as the standard, yet imposes financial penalties that force the institutions to forfeit money to the NCAA itself. In USC's case, it forfeited hundreds of thousands of dollars to the NCAA coffers. How can the NCAA act with complete independence when most of the revenues that are forfeited as part of compliance with the Infractions Reports are confiscated by the NCAA itself? Under the guise of protecting standards, it enriches itself. That is very much a conflict of interest and clouds the supposed impartiality of the committees.

In closing, it seems appropriate that the penalties imposed by the NCAA against USC athletics need to be revisited. The penalties have caused USC irreparable harm and have denied the athletic program significant revenue that can never be reclaimed.

The least the NCAA can do is revoke the invalidated games and request that the Heisman Trophy Trust reevaluate the vacated Heisman for Reggie Bush. The Trophy Trust recognizes that the university for which a Heisman Trophy winner played should also be a recipient and they back that up with a trophy for the university.

Reggie Bush is not the reason the author champions a return of his Heisman. He knowingly committed gross violations of NCAA rules and did it in disregard of the jeopardy in which he placed his own teammates. Heisman Trophies are a measure of the strength of a university's football program. USC's Heisman should be reinstated and to do so entails returning Bush's Heisman. The author's feelings are that USC has been violated and deserves recompense.

As previously mentioned, the NCAA needs to reevaluate its targets in the imposition of its penalties. Often universities are at fault and knowingly approve of illicit actions like Miami did under Dee. But, if it cannot be proved that a university is at fault, like USC was not, then the university should not be penalized.

With NIL, the floodgates have opened and, depending on the resolution of the NIL discussions, there may never again be a need for the NCAA to penalize athletes. If there is, they should target the perpetrators and not the institutions, unless they too were proved to be knowingly involved.

Chapter Fourteen

Trojan Coaches & Support Staff

Coaching a major college football program like USC has become a huge business. It was only a few short years ago that the author visited the Trojan website and read about the Trojan coaches. The number of assistant football coaches is limited by NCAA rules. At that time, a coaching staff would consist of a head coach, nine assistant coaches, (later changed to ten) and four graduate assistants.

While the numbers are still limited by the NCAA, many of those listed on the coaching staff are support personnel. It is the number of support staffers that has exploded these last few years.

The increases really started a brief seven years ago. According to Clemson Coach Dabo Swinney, "Saban changed the game" in 2016. "He changed it for everybody, changed the whole model. And you can see the results that they've (Alabama) had."

Well-funded major colleges have constructed on-campus TV broadcasting studios, indoor practice facilities, "grandiose player lounges," player nutrition programs, tutoring, conditioning centers, etc. The McKay Center provides much of that for Trojan student-athletes. It has managed to widen the divide between the few major programs and the rest of the college football world.

Now, the "athletic arms race has shifted to building cadres of football personnel, a less permanent but no less tangible resource." The NCAA "also sanctions five strength and conditioning coordinators. USC labels them as Sports Performance Directors or Assistant Directors.

TROJAN FOOTBALL SUPPORT STAFF:

The labels given to some of the staff make it seem that there must be some type of overlapping responsibilities: The reality is often quite different.

RECRUITING: Annie Hanson, wife of the Tight Ends Coach, has two assistants to handle recruiting support.

MARKETING and BRANDING: Five staff members oversee various aspects of the product that is released to the public.

ADMINISTRATION and OPERATIONS: Five staff members help in various aspects of direction and control.

PLAYER SUPPORT: Gavin Morris brings a wealth of experience as Assistant Athletic Director and Director of Player Relations. His staff includes two assistant directors of Player Personnel, a Director of Player Development, and a Director of Player Engagement.

TROJAN ASSISTANT COACHING STAFF:

Sports Performance is an area that has seen a lot of expansion on many college football staffs. They used to call those in charge directors of weight training or Strength and Conditioning Coaches. Now it is a whole new ballgame. According to national work recruitment experts "Indeed" a "sports performance coach helps athletes optimize their abilities through a unique approach to training. They combine psychological, mental, and physical elements that allow them to develop comprehensive career plans.

For instance, they might work focused on improving an athlete's individual performance or ability to work with their team. Their goal is to refine a client's natural skills and help them perform well in high-pressure situations. Sports performance coaches also specialize in risk management, injury prevention, and nutrition. In addition to relying on their own expertise, these professionals communicate with specialists like nutritionists and physiotherapists."

Coach Dennis Wylie came with Coach Riley from Oklahoma and oversees Football Sports Performance. Wylie has four assistants plus a Director of Sports Science.

Two assistant coaches are assigned to video operations.

Four are assigned as Defensive Analysts.

Two are assigned as Offensive Analysts, including Kliff Kingsbury, who starred at Texas Tech. He passed for over 12,000 yards, with 95 touchdowns. As an expert on the spread offense, Kingsbury was head coach of Arizona in the NFL. In our competitive world, to have an analyst with Kingsbury's experience is nothing short of amazing.

Two assistant coaches are assigned as Defensive Graduate Assistants and two are Offensive Graduate Assistants.

Ryan Dougherty is another who came with Riley from Oklahoma. The Trojan website lists Ryan as Senior Special Teams Analyst and Assistant Special Teams Coordinator. The question that immediately comes to mind is "assistant to whom?" No other coach is listed as Special Teams Coordinator. Either an oversight or Dougherty is really in charge of special teams without the coordinator title, which would be surprising with the current penchant for grandiose titles.

TROJAN COACHING STAFF:

DONTE WILLIAMS: Defensive Backs Coach / Defensive Passing Game Coordinator

Williams, the only holdover from the coaching staff of Coach Clay Helton, has more than a dozen years coaching defensive backs. He served as interim

Donte Williams. *clutchtown.com photo*

Head Coach for USC after the firing of Clay Helton. 24/7 Sports named Williams the best recruiter in the Pac-12 for three consecutive years (2020-2022) and the third-best recruiter in the nation for the 2022 season when he coached Trojan outside linebackers in addition to cornerbacks.

DENNIS SIMMONS: Assistant Head Coach / Outside Wide Receivers Coach / Offensive Passing Game Coordinator

Simmons spent seven seasons before coming to USC with Oklahoma. Rivals "named him one of the nation's Top 25 recruiters in 2019. While at Oklahoma, he coached the 2016 Biletnikoff Award winner, a Heisman Trophy finalist, Dede Westbrook, and Marquise Brown, who both were unanimous All-Americans. Additionally, he coached the 2019 Biletnikoff finalist.

Before assuming his duties at Oklahoma, he was outside receivers coach at Washington State from 2012 to 2014, when they led the nation in passing offense.

SHAUN NUA: Defensive Line Coach

Former Super Bowl-winning defensive end Nua coached Trojan Tuli Tuipulotu, voted the Pac-12 Defensive Player of the Year in 2022. Before coming to USC, he coached the Michigan defensive line, which included coaching the Big Ten Defensive Player of the Year.

Shaun got his football start at Tafuna High in American Samoa. He has coached many

All-Americans and was a semi-finalist for the Broyles Award, given annually to the nation's top assistant coach. It will be exciting to see how he fares with USC's NCAA Transfer Portal linemen.

Dennis Simmons. *youtube.com photo*

Shaun Nua. *on3.com photo*

BRIAN ODOM: Associate Head Coach for Defense / Inside Linebackers Coach

Brian Odom coached the dynamic duo of linebackers Shane Lee and Eric Gentry, both of whom had transferred through the Transfer Portal to USC from Alabama and Arizona. He coached them to become the second and third leading tacklers for SC in 2022.

He was instrumental in convincing Shane Lee to return to USC for his last eligible year and he recruited one of the best high school linebackers in the nation, Tackett Curtis from Louisiana. Odom also helped bring Mason Cobb from Oklahoma State. Cobb started 13 games for Oklahoma State and will have two years of eligibility remaining.

Brian Odom. *kansascity.com photo*

KIEL McDONALD: Running Backs Coach

McDonald coached Trojan Travis Dye to amass 844 yards on 145 carries for an average of 6.1 yards per carry. An untimely injury kept him from being the top runner in the Pac-12.

While at Utah for the five years prior to coming to SC, he coached the Pac-12 Offensive Player of the Year in 2019, who also set Utah's single-season touchdown record of 21. In four of his five years, his backs eclipsed 1,000 yards rushing with one becoming Utah's all-time leading rusher. In 2020, his runner Ty Jordan was awarded the Pac-12 Offensive Player of the Year.

Kiel McDonald. *on3.com photo*

ROY MANNING: Assistant Head Coach for Defense / Outside Linebackers Coach / Nickels (secondary) Coach

Manning also has duties coaching rushing defensive ends, which needs to be coordinated with the outside linebacker rushing the quarterback. His experience coaching linebackers includes Michigan, Washington State, and UCLA as well as Oklahoma. In 2020, the Oklahoma defense was third nationally in interceptions with 16 and the 2022 Trojans snagged 19. Linebackers played a large role in those interceptions.

Roy Manning. *youtube.com photo*

LUKE HUARD: Inside Wide Receivers Coach

Huard is brother to Damon and Brock Huard who both played quarterback for Washington. Luke was a North Carolina quarterback. As such, he knows a lot about wide receiving. He joined USC in 2022 as offensive analyst and by spring he was a full-time coach. Prior to USC, he was an offensive analyst for Texas A&M for three years. Before that, he was Offensive Coordinator and quarterbacks coach at Georgia State.

Luke Huard. *youtube.com photo*

JOSH HENSON: Offensive Coordinator / Offensive Line Coach

Josh Henson has the tough job of replacing most of the top-rated offensive lines in the nation. While USC missed on several 5-star recruits, he managed to bring in a lot of quality linemen. Henson's line in 2022 made possible the offensive explosion of Heisman winner Caleb Williams.

Henson has 24 years of coaching experience in the Big 12 and SEC. While Coach Riley acts as defacto Offensive Coordinator, his focus is on the QB and receivers, while Henson can help with blending the blocking and running. His previous 3 years were with Texas A&M.

Josh Henson. *on3.com photo*

ZACH HANSON: Tight Ends Coach

Previously coaching at North Carolina, Kansas State, Tulsa, and Oklahoma, Hanson is "regarded as one of the games' top young coaches." For the Trojans, he and his wife are doubly effective as she oversees Trojan Recruiting and has a staff to help. Hanson helped acquire the commitment of Duce Robinson for 2024, "the nation's top tight end prospect."

Zach Hanson. *youtube.com photo*

ALEX GRINCH: Defensive Coordinator / Safeties Coach

Coach Grinch has a lot to account for in the 2022 meltdown of the Trojan Defense, when they lost the last two games. But, doubters need to consider that the Trojans went from a 4-8 season in 2021 to an outstanding record of 11-3 in 2022. There were high expectations. Perhaps too high for a first-year team of coaches and players from such a wide range of universities.

So too was Grinch having to face a first-year recruit and transfer portal bias in favor of the offense. That should be righted, and the Trojans will have a stronger defense with which Grinch can prove his doubters wrong.

Trojan Defensive Coordinator
Alex Grinch. *usc.rivals.com photo*

LINCOLN RILEY: USC Trojans Head Football Coach / Effective Quarterbacks Coach

Riley engineered the Trojan improvement from a 4-8 record to 11-3 in his first year. His accolades speak for themselves: 3 Heisman Trophy winners and 1 runner-up in six years as head coach; 4 Big-12 Championships; 3 College Football Playoffs (CFP) appearances; and 2018 Big-12 Coach of the Year.

The eyes of the college football world will be on Riley during this, his sophomore season at USC. Will he coach Caleb Williams to a second straight Heisman in only his junior year? Will his offensive and defensive lines, largely constructed of transfer athletes, solidify the "trenches"? Will his solid class of freshmen blend with the transfers? Will he engineer a Trojan Pac-12 Conference championship in USC's last year in the conference? Will he manage to gain the Trojans a spot in the final four-team CFP? Will he?

Trojan Head Football Coach
Lincoln Riley.
saturdayoutwest.com photo

Chapter Fifteen
What the Future Holds

Author's Note: *With the volatility of the football conference realignment taking place in the fall of 2023, when this book was completed, writing a chapter about the future of the conferences is a very risky undertaking. Changes are coming so fast, as of this writing on September 1, 2023, that this chapter will be soon outdated.*

With that in mind, the reader is advised that there will be omissions in this chapter. One obvious omission is that a resolution of the question of what finally happened to the Pac-12 will have been decided, with Oregon State and Washington State either rebuilding the Pac-12 or finding a post-Pac-12 home.

UNIVERSITY of SOUTHERN CALIFORNIA (USC) in the BIG TEN:

It will be surreal. The realignment of the Pac-12 and Big Ten Conferences is happening. It has been decided and USC, UCLA, Oregon, and Washington will be moving from the Pac-12 to the Big Ten for the 2024 season.

In 1946, the Pac-8, the Big Ten, and the Tournament of Roses decided to make the annual Rose Bowl game strictly between the Pacific Coast teams and the Big Ten. That agreement still stands, although it has changed with the advent of the Bowl Championship Series (BCS) and the College Football Playoff (CFP). When the Rose Bowl is not part of the playoffs, it reverts to the traditional alignment of the Pac-12 and the Big 10. With the December 2024 expansion of the CFP from four to 12 teams, the entire national bowl situation will be drastically changed. It will no longer be potentially possible for the best in the West to play the best in the Midwest. Any conceivable best will be involved in the playoffs.

GEOGRAPHY of the CONFERENCES in 2023 and 2024:

The PAC-12 CONFERENCE in 2023:

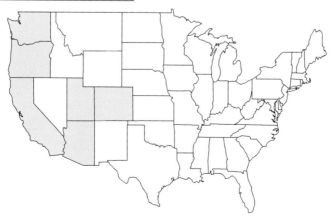

The PAC-12 CONFERENCE in 2024:

As of this writing, the Pac-12 Conference is down to only two teams and will, undoubtedly, cease to exist in any recognizable form for the 2024 season.

The BIG TEN CONFERENCE in 2023:

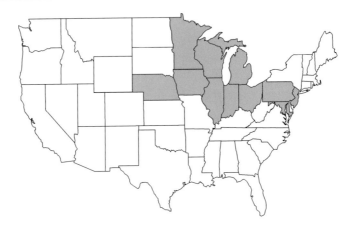

The BIG TEN CONFERENCE in 2024:

The Big Ten Conference will be adding four Pac-12 teams for the 2024 season: Washington, Oregon, USC, and UCLA. The additions will make the Big Ten a truly coast-to-coast conference, with Rutgers in New Jersey and the University of Maryland across the entire continent from the West Coast powers.

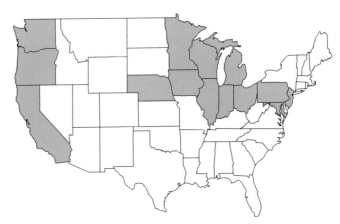

THE COLLEGE FOOTBALL PLAYOFFS (CFP):

It is now being determined how the bowl games will fit into the expanded playoff picture. For now, much is still speculation. The situation is so volatile, with the expanded playoffs and the accelerating conference realignment, that a good part of this chapter is speculation. By the time the reader picks up this book, additional changes will already have taken place that supersede information contained herein.

That USC and UCLA are jumping the Pacific ship at the same time as the CFP expansion to twelve teams, makes the situation even more intriguing. Also, the traditional powers from the Big 12 are moving. In 2024, Texas and Oklahoma will be in the SEC.

Movements of the type that USC, UCLA, Texas, and Oklahoma will be doing do not involve just football. They involve every athletic sport practiced by the universities. It has already been shown in this book that the Pac-12 will no longer be able to call itself the "Conference of Champions". With USC and UCLA having the second and third most NCAA Championships, that conference motto will be able to be shifted to the Big Ten.

The ATLANTIC COAST CONFERENCE (ACC) in 2023:

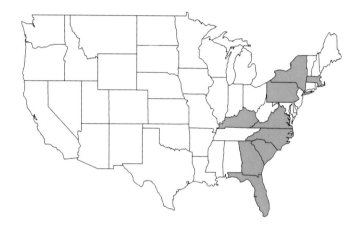

The ATLANTIC COAST CONFERENCE (ACC) in 2024:

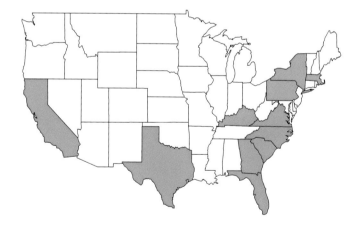

The ACC expanding to the West Coast does not make a lot of sense. The only sense it shows is a sense of desperation. Current out-of-conference or playoff games that require teams to travel across the entire country make sense in that they are occasional. But it ceases to make sense when forced to do it on a regular basis as part of a conference. The ACC is considering using Dallas as a mid-point to conduct conference games when the only Texas team in the conference is SMU. A mid-point game to reduce travel to half the time has the negative effect of causing all those games to be away games with fan participation being significantly reduced at the games. Do Stanford or Cal fans want to travel to Texas for every conference game with the only exception being those games against each other? It just does not make sense. What does make sense is for those two California teams to join the Big Ten. That would then increase the number of former Pac-12 teams to six and significantly reduce team and fan travel times as five conference games, instead of one, would then be played on the West Coast.

The BIG 12 CONFERENCE (Big XII) in 2023:

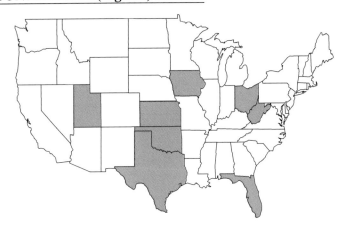

The BIG-12 CONFERENCE (Big XII) in 2024:

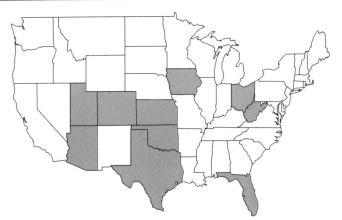

The ACC is currently, with the exceptions of Pennsylvania and Kentucky, strictly an Atlantic Coastal hugging conference. To add only two West Coast teams really creates travel headaches that will not go away. The Big Ten has five states located farther west than any ACC location and it added four West Coast teams instead of the two added by the ACC.

With the Pac-12 on life support, it does leave the four other Power Five Conferences a bit more viable. The aggressive moves of the Big 12 seem to ensure its survival, at least in the short run. If the Big Ten and the SEC expand further, teams in the Big 12 and the vulnerable ACC are ripe for poaching. If the Big Ten and SEC decide to conform to even greater geographical alignments, then the ACC is the most vulnerable conference and the Big 12 will also be in play. As it stands, the two best conferences will both be expanding. The Big Ten will have 18 teams in 2024, while the SEC will have 16.

The next great expansion might see both conferences heading for 24 members, with a possible interim stop at 20. If they choose to make the leap, then both the ACC and Big 12 will be losing teams. To reach the 24-team goal, at least one of the two, ACC or the Big XII, will be in danger of elimination. With the precarious state of the ACC, Notre Dame, which is aligned with the ACC, might look more favorably to joining the Big Ten, especially with two Indiana teams already in the conference and the advantages of a tighter-knit geography already mentioned. If the Big XII does eventually fold, where will the two Kansas teams end up?

It is in the surviving conference's best interest not to get too far ahead in admitting additional teams. The reason for teams to change conferences is all about revenue. The more teams are admitted to a conference, the greater the dilution of the conference money allocated to each member team derived from its media contract. The revenue value of additional teams, depending on the quality of the added team, is derived from additional revenue created due to the new teams in the following media contract.

The SOUTHEAST CONFERENCE (SEC) in 2023:

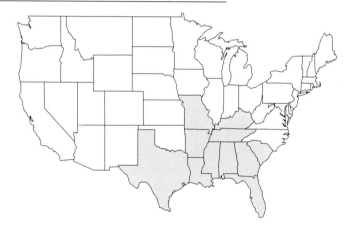

The SOUTHEAST CONFERENCE (SEC) in 2024:

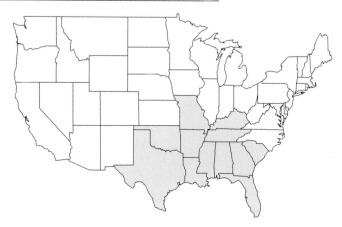

In addition, member universities don't like much disparity to exist if they are in a conference with more teams chasing a conference championship. As presently constituted, the champions of the ACC, SEC, Big Ten, and Big Twelve will all, with a high degree of probability, be automatically selected for the national playoffs. From that standpoint, university administrators want fewer teams chasing the championship. The determination of who will receive automatic invitations to the playoffs will have been decided by the time this book is read.

Make no mistake, the CFPs mean money to the participating universities and also mean greater exposure to potential recruits, which leads to better teams with greater chances to make the playoffs. For elite teams, it is a happy circle of success guaranteeing greater success.

The only change to the SEC map (previous page) is the addition of the State of Oklahoma. As can be seen, the SEC has the tightest geographical integration of any major conference. From that standpoint, the ACC looks to be the conference that will most likely provide teams in a future SEC expansion. In addition to adding teams within the existing states, the obvious thrust of expansion would be in the ACC direction of North Carolina, Virginia, and West Virginia. Movement west could include Big 12 territory in Arizona, Utah, Colorado, and Kansas.

The Rose Bowl, along with the other New Year's Six Bowls (Cotton, Fiesta, Orange, Sugar, and Peach Bowls) will be heavily involved in the newly expanded College Football Playoffs (CFP). Twelve teams involved in the playoffs will really change things. All the New Year's Six bowls will be part of the College Football Playoffs.

The teams, conferences, and alignments are undergoing such constant change that any determination of the eventual outcome is impossible to guess. Newly built stadiums in Los Angeles, Dallas, and elsewhere will be vying to be included in the best and most lucrative of the playoff venues, plus the various bowl games are also in limbo and fighting for revenue and relevancy.

With the amount of money that will be involved, the relegation of the games is vitally important to the bowls, the conferences, and the universities. Will the CFP rotate its title game to different stadiums or select one stadium? Highly likely that it will be rotated, but how will it be rotated and which bowls or stadiums will be involved? It is a huge problem, and the outcome will change everything.

For the Trojans and Bruins, their change will be even more drastic. The 77 years that the Rose Bowl has been traditional means that almost everyone alive on the West Coast only knows the Big Ten opponents of Pac-12 teams. After 2024, the opponents of the West Coast will include USC and UCLA, Oregon, and Washington. While the universities will, of course, not physically move, their mentality will move. But, the mental move coincides with the CFP changes, which will include the bowl changes. It will no longer be East plays West in the Rose Bowl.

The loss of the ten Pac-12 schools will either result in the final two choosing other conferences which is a likely scenario, or the Pac-12 will expand by adding Mountain West and American Conference teams.

The moves that started with the Texas and Oklahoma transfers, then followed by USC and UCLA plus the rest of those abandoning the Pac-12, will force further realignments of the conferences Most, if not all, of the five Power Five conferences (Pac-12, ACC, Big 10, SEC, and Big 12) will no longer represent regions. With the Big Ten becoming the first national (coast-to-coast) conference, which was quickly followed by the ACC doing the same, the Big 12 will be forced to conform. The SEC, on the other hand, will probably still just represent the Southeast, with some representation of the Southwest.

IN 2024, WITH a CONTINENTAL SCOPE, WHAT SHOULD the BIG TEN CALL ITSELF?

The Big Ten probably paid big money to marketers to come up with B1G. It might seem cute but it is perhaps too cute. The ACC, SEC, and PAC-12 are all regionally identified by their titles. Only the Big 10 and Big 12 are not. The numbers in their titles started out to be the number of teams in their respective conferences, as it was for the Pacific schools. That is no longer the case as the Big 10 will have 18 teams in 2024 and the Big 12 will have 16. Does that make any sense at all?

The fact that the Big Ten and ACC in 2024 will be the only coast-to-coast conferences creates a significant marketing advantage. With the Big XII stretching from Florida to Arizona, it is also close to being a coast-to-coast conference. Why don't the conferences take advantage of that uniqueness and advertise the fact in their titles?

Suggestions of possible conference titles are as follows:

North American Continental Conference (NACC)

Conference of North America (CNA)

National Athletic Conference (NAC)

American Athletic Conference (AAC)

Continental Conference (CC)

Continental Conference of America (CCA)

Pacific-Atlantic Athletic Conference (PAAC)

American Continental Conference (ACC)

Coast to Coast Conference (CCC)

Athletic Union of American Universities (AUAU)

Continental Athletic Union (CAU)

Continental Union of America Universities (CUAU)

National Conference of America (NCA)

Continental Athletic Conference (CAC)

These are just some of the names that could be considered.

The current turmoil is occurring while USC is experiencing a football resurgence in influence, power, structure, and regional recruiting. Riley is one of the smart innovators in football and he seems to be continually refining what was started by Trojan coach Gus Henderson, that being the spread offense. How will Riley fit within the new landscape?

PROBABLE ALIGNMENT of BIG TEN DIVISIONS with ADDITION of USC, UCLA, OREGON & WASHINGTON:

It seems that the Big Ten will not align their teams in divisions. However, if they do, the following chart suggests the most probable division alignment. The number on the left for each university is the number of total NCAA national championships won, as of April 4, 2023.

WEST DIVISION			EAST DIVISION		
112	**USC**	California		RUTGERS	New Jersey
121	**UCLA**	California	32	MARYLAND	Maryland
21	NEBRASKA	Nebraska	53	PENN STATE	Pennsylvania
25	IOWA	Iowa	31	OHIO STATE	Ohio
19	MINNESOTA	Minnesota	39	MICHIGAN	Michigan
32	WISCONSIN	Wisconsin	20	MICHIGAN STATE	Michigan
18	ILLINOIS	Illinois	24	INDIANA	Indiana
34	**OREGON**	Oregon	3	PURDUE	Indiana
8	**WASHINGTON**	Washington	10	NORTHWESTERN	Illinois

POSSIBLE ACQUISITIONS by the BIG TEN:

With the additions of USC, UCLA, Oregon, and Washington in 2024, the Big Ten will increase to 18 teams. It is already known that they have an interest in further expansion. A requirement of admission is membership in the AAU. A June 6, 2023, report states that the Big Ten has vetted at least seven other teams in addition to those that are joining in 2024. Those seven teams are California, Stanford, Duke, North Carolina, Virginia, Georgia Tech, and Miami.

From an ease of scheduling standpoint, California and Stanford make the most sense as Big Ten additions. Their fan bases will not allow the travel situation with the ACC to last more than several years. The rest of the vetted teams make more sense joining the SEC, unless the Virginia schools might select the Big Ten.

Notre Dame is always the big question mark. The desirability of Notre Dame coming into the conference has always been the #1 priority of the Big Ten. With Notre Dame's affiliation with NBC, it is always a question of money and independence for the Irish. To balance any conference it is far better to add two instead of just one, but the Big Ten would bend over backward to make an accommodation with the Irish. Of interest, Notre Dame recently became a member of the AAU. Whether that indicates a genuine interest on their part in eventually joining the Big Ten, or just creating options, is anybody's guess.

If Notre Dame does not come, and that is a probability, then the Big Ten would have a greater interest in Stanford and California. Both have extremely high academic standards and Stanford has been first in the number of NCAA National Championships in the nation for quite some time. As is evident on the NCAA website, Stanford's athletic teams just keep on winning at a fast pace.

While the ACC is processing the entry of Stanford and Cal into its conference, the two Bay Area schools are a natural for the Big Ten as currently constituted. As previously mentioned, from a team travel and rivalry standpoint, the Big Ten makes far more sense because five of the nine conference games for Stanford and Cal in the Big Ten would likely be with teams formerly in the Pac-12.

Stanford and California are likely to move together, wherever they might go. The same for Oregon State and Washington State. An unknown wildcard is that California is in the same University system as UCLA and the Regents have already given their blessing to the movement of UCLA and California, although their preference is to have both schools in the same conference. California is really the University of California, Berkeley, while UCLA is the University of California, Los Angeles.

While the Pac-12 is at death's door, the ACC is also in trouble. Almost half of their 14 former teams are reportedly upset about an internal issue and may be looking for other conferences. Those include Miami, Clemson, Florida State, North Carolina State, and Virginia Tech.

In 2023, the Big 12 Conference added Cincinnati, Houston, University of Central Florida (UCF), and BYU. The loss of Texas and Oklahoma would have dropped them to 8 in 2024, but the four mentioned will increase them to 12 and the four Pac-12 teams (Arizona, Arizona State, Colorado, and Utah) will further increase them to 16 members by 2024.

All of this is of great interest to football fans and the stuff of excitement. But it is still speculation and from the outside looking in. The only obvious likelihood of happening is that there will be further major changes in the conference alignments.

HISTORICAL USC RECORDS AGAINST BIG-10 TEAMS (as of 9-1-2023):

If the Big Ten creates divisions in 2024 and the divisions are aligned as envisioned on the previous pages, then the historical records of USC, included below, will apply. They are printed below with the historical football records of USC against every other Big Ten team.

PROBABLE WEST DIVISION			PROBABLY EAST DIVISION		
UCLA	50-33-7	(+17)	Rutgers & Maryland	No record	
Iowa	7-2-0	(+5)	Purdue	3-1-0	(+2)
Minnesota	6-1-1	(+5)	Penn State	6-4-0	(+2)
Nebraska	3-0-1	(+3)	Ohio State	13-10-1	(+3)
Wisconsin	6-1-0	(+5)	Michigan	6-4-0	(+2)
Illinois	11-2-0	(+9)	Michigan State	4-4-0	(+0)
Northwestern	5-0-0	(+5)	Indiana	4-0-0	(+4)
Total (minus UCLA):	**38-6-2**	**(+32)**	**Total:**	**36-23-1**	**(+13)**

HISTORICAL USC RECORDS AGAINST OTHER CONFERENCES:

Records against Power Five Conferences, other than the Pac-12, are in red.

ACC	24-12-0	(+12)	Big 12	18-10-1	(+8)
Conference USA	3-0-1	(+3)	Independents	19-4-0	(+15)
Big Sky	6-0-0	(+6)	(without Notre Dame)	6-4-0	(+2)
Sun Belt	10-0-0	(+10)	Mountain West	31-1-1	(+30)
American Athletic	9-4	(+5)	SoCal (Southland)	62-15-8	(+47)
SEC	22-12-1	(+10)	Big 10	74-29-3	(+45

Over its entire history, USC has played 88 different colleges and universities. Of those, it has only nine losing records, with seven by only one or two games. Notre Dame (90 games played) and Alabama (8 games played) are USC's two nemesis teams:

Notre Dame	37-48-5	(-11)	Alabama	2-6-0	(-4)
TCU	2-3-0	(-1)	North Carolina	0-2-0	(-2)
Kansas	0-1-0	(-1)	Florida	0-1-0	(-1)
Kansas State	0-2-0	(-2)	Florida State	0-2-0	(-2)
Memphis	0-1-0	(-1)			

HISTORICAL USC RECORDS AGAINST PACIFIC COAST CONFERENCE TEAMS:

UCLA	50-33-7	(+17)	Arizona	36-7-0	(+29)
California	72-31-5	(+41)	Arizona State	24-14-0	(+10)
Stanford	63-34-3	(+29)	Colorado	16-0-0	(+16)
Oregon	38-22-2	(+16)	Utah	13-9-0	(+4)
Oregon State	64-12-4	(+52)	Washington	51-30-4	(+21)
Washington State	62-10-4	(+52)			

THE ROSE BOWL and the COLLEGE FOOTBALL PLAYOFFS (CFP):

The Rose Bowl has contracted with the CFP that it will be part of the 12-team playoff picture either hosting quarterfinal games on January 1st or hosting one of two semi-final games the following week. Compared to its illustrious history, the Rose Bowl has already been tarnished. It will be further tarnished when it becomes an annual part of the College Football Playoffs.

The latest update on the CFP has it that the top four teams selected will have first-round byes with the bottom eight teams playing each other. The first game will be played on December 20

2024, and the final three games of the first round will be on the following day. All four games of the first round will be played in on-campus stadiums.

On New Year's Day, January 1, 2025, the four first-round winners will play the top four teams in the quarterfinals in the following bowls: Fiesta, Peach, Rose, and Sugar. The participants in the various bowl games will be selected in order of seed by the participating teams. The following week the remaining four teams will play the semifinals in the Cotton and Orange Bowls. The participants will again choose which bowls to play by order of their rankings.

As of this writing, the location of the national championship game has not been decided but will probably be selected as it has been previously done. The competition will be high among the few national stadiums with amenities and locations to satisfy NCAA requirements. That game will be played on January 20, 2025.

FOLLOW the MONEY:

It is sad that money has played such an important part in university decisions to change conferences. In the majority of cases, it seems that has been the only criteria used. There are more important things than money, which tends to tarnish the histories of intense competition and rivalries. It lessens the essence of sportsmanship, the beauty of the game, and takes precedence over its wonderful traditions. The entire concept of amateurism is being eroded.

College sports started out on a strictly amateur basis. In most college sports, that is still the case. However, football has changed and is obviously becoming more professional. Club or team sports teach the importance of working together and have always been considered an important part of any college curriculum. Team sports teach loyalty to the team, but the NCAA Transfer Portal has lessened that sense of team loyalty and now resembles a form of free agency. NIL (Name, Image, and Likeness) has destroyed any semblance of amateurism in college football by providing money and benefits to college players. Student-athlete recipients of NIL money are not just preparing for jobs in the NFL, they already have jobs.

THE GREATEST FOOTBALL ACHIEVEMENTS of any AMERICAN UNIVERSITY:

When every superlative of USC is considered, it has arguably the best college record in the fabled history of American football. The following is a reminder of the information included in this book. Records themselves tell a story, but to make it complete, the quality of opponents must be considered. USC is the only American Division One football program that has never scheduled a non-Division One program in its illustrious history. The superlatives follow:

(1) The winningest team in Rose Bowl history with 25 victories and only nine losses. The closest other team to USC is Ohio State with nine victories.

(2) Thirty-nine (39) Conference Championships, which ranks 5th nationally.

(3) The most Heisman Trophy winners in history: 8 (the Bush Heisman included); four players were second place in the Heisman voting and three players were third.

(4) Twenty-Nine (29) 10-win seasons

(5) First Trojan All-American was African American (1925)

(6) If a nation, USC would have the 12th highest number of Olympic Gold Medals: 153

(7) Third in the nation in the number of National Championships in all NCAA sports. Stanford is #1 and UCLA is #2.

(8) For overall national championships, including the NCAA, the Trojans have won 135 championships, the most in history for any school.

(9) If just considering men's National Championships, USC has 98, of which 85 are NCAA championships, both national records.

(10) Third highest number of actual (not claimed) football National Championships (9), only behind Alabama (14) and Notre Dame (10). USC claims 11

(11) The second highest number of second-place finishes (7) in the football National Championship historical selections. Ohio State is first with eight and Notre Dame is third with six.

(12) The 1972 Trojan team had 13 All-Americans, with 33 players going to the NFL.

(13) The 1979 Trojan team had 10 Consensus 1st String All-Americans, had 34 team members go to the NFL, and had 4 of the 14 Trojans in the NFL Hall of Fame.

(14) The 14 Trojan members of the NFL Hall of Fame are the most for any university.

(15) USC has had more team members go to the NFL than any other college or university in America: 325

NEW SPORTS FACILITIES PLANNED:

On Thursday, June 15, 2023, USC announced plans to upgrade Trojan sports facilities. It will be a huge investment in time and money.

The UPGRADING of DEDEAUX FIELD:

The proposed new baseball stadium, pictured next page, will be repositioned in roughly the same area as the current Dedeaux Stadium. It will be slightly moved to the west, closer to Vermont Avenue.

NEW TRI-LEVEL FOOTBALL PERFORMANCE CENTER:

The capacity of the new (baseball) stadium will be 2,500, "with new seating options, outdoor social spaces, an indoor hospitality space, multiple concession locations, expanded restrooms, a video board, and an audio system. The new stadium will also include a brand-new press box, coaching and support staff offices, and a team meeting space."

The Football Performance Center, pictured next page, will be built on existing football practice fields. It will feature two full-length practice fields that can be accessed directly from the new center. The Performance Center will include a featured rooftop hospitality lounge, a new weight room, which will free up space for other sports athletes using the McKay Center weight room

Artist rendering of the proposed new baseball stadium. *HNTB rendering*

New tri-level USC Football Performance Center to be built on existing football practice fields.
photos courtesy of HNTB

Artist view of the future Trojan Football Performance Center. An on-campus view of the current Trojan football practice fields is included below. The Loker Track & Field Stadium is lower right in peach color.

Current view of USC on-campus football practice field, lower left, and the Loker Track and Field Stadium, center. The practice field (with USC etched in the turf) will be replaced with the Football Performance Center.

multiple player lounges, a recovery hub, nutritional support, a new locker room, sports sciences services, a training room, and an equipment room.

The Center will also feature a team auditorium, position meeting rooms, recruiting areas, much-needed staff offices for an expanded staff, and flexible space for future growth.

NEW RAWLINSON STADIUM for WOMEN'S SOCCER and LACROSSE:

Like all the recent and proposed athletic additions, Rawlinson Stadium will be state-of-the-art. The 2,500-seat facility, which opens in 2025, will be extremely fan-friendly, with similar capacity and amenities as the proposed new Dedeaux Stadium.

Rawlinson Stadium will replace the existing Soni McAlister Field at the same location. "The stadium will feature a total capacity of 2,500, and include spectator viewing decks and social spaces, a state-of-the-art press box, spectator restrooms, a box office, concession stands, and a formal entry plaza."

The $38 million stadium "will have new, dedicated locker rooms for the soccer and lacrosse teams, as well as a team meeting area, a sports medicine space, a nutrition fueling bar, and meeting spaces for coaches. Additionally, it will include an LED video board and a natural grass playing surface."

The new facilities are a continuance of the major renovation of the entire Trojan package of athletic facilities to go along with the current and past upgrades to the Los Angeles Memorial Coliseum and the renovations to the on-campus Loker Track and Field Stadium. The facilities

The proposed Rawlinson Stadium will be at the same location as McAlister Field, which is just to the NE of the USC University Village.

New Rawlinson Stadium for Women's Soccer and Lacrosse. *HNTB photos*

The artist renderings in this entire section are credited to HNTB Architecture, a Los Angeles firm. It has done significant work for USC and specializes in historic preservation, program management, and structural engineering. *www.hntb.com*

program goes along with a doubling of the number of meals offered to student-athletes, plus a doubling of the number of sport psychology clinicians.

On top of the above, USC has launched "the Trojan Enrichment Program, which allows for the maximum amount of education-related financial support to all student-athletes."

This initiative also includes plans "for future renovations to the John McKay Center, a significantly expanded student-athlete dining facility, an upgraded golf practice facility, and enhancements to the Galen Basketball Center arena."

USC BIG TEN OPPONENTS ANNOUNCED for 2024 and 2025:

The Trojan Big 10 listing of opponents for 2024 has been announced. It is somewhat confusing as it does not seem based on an east-west division alignment. Perhaps the Big 10 wants to fill the stadiums throughout their domain with the novelty of watching the LA schools or, more likely, they want to eliminate their divisions to ensure that the best two teams are selected for the Big Ten playoff.

2024: Illinois, Iowa, Michigan, Wisconsin, Maryland, Northwestern, Penn State, Purdue, and UCLA

2025: Indiana, Michigan State, Nebraska, Penn State, Minnesota, UCLA, Indiana, Ohio State, Rutgers, and Wisconsin.

The only common opponents during both years are listed in purple: Penn State, UCLA, and Wisconsin. Game times and locations are to be announced (TBA).

FUTURE GAMES – the TIME ZONES:

The Pac-12 had four teams with a one-hour difference between them and USC's time zone: Arizona, Arizona State, Utah, and Colorado, which are all on mountain time. When USC is in the Big 10, that will all change.

A benefit will be that Big 10 games telecast to the West Coast will be earlier. Both USC and UCLA games should have more favorable schedules for local and East Coast viewing. It is no secret that the networks give preference to the Big 10 and the SEC when it comes to prime-time scheduling. That will benefit USC. Below is a listing of time zones for every Big 10 team:

> **PACIFIC TIME ZONE:** USC, UCLA, Oregon, and Washington.
>
> **CENTRAL TIME ZONE:** Iowa, Minnesota, Wisconsin, Nebraska, Northwestern, and Illinois,
>
> **EASTERN TIME ZONE:** Indiana, Purdue, Rutgers, Maryland, Penn State, Ohio State, Michigan, and Michigan State

CONCLUSION:

Change is inevitable and often unremarkable. What is remarkable is that the Rose Bowl structure of pitting the West against the Midwest, was able to remain intact for as long as it did.

Change can be exciting. The unknown can be tantalizing, and right now, there is an awful lot that is unknown. This book is being written from May through August of 2023. Even as it is being written, changes are being discussed and decisions are being made in meetings and boardrooms in every athletic conference across the country.

Whatever the changes, USC seems to be on the cusp of something great. Los Angeles can feel it. The USC students can feel it. The student-athletes can feel it. We fans can feel it.

Jennifer Cohen, the new Athletic Director who came to USC from the University of Washington in late August of 2023, is most assuredly a person with vision. Reportedly, she has a "see-it-through" determination, flexibility, and the capability of meeting the challenges of change. USC will need that capability in the new environment of the Big Ten.

The Lincoln Riley Coaching Era holds promise that it could eventually become the most dominant of any Trojan coaching era that proceeded it. Riley realizes that the step, from promise to realization of that promise, will be huge.

If he can realize the promise, the question remains: Will Lincoln Riley stay to establish and entrench the greatest legacy in American college football history, or will he succumb to the siren call of the NFL as have other great Trojan coaches: John McKay, John Robinson, and Pete Carroll? It seems that McKay, Robinson, and Carroll are all remembered more for what they accomplished with USC than any association with NFL teams. Nick Saban will be remembered far more for what he accomplished at Alabama, than he will for his work in the NFL.

As we approach the coming dawn that is wrought by change, we must never forget that football is still just a game. A game that offers opportunities for those involved and a fun and rewarding

Offensive genius and master of the spread, Coach Lincoln Riley with quarterback and Heisman winner Caleb Williams (13). *reignoftroy.com photo*

experience for both the players and those of us who consider ourselves fans.

Most of all, the university must continue to stand for values. If it does not stand for values, then what is the purpose?

Over the many years, Trojan teams have given us all (the university, the students, the faculty, the fans, and residents of Southern California) pride in their many victories and accomplishments, but also pride in how it has all been accomplished.

USC must never forget that it represents a standard for us all. The university is a teacher, not just of its students, but for all of us. That Trojan standard for many has been true sportsmanship, strong perseverance, and steadfast determination. No matter what the odds, our collective determination is the standard that we represent, and that is to…**FIGHT ON.**

Breaking News

August 23, 2023: Reggie Bush has filed a defamation suit against the NCAA and is demanding the return of his Heisman Trophy.

August 24, 2023: On the same day that this book was being formatted for upload preparation to Amazon, it was reported that Cal, Stanford, and Southern Methodist (SMU) were finalizing an agreement with the ACC for inclusion in the ACC in football, and men's and women's basketball. This will make the ACC another coast-to-coast conference and will cut the former Pac-12 down another notch.

With only two teams left, it will be very difficult for the Pac-12 to rebound after the 2023 season. Washington State and Oregon State will have to find another home, although that home may call itself the Pac-12. It also strengthens the ACC, giving it a cushion in the event it is poached of any teams. The ACC is also protected by a hefty cash penalty that will be imposed on any departing university.

September 1, 2023: The news about SMU, Cal, and Stanford joining the Atlantic Coast Conference (ACC) was confirmed.

September 8, 2023: Washington State and Oregon State Universities have filed suit against the Pac-12 and the ten universities that will depart the Pac-12 in 2024.

September 11, 2023: A judge ruled in favor of Washington State and Oregon State, stating that they should have the primary say in what happens to the Pac-12 in 2024, and perhaps beyond, instead of the ten departing universities.

Dominant Trojan Coaching Eras

Support Information

Bibliography

BOOKS & ENCYCLOPEDIAS:

"Turning of the Tide"
— Don Yaeger w/ Sam Cunningham & John Papadakis . . . . . . www.centerstreet.com

"Tom Kelly's Tales from the USC Trojans"
— Tom Kelly w/Tom Hoffarth . . . . .www.sportspublishingllc.com

"Conquest" — David Wharton & Gary Klein . . . . Triumph Books

"No Doubt! USCs 2004 Championship Season" . . . . .www.sportspublishingllc.com

"2017 USC Media Guide" — USC Athletic Department . . . . www.USCTrojans.com

"Cardinal and Gold" — Steve Delsohn . . . . .www.crownpublishing.com

"USC Trojans – Team of Destiny" — Russ Goodenough . . . . Unpublished

"What it Means to be a Trojan" — Steven Travers . . . . Triumph Books

"Trojans Essential" — Steven Travers . . . . Triumph Books

"USC Trojans – College Football's All-Time Greatest Dynasty"
— Steven Travers. . . . . .Taylor Trade Publishing

"USC Trojans – College Football's All-Time Greatest Dynasty – Revised"
— Stephen Travers . . . . Taylor Trade Publishing

"Trojan War" . . . . World History Encyclopedia

DVDs:

"2004 Rose Bowl" . . . . DVD Marketing Inc.

"2005 FedEx Orange Bowl" . . . . DVD Marketing Inc.

"History of USC Football" . . . . Warner Brothers Entertainment

"Undisputed" . . . . .Bayview

"Class of 2005 – Sudden Impact". . . . . www.USCFootball.com

INTERNET:

"Gus Henderson" . . . . wikipedia.com

"1922 USC Trojans Football Team" . . . . wikipedia.com

"Occidental College" . . . . wikipedia.com

"Metro League (Seattle)" . . . . wikipedia.com

"Dean Cromwell" . . . . wikipedia.com

"Summer Olympic Games" . . . . wikipedia.com

"1926 USC Trojans Football Team" . . . . wikipedia.com

"Rose Bowl" . . . . wikipedia.com

"Dean Cromwell" . . . . wikiwand.com

"Jess Hill" . . . . wikipedia.com

"Jeff Cravath" . . . . wikipedia.com

"Paul H. Helms" . . . . wikipedia.com

"List of Pac-12 Conference Football Champions" . . . . wikipedia.com

"List of Oklahoma Sooners Bowl Games" . . . . wikipedia.com

"List of USC Trojans Bowl Games" . . . . wikipedia.com

"1972 USC Trojans Football Team" . . . . wikipedia.com

"List of USC Trojan Football Seasons" . . . . wikipedia.com

"Bowl Championship Series" . . . . wikipedia.com

"Troy" . . . . wikipedia.com

"New Year's Six" . . . . wikipedia.com

"USC Trojans Football Statistical Leaders" . . . . wikipedia.com

"Clay Mathews Jr." . . . . wikipedia.com

"Ashley Nick" . . . . wikipedia.com

"Troy Niklas" . . . . wikipedia.com

"John McKay" . . . . wikipedia.com

"Marcus Allen" . . . . wikipedia.com

"John Robinson" . . . . wikipedia.com

"Bruce Mathews" . . . . wikipedia.com

"1978 USC Trojans Football Team" . . . . wikipedia.com

"Mathews Family" . . . . wikipedia.com

"National Federation of State High School Associations" . . . . wikipedia.com

"2011 University of Miami Athletics Scandal" . . . . wikipedia.com

"University of Southern California Athletics Scandal" . . . . wikipedia.com

"List of USC Trojan Head Football Coaches" . . . . wikipedia.com

BIBLIOGRAPHY

"List of United States High School National Records in Track & Field" . . . . . wikipedia.com

"College Football National Championships in NCAA Division 1 FBS" . . . . . . wikipedia.com

"USC Trojans Football Statistical Leaders" . . . . wikipedia.com

"ROTC at USC Price" . . . . priceschool.usc.edu

"Pasadena Bowl" . . . . americanfootballdatabasefandom.com

"Dean Cromwell" . . . . oxyathletics.com

"John Wayne: The Iconic Actor Was Once a College Football Star" . . . . outsider.com

"Centennial (Corona, CA) Alumni Pro Stats" . . . . www.pro-football-reference.com

"Top 10 NFL-Producing High Schools in Pac-12 States" . . . . . . www.superwestsports.com

"USC Players/Alumni" . . . . www.pro-football-reference.com

"Greatest Mater Dei High School Football Players of All Time"
— By Tony Adame, September 30, 2022 . . . . .www.stadiumtalk.com

"How the College Football Playoff Works". . . . . www.ncaa.com

"Jimbo Fisher: Aggies OL Luke Mathews "Medically Done" . . . . .www.si.com

"The 50 Greatest USC Football Players of All Time . . . . www.bleacherreport.com

"USC Traditions" . . . . www.about.usc.edu

"Trojans Marching Band". . . . . www.about.usc.edu

"About USC – History" . . . . www.abot.usc.edu/history/

"What are the colors of Oberlin College". . . . . www.answers.com

"Gus Henderson" . . . . American Football Database

"USCs Olympic History" . . . . usctrojans.com

"USCs Olympians By The Numbers" . . . . usctrojans.com

"Broadway High School, Seattle's First Dedicated High School, Opens in 1902". historylink.org

"Seattle Public Schools, 1862-2000: Broadway High School". . . . . historylink.org

"Oldest Bowl Games". . . . . oldest.org

"USC History Collection". . . . . specol@usc.edu

"Trojan Statistics" . . . . .trojanforcestats.us

"USC Images of Logos & Banners" . . . . sportslogos.net

"John Robinson, Pro Football History". . . . . duckduckgo.com

"Those USC Tailbacks" . . . . collegefootballcrazy.om

"The History of the College Football National Championships" . . . . asipofsports.com

NEWSPAPERS, NEWS MAGAZINES, NEWS OUTLETS and ARCHIVES:

"Past Glories: USC Celebrates 100 Years of Football Full of Memories and 8 National Titles"
— Mal Florence, August 25, 1988 . . . .*Los Angeles Times*

"The Evolution of Oklahoma's Air Raid under Lincoln Riley" . . . .*USA Today* Sports

"USC Football Coaches: Glory and Gaffes, from Gloomy Gus to Lincoln Riley". . .Yahoo News

"When Charlie Dumas Jumped, the Barrier Fell"
— Earl Gustkey, June 29, 1986 . . . .*Los Angeles Times*

"Traveler" . . . . USC Archives, About USC

"USCs Other Loyal Mascot"
— By Ronald L. Olson Jr, and Dustin Jacobs, Spring 2015 . . . . .USC Archives

"USC National Championships" . . . . .USC Archives

"Inside the 'Secret' Baseball Academy the Dodgers are Running in Uganda"
— By Kevin Baxter, May, 2023 . . . .*Los Angeles Times*

"How Osi Umenyiora is Finding NFL Players in Africa"
— By Alex Prewitt, June 22, 2022 . . . . *Sports Illustrated*

"The 25 Longest Winning Streaks in High School Football History"
— By Tyler Calvaruso, November 18, 2021

"List of USC Trojan Starting Quarterbacks" . . . . American Football Database

"*USA Today* Sports Super 25 High School Football Rankings"
— *USA Today* HSS Staff, December 20, 2022 . . . .*USA Today*

"Trinity (League) Football Standings" . . . . MaxPreps

"2022 Football Standings" . . . . Big Ten Archive

"The Noble Trojan: CBS Movie Tells the Story of USCs Tailback Ricky Bell"
— Mal Florence, March 31, 1991 . . . .*Los Angeles Times*

"Ricky Bell: 'The Bulldog'" — September 12, 2001. . . . . SC Football Archive

"USC Football Coaches: Glory & Gaffes, from Gloomy Gus to Lincoln Riley"
— Steve Henson, November 28, 2021 . . . .*Los Angeles Times*

"We Were the Greatest Team Ever': Anthony Davis, 1972 USC Trojan's Savor Their Legacy"
— Ryan Kartje, November 24, 2022 . . . .*Los Angeles Times*

"USC Rising from the Dead: The Anthony Davis Game in 1974"
— Matt Zemek, April 12, 2020. . . . .*Los Angeles Times*

"The Most Memorable Rose Bowl: The 1963 Game"
— Earl Gustkey, January 1, 1992 . . . .*Los Angeles Times*

"John Robinson" . . . . Sports Reference CFB

BIBLIOGRAPHY

"The Trojan Way: USCs 14 NFL Hall of Fame Players
— Matt Zemek, February 12, 2022 . . . . *USA Today*

"Kevin Williams, Former USC Football Star, Killed in Train Wreck"
— February 3, 1996 . . . . AP News

"Former USC Defensive Back Kenny Moore Dies"
— Scott Wolf, August 16, 2020 . . . . .Fan Nation

"Family, Friends Recall Ex-USC Star Williams"
Joh Glionna, February 4, 1996 . . . . *Los Angeles Times*

"1979 USC Trojans Roster . . . . SRCFB

"What is NIL?: Everything you need to know about the NCAA and Name, Image, and Likeness"
. . . . The Athletic

"Court Slams NCAA in Reggie Bush USC Violations Case"
— Brent Schrotenboer, December 7, 2015. . . . .*USA Today*

"USC says Unsealed Documents in McNair Defamation Case Prove NCAA bias"
— Gary Klein, March 25, 2015. . . . . *Los Angeles Times*

"Steve Sarkisian Coaching Timeline"
— Zac Al-Khateeb, September 10, 2022 . . . . The Sporting News

"Lane Kiffin Coaching Timeline"
— Zac Al-Khateeb, October 2, 2021 . . . . The Sporting News

"Lane Kiffin – Football Coach – Ole Miss Athletics" . . . . olemisssports.com

"Pete Carroll shows Sadness for Friend Steve Sarkisian"
— Gregg Bell, October 13, 2015 . . . . The News Tribune

Photo & Map Credits

FAIR-USE DOCTRINE: This book contains new historical information and a new approach to the history of USC football that has not been previously published.

Since all royalties of any kind and any monies gained through sales of any kind will be donated, regardless of any expenses incurred, and that the purpose of this book in also to provide the reader a better understanding of that untold history, this document and its included photos and maps are protected from copyright action under the Fair Use Doctrine of the United States Copyright Act.

AUTHOR'S THANKS: The author thanks the providers for all the photos and maps included herein. Photos go a long way toward telling a story in ways that words cannot.

CHAPTER ONE:

Photo of Coach Dean Cromwell . . . . .www.wikipedia.com

CHAPTER TWO:

Photo of Coach Gus Henderson. . . . . .www.wikipedia.com

Photo of All-American Brice Taylor . . . . www.e-bay.com

Photo of Coach Gus Henderson www.tiptop25.com

Photo of Coach Howard Jones . . . . www.newsday.com

CHAPTER FOUR:

Photo of Coach Jeff Cravath . . . . .www.wikipedia.com

Photo of Coach Jess Hill . . . . .www.wikipedia.com

Photo of Athletic Director Willis Hunter . . . . .www.wikipedia.com

PHOTO GALLERY #1:

Photo of Memorial Coliseum . . . . www.neontommy.com

Photo of Uytengsu Aquatics Center . . . . www.news.usc.edu

Photo of Galen Center. . . . . www.pinterest.com

Photo of Aquatics Center Pool . . . . www.pinterest.com

Photo of Loker Track Stadium . . . . www.usc.edu

Photo of McCallister Field . . . . www.uscannenbergmedia.com

Photo of Trojan football players . . . . www.pinterest.com

Photo of USC baseball stadium . . . . www.usc.edu

Photo of Lasorda & Dedeaux . . . . www.dartentitles.com

Photo of Dedeaux Stadium . . . . www.dedeauxfoundation.com

Photo of Dedeaux statue . . . . www.offbeat.group.shef.au.uk

Photo of Engemann Health Center . . . . www.pinterest.com

Photo of marching band . . . . www.ncaa.com

Photo of USC cheerleaders . . . . www.si.com

Photo of Traveler . . . . www.mysantonio.com

Photo of Matt Leinart . . . . www.theheismanwinners.com

CHAPTER SIX:

Photo of Rose Bowl Stadium . . . . www.youtube.com

Photo of Rose Bowl game . . . . www.espn.com

Photo of 2004 Rose Bowl . . . . www.espn.com

Photo of Rose Bowl Stadium . . . . www.insideworldfootball.com

Photo of Rose Bowl construction . . . . www.wikipedia.com

Photo of Rose Bowl Stadium . . . . www.wikipedia.com

PHOTO GALLERY #2:

Photo of Los Angeles Memorial Coliseum . . . . Adobe Stock image

Photo of UCLA in Rose Bowl . . . . www.sbnation.com

Photo of Dodger Stadium at night . . . . www.wallpapercave.com

Photo of Angel Stadium . . . . www.thegreatgame.com

Photo of SoFi Stadium . . . . www.teazilla.com

Photo of interior of SoFi Stadium . . . . www.stadionwelt.de

Photo of Dodger Stadium . . . . www.abcnew.delaugher.org

Photo of Banc of California Stadium . . . . www.reddit.com

Artist rendering of Exposition Park . . . . www.cnu.org

Photo of Dignity Health Sports Park . . . . www.dignityhealthsportspark.com

Photo of Intuit Dome under construction . . . . .www.msn.com

Photo of Pauley Pavilion . . . . .www.kovach.net

Photo of Galen Center. . . . . www.clarkconstruction.com

CHAPTER ELEVEN:

Photo of Traveler . . . . .www.uscarchives.com

Photo of Tirebiter . . . . .www.uscarchives.com

CHAPTER FOURTEEN:

Maps of the United States . . . . www.printable-us-map.com

AUTHOR'S NOTE: *As usual, Wikipedia has played a large part in the creation of a book by the author. They not only provide a huge amount of information; they also provide photographs. They have undertaken an enormous task of providing information on everything. If readers feel so inclined, they need donations to continue.*

Dominant Trojan Coaching Eras

Historical Trojan Coaching Records

CHRONOLOGICAL:

COACH	YEARS		RECORD	% WINS
Henry Goddard	1888	1	2-0	1.000
Frank Suffel	1888	1	2-0	1.000
Lewis Freeman	1897	1	5-1	0.833
Clair Tappaan	1901	1	0-2	0.000
John Walker	1903	1	4-2	0.667
Harvey Holmes	1904-1907	4	19-5-3	0.759
William Traeger	1908	1	3-1-1	0.700
Dean Cromwell	1909-1910	2		
	1916-1918	3 (5)	21-8-6	0.686
Ralph Glaze	1914-1915	2	7-7-0	0.500
Gus Henderson	1919-1924	5	45-7-0	0.865
Howard Jones	1925-1940	16	121-36-13	0.750
Sam Berry	1941	1	2-6-1	0.278
Jeff Cravath	1942-1950	9	54-28-8	0.644
Jess Hill	1951-1956	6	45-17-1	0.722
Don Clark	1957-1959	3	13-16-1	0.450
John McKay	1960-1975	16	127-40-8	0.749
John Robinson	1976-1982	7		
	1993-1997	5 (12)	104-35-4	0.741
Ted Tollner	1983-1986	4	26-20-1	0.564
Larry Smith	1987-1992	6	44-25-3	0.632
Paul Hackett	1998-2000	3	19-18	0.514
Pete Carroll	2001-2009	9	97-19	0.836
Lane Kiffin	2010-2013	3.25	28-15	0.651

COACH	YEARS		RECORD	% WINS
Ed Orgeron	2013	.67	6-2	0.750
Clay Helton	2013	.08	46-24	0.657
	2015-2021	6.75		
Steve Sarkisian	2014-2015	1.3	12-6	0.667
Donte Williams	2021	.83	3-7	0.300
Lincoln Riley	2022	1	11-3	0.786

HIGHEST PERCENTAGE of WINS (Two years or more coaching):

COACH	YEARS	% OF WINS	COACH	YEARS	% OF WINS
Gus Henderson	5	0.865	Clay Helton	6.75	0.657
Pete Carroll	9	0.836	Lane Kiffin	3.25	0.651
Harvey Holmes	4	0.759	Jeff Cravath	9	0.644
Howard Jones	16	0.750	Larry Smith	6	0.632
John McKay	16	0.749	Ted Tollner	4	0.564
John Robinson	12	0.741	Paul Hackett	3	0.514
Jess Hill	6	0.722	Don Clark	3	0.450
Dean Cromwell	5	0.686			

MOST WINS & MOST YEARS (Two years or more coaching):

COACH	MOST WINS	MOST YEARS	COACH	MOST WINS	MOST YEARS
John McKay	127	16	Larry Smith	44	6
Howard Jones	121	16	Lane Kiffin	28	3.25
John Robinson	104	12	Ted Tollner	26	4
Pete Carroll	97	9	Dean Cromwell	21	5
Jeff Cravath	54	9	Harvey Holmes	19	4
Clay Helton	46	6.75	Paul Hackett	19	3
Jess Hill	45	6	Don Clark	13	3
Gus Henderson	45	5			

Dominant Trojan Coaching Eras

Historical Trojan
1st Team All-Americans

For those among the readers who might like to take a trip down the Trojan memory lane, below are the names of those All-Americans by era. Enjoy the trip.

HENDERSON-JONES ERA: (24 in 16 years):

YEAR	ALL-AMERICAN	# OF 1ST TEAMS SELECTIONS	YEAR	ALL-AMERICAN	# OF 1ST TEAMS SELECTIONS
1925	Brice Jones	2	1931	Stan Williamson	2
1926	Mort Kaer	9	1931	Gus Shaver	6
1927	Morley Drury	10	1931	Johnny Baker	9
1927	Jess Hibbs	8	1932	Tay Brown	1
1928	Jess Hibbs	3	1932	Aaron Rosenberg	1
1928	Don Williams	2	1932	Ernie Smith	10
1929	Nate Barragar	1	1933	Aaron Rosenberg	8
1929	Francis Tappaan	5	1933	Larry Stevens	1
1930	Garrett Arbelbide	1	1933	Cotton Warburton	10
1930	Orv Mohler	1	1938	Harry Smith	3
1930	Erny Pinckert	9	1939	Harry Smith	10
1931	Erny Pinckert	4	1939	Grenny Lansdell	2

CRAVATH-HILL ERA: (9 in 15 years):

YEAR	ALL-AMERICAN	# OF 1ST TEAMS SELECTIONS	YEAR	ALL-AMERICAN	# OF 1ST TEAMS SELECTIONS
1943	Ralph Heywood	6	1951	Pat Cannamela	4
1944	John Ferraro	10	1952	Jim Sears	6
1947	John Ferraro	5	1952	Elmer Willhoite	8
1947	Paul Cleary	7	1955	Jon Arnett	3
1951	Frank Gifford	1			

DON CLARK: (3 in 3 years):

YEAR	ALL-AMERICAN	# OF 1ST TEAMS SELECTIONS	YEAR	ALL-AMERICAN	# OF 1ST TEAMS SELECTIONS
1959	Ron Mix	1	1959	Marlin McKeever	4
1959	Mike McKeever	1			

McKAY-ROBINSON ERA: (60 in 23 years):

YEAR	ALL-AMERICAN	# OF 1ST TEAMS SELECTIONS	YEAR	ALL-AMERICAN	# OF 1ST TEAMS SELECTIONS
1960	Marlin McKeever	1	1972	Pete Adams	1
1962	Hal Bedsole	10	1972	John Grant	1
1962	Damon Bame	2	1973	Lynn Swann	7
1963	Damon Bame	3	1973	Steve Riley	1
1964	Bill Fisk	2	1973	Artimus Parker	3
1964	Mike Garrett	2	1973	Booker Brown	4
1965	Mike Garrett	11	1973	Richard Wood	4
1966	Nate Shaw	8	1974	Anthony Davis	6
1966	Ron Yary	8	1974	Richard Wood	4
1967	Ron Yary	11	1974	Charles Phillips	1
1967	O.J. Simpson	11	1974	Bill Bain	1
1967	Adrian Young	9	1974	Jim Obradovich	1
1967	Tim Rossovich	5	1975	Ricky Bell	6
1968	O.J. Simpson	10	1975	Marvin Powell	1
1968	Mike Battle	3	1976	Marvin Powell	3
1969	Jimmy Gunn	8	1976	Ricky Bell	8
1969	Al Cowlings	3	1976	Dennis Thurman	3
1969	Sid Smith	4	1976	Gary Jeter	3
1969	Clarence Davis	1	1977	Dennis Thurman	6
1970	Marv Montgomery	1	1977	Clay Mathews Jr.	1
1971	John Vella	4	1978	Pat Howell	7
1971	Willie Hall	2	1978	Charles White	6
1972	Charles Young		1979	Charles White	7
1972	Richard Wood	2	1979	Dennis Johnson	2
1972	Sam Cunningham	2	1979	Paul McDonald	1

McKAY-ROBINSON ERA: (60 in 23 years) *continued*:

YEAR	ALL-AMERICAN	# OF 1ST TEAMS SELECTIONS	YEAR	ALL-AMERICAN	# OF 1ST TEAMS SELECTIONS
1979	Brad Budde	7	1981	Chip Banks	3
1980	Ronnie Lott	8	1981	Roy Foster	5
1980	Roy Foster	1	1982	Don Mosebar	7
1980	Keith Van Horne	6	1982	Bruce Mathews	8
1981	Marcus Allen	8	1982	George Achica	6

SMITH-TOLLNER-ROBINSON II ERA: (15 in 15 years):

YEAR	ALL-AMERICAN	# OF 1ST TEAMS SELECTIONS	YEAR	ALL-AMERICAN	# OF 1ST TEAMS SELECTIONS
1983	Tony Slaton	5	1989	Tim Ryan	5
1984	Jack Del Rio	7	1989	Junior Seau	1
1984	Duane Bickett	4	1989	Mark Tucker	1
1985	Jeff Bregel	8	1989	Mark Carrier	8
1985	Tim McDonald	1	1990	Scott Russ	1
1986	Jeff Bregel	8	1992	Curtis Conway	1
1987	Dave Cadigan	5	1992	Tony Boselli	1
1988	Erik Affholter	2	1993	Johnnie Morton	5
1988	Mark Carrier	2	1994	Tony Boselli	7
1988	Rodney Peete	1	1995	Keyshawn Johnson	10
1988	Tim Ryan	1	1998	Chris Claiborne	7
1988	Cleveland Colter	1			

PETE CARROLL ERA: (35 in 9 years):

YEAR	ALL-AMERICAN	# OF 1ST TEAMS SELECTIONS	YEAR	ALL-AMERICAN	# OF 1ST TEAMS SELECTIONS
2001	Troy Polamalu	2	2005	Darnell Bing	2
2002	Troy Polamalu	5	2005	Matt Leinart	2
2002	Carson Palmer	6	2006	Steve Smith	1
2003	Tom Malone	3	2006	Sedrick Ellis	1
2003	Matt Leinart	1	2006	Ryan Kalil	2
2003	Kenechi Udeze	7	2006	Sam Baker	4
2003	Jacob Rogers	7	2006	Dwayne Jarrett	5
2003	Mike Williams	9	2007	Sedrick Ellis	9
2004	Lofa Tatupu	1	2007	Sam Baker	2
2004	Mike Patterson	3	2007	Fred Davis	2
2004	Reggie Bush	8	2007	Keith Rivers	2
2004	Matt Leinart	6	2007	Taylor Mays	1
2004	Matt Grootegoed	4	2008	Rey Maualuga	10
2004	Shaun Cody	6	2008	Taylor Mays	10
2005	Reggie Bush	10	2008	Brian Cushing	1
2005	Dwayne Jarrett	8	2009	Taylor Mays	2
2005	Taitusi Lutui	7	2009	Charles Brown	2
2005	Sam Baker	1			

POST-CARROLL ERA: (12 in 13 years):

YEAR	ALL-AMERICAN	# OF 1ST TEAMS SELECTIONS	YEAR	ALL-AMERICAN	# OF 1ST TEAMS SELECTIONS
2011	Robert Woods	4	2014	Nelson Agholor	1
2011	Matt Kalil	5	2016	Adoree' Jackson	11
2011	T.J. McDonald	2	2016	Zach Banner	2
2012	Marqise Lee	11	2016	Chad Wheeler	1
2013	Leonard Williams	1	2017	Ronald Jones II	1
2014	Leonard Williams	5	2017	Ucenna Nwosu	1

National Championships in Football

"The concept of a national championship in college football dates to the early years of the sport in the 19th century." However, recognized early authority on college football, Walter Camp, stated this in 1919: "Football…is not a game where a great national championship is possible or desirable. The very nature of the sport would forbid anything like a series of contests as are played in baseball."

While Camp may be right, "the very nature" of Americans is that they will constantly try.

The first listing of a national champion was in 1869, when Princeton won the mythical crown. However, there was no coach for that first team and the absence of a coach continued for national champs until Princeton again won the title in 1878. Strangely enough, their coach was Woodrow Wilson, who would later become President of Princeton and President of the United States.

Early-day football was mostly a club type sport that often did not include a coach. The ten-year break in coaching from the 1869 Princeton team to the 1878 Princeton team continued until Yale won the title in 1888, with the above-mentioned Walter Camp as its coach.

The author has chosen to start the listing of national champions with that 1888 season, which coincides with the Trojans first season playing football. Those early years were dominated by the Ivy League as they were the first and often the only teams playing the sport. The reconstruction of those early years by naming a champion was done in more modern times. Much of the reconstruction was done by Bill Schroeder of the Helms Foundation. Schroeder was a very fair and knowledgeable man.

Author's Note: *The author's father, who is in the Helms Foundation Hall of Fame, knew Schroeder and commented favorably on him to the author.*

Major Selectors: **HAF** (Helms Athletic Foundation); **NFF** (National Football Foundation); **FWAA** (Football Writers Association of America); **AP** (Associated Press). **COACHES** includes **UPI** (United Press); **ESPN**; **CNN**; **USAT** (*USA Today*); BRC (Blue Ribbon Commission); and **NCF** (National Championship Foundation).

Other organizations made selections, but the below listing only includes major selectors. This listing, because it relies strictly on major selectors, may differ from other listings.

The following listing is based on the Wikipedia listing titled: "College Football National Championships in (the) NCAA Division 1 FBS." The listing of majors is also the Wikipedia listing, with the exception of NCF, which was selected by another source.

DISCLAIMER: The author has found several mistakes in Wikipedia documents which involved events in which the author was first person. While he has faith in the veracity of Wikipedia reporting mistakes may have been made in the following document?

YEAR	TEAM SELECTED	RECORD	COACH(ES)	MAJOR SELECTORS
1888	Yale	13-0	Walter Camp	Helms, NCF
1889	Princeton	10-0		Helms, NCF
1890	Harvard	11-0	George Adams	Helms, NCF
1891	Yale	13-0	Walter Camp	Helms, NCF
1892	Yale	13-0	Walter Camp	Helms, NCF
1893	Princeton	11-0		Helms, NCF
1894	Yale	16-0	William Rhodes	Helms, NCF
1895	Penn	14-0	George Woodruff	Helms, NCF
1896	Princeton	10-0-1	Franklin Morse	Helms, NCF
1897	Penn	15-0	George Woodruff	Helms, NCF
1898	Harvard	11-0	William Forbes	Helms, NCF
1899	Harvard	10-0-1	Benjamin Dibblee	Helms, NCF
1900	Yale	12-0	Malcolm McBride	Helms, NCF
1901	Michigan	11-0	Fielding H. Yost	Helms, NCF
1902	Michigan	11-0	Fielding H. Yost	Helms, NCF
1903	Princeton	11-0	Art Hillebrand	Helms, NCF
1904	Penn	12-0	Carl S. Williams	Helms, NCF
1905	Chicago	10-0	Amos Alonzo Stagg	Helms, NCF
1906	Princeton	9-0-1	William Roper	Helms, NCF
1907	Yale	9-0-1	William F. Know	Helms, NCF
1908	Penn	11-0-1	Sol Metzger	Helms, NCF
1909	Yale	10-0	**Howard Jones**	Helms, NCF
1910	Harvard	8-0-1	Percy Haughton	Helms, NCF
1911	Princeton	8-0-2	William Roper	Helms, NCF
1912	Harvard	9-0	Percy Haughton	Helms, NCF
1913	Harvard	9-0	Percy Haughton	Helms, NCF
1914	Army	9-0	Charles Daly	Helms, NCF
1915	Cornell	9-0	Albert Sharpe	Helms, NCF
1916	Pittsburgh	8-0	Glenn "Pop" Warner	Helms, NCF
1917	Georgia Tech	9-0	**John Heisman**	Helms, NCF

YEAR	TEAM SELECTED	RECORD	COACH(ES)	MAJOR SELECTORS
1918	Pittsburgh	4-1	Glenn "Pop" Warner	Helms, NCF
Season cut short due to World War I				
1919	Harvard	9-0-1	Bob Fisher	Helms, NCF
1920	California	9-0	Any Smith	Helms, NCF
1921	Cornell	8-0	Gil Dobie	Helms, NCF
*Iowa, coached by **Howard Jones**, came in tied for third.*				
1922	California	9-0	Andy Smith	NCF
1923	Illinois	8-0	Robert Zuppke	Helms, NCF
1924	Notre Dame	10-0	Knute Rockne	Helms, NCF
1925	Alabama	10-0	Wallace Wade	Helms, NCF
1926	Alabama	9-0-1	Wallace Wade	Helms, NCF
1926	Stanford	10-0-1	Glenn "Pop" Warner	Helms, NCF
1927	Illinois	7-0-1	Robert Zuppke	Helms, NCF
1928	Georgia Tech	10-0	William Alexander	Helms, NCF
USC claims this year as a national championship year. Georgia Tech was selected by two majors and eight minors, while USC (9-0-1), which was second, was only selected by two minors.				
1929	Notre Dame	9-0	Knute Rockne	Helms, NCF
USC (10-2) was selected second on-the-basis of three minor selectors.				
1930	Notre Dame	10-0	Knute Rockne	Helms, NCF
1931	**USC**	10-1	**Howard Jones**	Helms, NCF
USC was selected by two majors and nine minors, while two other teams only received a single minor selection.				
1932	**USC**	10-0	**Howard Jones**	Helms, NCF
USC additionally was selected by ten minor selectors, for an overwhelming selection, like 1931.				
1933	Michigan	7-0-1	Harry Kipke	Helms, NCF
USC, tied for second, which was the third second selection in six years, starting in 1928.				
1934	Minnesota	8-0	Bernie Bierman	Helms, NCF
Alabama claims this year (10-0), but only was selected by five minor selectors.				
1935	Minnesota	8-0	Bernie Bierman	Helms, NCF
1936	Minnesota	7-1	Bernie Bierman	AP, Helms, NCF
1937	Pittsburgh	8-1-1	Jack Sutherland	AP, NCF
1938	TCU	11-0	Dutch Meyer	AP, Helms, NCF

Tennessee (11-0) claims this year as its National Championship. While it received ten minor selections, it had no majors and TCU had three.

YEAR	TEAM SELECTED	RECORD	COACH(ES)	MAJOR SELECTORS
1939	Texas A&M	11-0	Homer Norton	AP, Helms, NCF

USC claims this year, but only received one minor while A&M received all three majors and ten minors.

YEAR	TEAM SELECTED	RECORD	COACH(ES)	MAJOR SELECTORS
1940	Minnesota	8-0	Bernie Bierman	AP, NCF
1941	Minnesota	6-0	Bernie Bierman	AP, Helms, NCF
1942	Ohio State	9-1	Paul Brown	AP, NCF

Georgia claims this year, but received no majors and only eight minors.

YEAR	TEAM SELECTED	RECORD	COACH(ES)	MAJOR SELECTORS
1943	Notre Dame	9-1	Frank Leahy	AP, Helms, NCF
1944	Army	9-0	Earl Blaik	AP, Helms, NCF
1945	Army	9-0	Earl Blaik	AP, Helms, NCF
1946	Notre Dame	8-0-1	Frank Leahy	AP, Helms, NCF
1947	Michigan	10-0	Fritz Crisler	Helms, NCF

AP selected Notre Dame (9-0)

YEAR	TEAM SELECTED	RECORD	COACH(ES)	MAJOR SELECTORS
1948	Michigan	9-0	Bennis Oosterbaan	AP, Helms, NCF
1949	Notre Dame	10-0	Frank Leahy	AP, Helms, NCF
1950	Oklahoma	10-1	Bud Wilkinson	AP, Helms
1951	Tennessee	10-1	Robert Neyland	AP, UP
1952	Michigan State	9-0	Biggie Munn	AP, UP, Helms, NCF
1953	Maryland	10-1	Jim Tatum	AP, UP

Notre Dame was selected by Helms and NCF

YEAR	TEAM SELECTED	RECORD	COACH(ES)	MAJOR SELECTORS
1954	Ohio State	10-0	Woody Hayes	AP, Helms, NCF
	UCLA	9-0	Red Sanders	UP, FWAA
1955	Oklahoma	11-0	Bud Wilkinson	AP, UP, Helms, NCF, FWAA
1956	Oklahoma	10-0	Bud Wilkinson	AP, UP, Helms, NCF, FWAA
1957	Auburn	10-0	Ralph Jordan	AP, Helms, NCF
	Ohio State	9-1	Woody Hayes	UP, FWAA
1958	LSU	11-0	Paul Dietzel	AP, UPI, Helms, NCF
1959	Syracuse	11-0	Ben Schwartzwalder	AP, UPI, Helms, NCF, NFF, FWAA
1960	Minnesota	8-2	Murray Warmath	AP, UPI, NFF
	Ole Miss	10-0-1	Johnny Vaught	FWAA, NCF
1961	Alabama	11-0	Paul "Bear" Bryant	AP, UPI, NFF, Helms, NCF
1962	**USC**	11-0	John McKay	AP, UPI, NFF, Helms, FWAA, NCF
1963	Texas	11-0	Darrell Royal	AP, UPI, NFF, Helms, FWAA, NCF

YEAR	TEAM SELECTED	RECORD	COACH(ES)	MAJOR SELECTORS
1964	Alabama	10-1	Paul "Bear" Bryant	AP, UPI
	Arkansas	11-0	Frank Broyles	FWAA, Helms, NCF
1965	Alabama	9-1-1	Paul "Bear" Bryant	AP, FWAA, NCF
	Michigan State	10-1	Duffy Daugherty	UPI, FWAA, NFF, Helms
When major selectors are listed twice, it means that they selected both.				
1966	Notre Dame	9-0-1	Ara Parseghian	AP, UPI, FWAA, NFF, Helms, NCF
1967	**USC**	10-1	John McKay	AP, UPI, FWAA, NFF, Helms, NCF
1968	Ohio State	10-0	Woody Hayes	AP, UPI, FWAA, NFF, Helms, NCF
1969	Texas	11-0	Darrell Royal	AP, UPI, FWAA, NFF, Helms, NCF
1970	Texas	10-1	Darrell Royal	UPI, NFF
	Nebraska	11-0-1	Bob Devaney	AP, FWAA, Helms, NCF
1971	Nebraska	13-0	Bob Devaney	AP, FWAA, Helms, NFF, UPI, NCF
1972	**USC**	12-0	John McKay	AP, UPI, FWAA, NFF, Helms, NCF
1973	Notre Dame	11-0	Ara Parseghian	AP, FWAA, NFF, Helms, NCF
1974	**USC**	10-1-1	John McKay	FWAA, UPI, NFF, Helms, NCF
	Oklahoma	11-0	Barry Switzer	AP, Helms, NCF
When major selectors are listed twice, it means that they selected both.				
1975	Oklahoma	11-1	Barry Switzer	AP, FWAA, NFF, UPI, Helms, NCF
1976	Pittsburgh	12-0	Johnny Major	AP, FWAA, NFF, UPI, Helms, NCF
USC under John Robinson was selected second. They were the choice of six minor selectors, but no majors.				
1977	Notre Dame	11-1	Dan Devine	AP, FWAA, UPI, NFF, Helms, NCF
1978	**USC**	12-1	John Robinson	UPI, Helms, NCF
	Alabama	11-1	Paul "Bear" Bryant	AP, FWAA, NFF, Helms, NCF
1979	Alabama	12-0	Paul "Bear" Bryant	AP, FWAA, NFF, UPI, Helms, NCF
USC (11-0-1) under John Robinson, finished second among selectors.				
1980	Georgia	12-0	Vince Dooley	AP, FWAA, NFF, UPI, Helms, NCF
1981	Clemson	12-0	Danny Ford	AP, UPI, FWAA, NFF, Helms, NCF
1982	Penn State	11-1	Joe Paterno	AP, UPI, FWAA, NFF, USAT, Helms, NCF
1983	Miami	11-1	Howard Schnellenberger	AP, UPI, FWAA, NFF, NCF, USAT/CNN
1984	BYU	13-0	LaVell Edwards	AP, UPI, FWAA, NFF, NCF, USAT/CNN
1985	Oklahoma	11-1	Barry Switzer	AP, UPI, FWAA, NFF, NCF, USAT/CNN
1986	Penn State	12-0	Joe Paterno	AP, UPI, FWAA, NFF, NCF, USAT/CNN

YEAR	TEAM SELECTED	RECORD	COACH(ES)	MAJOR SELECTORS
1987	Miami	12-0	Jimmy Johnson	AP, UPI, FWAA, NFF, NCF, USAT/CNN
1988	Notre Dame	12-0	Lou Holtz	AP, UPI, FWAA, NFF, NCF, USAT/CNN
1989	Miami	11-1	Dennis Erickson	AP, UPI, FWAA, NFF, NCF, USAT, CNN
1990	Colorado	11-1-1	Bill McCartney	AP, FWAA, NFF, NCF, USAT/CNN
1991	Washington	12-0	Don James	UPI/NFF, FWAA, NCF, USAT/CNN
1992	Alabama	13-0	Gene Stallings	AP, UPI/NFF, FWAA, NCF, USAT/CNN
1993	Florida State	12-1	Bobby Bowden	AP, UPI, FWAA, NCF, USAT/NFF/CNN
1994	Nebraska	13-0	Tom Osborne	AP, UPI, FWAA, NCF, USAT/CNN/NFF
1995	Nebraska	12-0	Tom Osborne	AP, UPI, FWAA, NCF, NFF, USAT/CNN
1996	Florida	12-1	Steve Spurrier	AP, FWAA, NFF, NCF, USAT/CNN
1997	Michigan	12-0	Lloyd Carr	AP, FWAA, NFF, NCF
	Nebraska	13-0	Tom Osborne	USAT/ESPN, NCF
1998	Tennessee	13-0	Phillip Fulmer	AP, FWAA, NFF, NCF, USAT/ESPN
1999	Florida State	12-0	Bobby Bowden	AP, FWAA, NFF, NCF, USAT/ESPN
2000	Oklahoma	13-0	Bob Stoops	AP, FWAA, NFF, NCF, USAT/ESPN
2001	Miami	12-0	Larry Coker	AP, FWAA, NFF, USAT/ESPN
2002	Ohio State	14-0	Jim Tressel	AP, FWAA, NFF, USAT/ESPN

USC (11-2) was selected second in this year's championship, with three minor selectors.
The Trojans came on strong the second half of the season, promoting the selection.

2003	**USC**	12-1	Pete Carroll	AP, FWAA
	LSU	13-1	Nick Saban	NFF, USAT/ESPN

While both teams qualified, the AP recognition was usually considered the strongest.

2004	**USC**	11-0	Pete Carroll	AP, NFF

Another team garnered selection from FWAA & USAT/ESPN, but was forced to vacate giving the Trojans sole title.

2005	Texas	13-0	Mack Brown	AP, NFF, FW, USAT

USC came in second by virtue of losing, in overtime, the incredibly exciting Rose Bowl game for the national championship

2006	Florida	13-1	Urban Meyer	AP, FWAA, NFF, USAT
2007	LSU	12-2	Les Miles	AP, FWAA, NFF, USAT

USC (11-2) came in tied for second.

2008	Florida	13-1	Urban Meyer	AP, FWAA, NFF, USAT
2009	Alabama	14-0	Nick Saban	AP, FWAA, NFF, USAT

NATIONAL CHAMPIONSHIPS IN FOOTBALL

YEAR	TEAM SELECTED	RECORD	COACH(ES)	MAJOR SELECTORS
2010	Auburn	14-0	Gene Chizik	AP, FWAA, NFF, USAT
2011	Alabama	12-1	Nick Saban	AP, FWAA, NFF, USAT
2012	Alabama	13-1	Nick Saban	AP, FWAA, NFF, USAT
2013	Florida State	14-0	Jimbo Fisher	AP, FWAA, NFF, USAT
2014	Ohio State	14-1	Urban Meyer	AP, FWAA/NFF, USAT/AMWAY
2015	Alabama	14-1	Nick Saban	AP, FWAA/NFF, USAT/AMWAY
2016	Clemson	14-1	Dabo Sweeney	AP, FWAA/NFF, USAT/AMWAY
2017	Alabama	13-1	Nick Saban	AP, FWAA/NFF, USAT/AMWAY
2018	Clemson	15-0	Dabo Sweeney	AP, FWAA/NFF, USAT/AMWAY
2019	LSU	15-0	Ed Orgeron	AP, FWAA/NFF, USAT/AMWAY
2020	Alabama	13-0	Nick Saban	AP, FWAA/NFF, USAT/AMWAY
2021	Georgia	14-1	Kirby Smart	AP, FWAA/NFF, USAT/AMWAY
2022	Georgia	15-0	Kirby Smart	AP, FWAA/NFF, USAT/AMWAY

About the Author

The author, Russ Goodenough, was both a military and civilian pilot prior to concentrating on the writing of books. In the military, he flew the then-fastest operational fighter in the world, the F-4C Phantom II, Prior to that, he attended the United States Air Force Academy. During his wartime, he flew 148 combat missions over much of Southeast Asia, including North Vietnam, China, Laos and the Gulf of Tonkin.

In combat, he won the Distinguished Flying Cross (DFC), the Purple Heart, (9) Air Medals, the Air Force Commendation Medal for commanding the 12th TFW Command Post for the visits to Vietnam of Secretary McNamara and President Johnson, the Combat Readiness Medal, the U.S. National Defense Service Medal, the Small Arms Marksmanship Award, the Vietnam Service Medal with two Bronze Service Stars, the Republic of Vietnam awarded Civil Action Campaign Medal, the Republic of Vietnam awarded Civil Action Outstanding Unit Citation with Order of the Palm and the United States Air Force Outstanding Unit Award with an Oak Leaf Cluster.

Additionally, he wore the U.S. Army Paratrooper Wings as a jump-qualified Forward Air Controller. He was an F-4 Aircraft Commander, F-4 Combat Flight Leader, F-4 Instructor Pilot and Maintenance Test Pilot. While flying the F-4 for NATO as part of the European War Plan, he was also a nuclear bomb commander in charge of five bombs. The Martin Baker Company of London, England, maker of the Phantom ejection seats, honored him as the only airman in the world to have successfully ejected from both the front and back seats of the F-4 Phantom.

For 15 years, Goodenough flew as pilot for Continental Airlines, the last four of which were in the South Pacific. His destinations included Hawaii, Samoa, Fiji, New Zealand, Australia, Guam, Okinawa, Taiwan, and Hong Kong. He flew the inaugural flight for Continental in the South Pacific and retired as a Captain on the DC-10.

For 34 years, he owned and was President and CEO of Cal U-Rent and Cal Party Rent of Thousand Oaks, and Ventura, California. Cal U-Rent was a homeowner and contractor rental company featuring tools and equipment up to large-sized loaders, dozers, skid steers, excavators, backhoes, tractors, and lifts. He rented many different types of trucks and trailers and was the largest retailer of propane in the tri-county region of Ventura, Santa Barbara, and San Luis Obispo Counties.

He started his writing career in high school, when he wrote articles about his Fillmore High football team. He was team quarterback and would write a column after the completion of each game. While at the Air Academy, the USAF published an essay of his concerning immigration. While with Cal U-Rent, he was lead-writer and Editor of the Conejo Business Times, a Chamber of Commerce newspaper widely read in the Conejo Valley of Southern California's Ventura County.

Russ, a lifetime Trojan fan, is now retired in Thousand Oaks, California with his wife Carolyn and busy writing books plus caring for his extensive yard. This is his sixth book.

PERSONAL COMMENTS and RICH MEMORIES of USC & ATHLETICS
by the AUTHOR:

My personal history is interwoven with the athletic histories of USC, the Los Angeles Memorial Coliseum, and Occidental College. Even though I did not attend USC or Occidental, I consider them as part of my own heritage. Growing up in Southern California, before the football, basketball, and baseball major league teams arrived in California, was quite different than it is today.

Instead of the Rams and Chargers, we had USC and UCLA in football. Instead of the Lakers we had UCLA under John Wooden. Instead of the Dodgers, we had the minor league Los Angeles Angels and the Hollywood Stars. To the south we had the minor league San Diego Padres and to the north it was the San Francisco Seals.

From my earliest recollections, I have been a Trojan fan. My father got his teaching administration certificate from USC and attended the USC School of Law for two years. In SoCal, USC was the standard of excellence in football and in all athletics. Today, USC and UCLA share that SoCal excellence. California culture in those days was often looked down upon by many in the East of the US. Our SoCal athletic teams were a source of pride and showed the rest of the country that those of us residing on the West Coast, also belonged.

The Coliseum was in our blood. My father attended the opening and closing ceremonies of the 1932 Olympic Summer Games held in the Coliseum. I was fortunate to win the lottery and was also able to attend both the opening and closing ceremonies for the 1984 Olympic Summer Games held in the Coliseum. God willing, I hope to attend the 2028 Summer Olympics to be hosted by both the Coliseum and the Ram's Stadium in the Inglewood part of Los Angeles.

USC has been an institution in Southern California a long time. With USCs inaugural football game being played in 1888, it was the only football team of note and that remained for another 3 years until UCLA played its first game in 1919. Small liberal-arts colleges like Occidental played better football in those days. The Los Angeles Rams came to Southern California from Cleveland Ohio. They did not play their first game in Los Angeles until 1946. Other professional sports team that now call Los Angeles home also came from other cities. Notably, the Dodgers came from the Brooklyn Borough of New York City and the Lakers moved from Minneapolis, Minnesota, the land of 10,000 lakes, which is how they got their name.

With the not-so-distant move by USC and UCLA to the Big Ten, perhaps it is a good time to recollect what the PAC-12 and its predecessors have meant to California. Things will be quite different when we leave the PAC-12 for the unknown of a stronger conference.

The PAC-12 had always prided itself and continually states that the PAC-12 is the conference of champions. What does that really mean? When they portray it during many conference football games some wonder how we can make that claim when we have not competed for a national championship in football for a long time. While USC has won 11 national championships in football, the rest of the west has never won more than one. But, there are many other sports that create champions.

The listing of conference champions in Track and Field for the Trojans brings back many memories. Many of us who were born in Southern California have similar memories.

In the listing of the 1949 USC Track Conference Champions is the name Mel Patton. In addition to a relay team, six individual championships were won by Trojans that year. Patton won the 100-yard and 220-yard dashes. In those days, we used yards instead of meters in race distances. A vivid memory of mine is sitting beside my father in the Coliseum and watching Mel Patton set the world record of 9.3 seconds in the 100.

Parry O'Brien from Santa Monica and USC won the conference shot put championships in 1951, 1952 and 1953. O'Brien created a new style of putting the shot and was a hero to many Trojan fans. He was the best in the country and an Olympic gold medalist in 1952, 1956 and a silver medalist in 1960. O'Brien placed 4th in the 1964 Olympics. For his accomplishments, he was inducted into the U.S. Olympic Hall of Fame.

In the 1954 conference championships, Jon Arnett was one of six Trojan champions, winning the Long Jump. Who can forget his gridiron exploits as one of the greatest tailbacks in Trojan football history.

Max Truex won the conference championship in the 2 Mile in both 1957 and 1958. I remember meeting Truex at Oxnard Air Force Base in 1958 as he was then a member of the USAF track team. I was still in high school and competing at Oxnard to attend the new USAF Academy.

On June 29, 1956, my father and I attended the Olympic Trials being held at the Coliseum. A 19-year-old freshman from Compton Junior College slowly approached the bar in the high jump competition. We had waited in the stadium for Charlie Dumas to jump. The competition was taking too long and we decided to leave. As we walked along beside the Coliseum on the USC campus side, we heard a mighty roar from the 20,000 attending. Dumas had finally cleared the 7-foot barrier that had repelled world jumpers for so long. It was similar when the Brit Roger Bannister finally eclipsed the four-minute mile barrier.

Dumas later became a Trojan and won the conference high jump in 1958, 1959, and 1960. When a young teen in junior high school, I used to ride in the back seat of cars that went to see my brother put the shot put. My oftentimes companion on those trips was going to see his brother Harry compete in shuttle hurdles for Mount Sac (Mt. San Antonio College). We used to drive to the Avant's home near Castaic Junction, which is now on Interstate Route 5 going from Los Angeles to the Central Valley.

The next time I saw Bobby Avant was at our Ventura County track and field championships. He was then using the Fosbury Flop in the high jump. That was in 1958. In 1959, Bobby was a Trojan and apparently tied Charlie Dumas for the conference championship. Dumas won in 1960 but Bobby won the conference championship all by himself in 1961. In that same year, Bobby won the AAU Championship with a leap of 7 feet. In that meet, he beat John Thomas who set the world outdoor high jump record in 1959 and later set the world indoor record. On July 5, 1961, Avant continued his mastery by winning the World Games held at Olympic Stadium in Helsinki, Finland. While jumping for the Southern California Striders at Helsinki, most of his competitive meets were as a Trojan.

Any SoCal residents who have lived here for long periods can relate many such incidents. Our connection to the Trojans has been important. I recall many years as a season ticket holder for Trojan football, both as a business owner and with personal tickets. Years of membership in the Trojan Club furthered my interest and was a bonding experience with other Trojan fans.

Another conference champion on that 1961 USC team was Dallas Long, winner of the shot put. He also won in 1962. My brother had followed our father's footsteps and graduated from Occidental. The biography of Trojan track and football coach Dean Cromwell includes references to his graduation from Occidental. My father had gotten to know Cromwell well. Cromwell had tried to recruit him to USC.

As a teen, I attended a ceremony at Occidental College when my father presented the Helms Trophy for the Best Athlete in North America to the then-world record holder in the pole vault, Bob Gutowski. It was on that occasion that Occidental College stated its research had determined that my father had been the first high school pole vaulter in the world to have cleared 12 feet in the era of bamboo vaulting poles. Due to his excellence in track, football, and baseball at Occidental College he got to know Cromwell, another Oxy alumnus who had tried to recruit him to USC. He won the California State Meet that year (1920), setting a record in the process.

Bob "Guts" Gutowski was part of the Occidental Track Team. My memories include a track meet at Stanford and watching Gutowski break the world vault record. Gutowski belonged to the ATO fraternity at Oxy. It was the "jock" fraternity with maybe 40 guys belonging. My brother Dave was an ATO and invited me down to spend the night .I have a vivid memory of seeing the massive silhouette of Dallas Long standing in the backlit door to our bedroom. Long was an ATO from USC and was visiting his frat brothers. Long was a typical Trojan. Between 1959 and 1964, Long set six official and five unofficial world records in the shot put. His last record was set at the USA vs. USSR dual meet in 1964.

Gutowski was not the only notable at the ATO House. I was only a high school freshman at the time that I met Jim Mora, another brother. Mora later served as head coach for the New Orleans Saints from 1986 to 1996 and the Indianapolis Colts from 1998 to 2001. Two year later, as a high school junior, my brother introduced me to another ATO, Jack Kemp, under the Oxy Tiger football stadium seats. That year I started for my high school football team as a quarterback and I was awestruck at meeting Kemp. Kemp later starred as quarterback for San Diego and Buffalo in the NFL and served as congressman from Buffalo. He later ran for president.

Kemp had another connection. The superintendent of schools and the high school principal for our little hometown of Fillmore were Occidental graduates. The superintendent, Donovan Main, sent his daughter, Joanne, to Oxy the same year my brother went. She later married Kemp.

Occidental was a national power in track in 1924. My father was one of the favorites to win the pole vault in the Olympic Trials to be held later in the year. The Occidental Track Team toured the eastern United States and my father broke his ankle falling into the vaulting pit that had been filled with sand. He was unable to compete in the Olympic Trials and lost his chance to represent the United States in the 1924 Paris "Chariots of Fire" Olympics.

My brother had a vested interest in Parry O'Brien and Dallas Long, shot putters from USC. Dave was a shot putter himself. Dave set a shot-put record at our high school in 1953 that still stands. H won Ventura County and won second in the Southern California meet to qualify for the California State Track Championships. As a college freshman, he was among the ten top freshmen shot putters in the United States. Unfortunately, he married his sophomore year and had to quit track to devote to several jobs to support his family, which included a child. His promising track carrier was thus cut short.

I had another memorable event regarding the shot put. I flew South Pacific as a pilot for Continental Airlines. One of our destinations out of Honolulu was Nandi, Fiji. In May of 1979, American Airlines lost a DC-10 at Chicago when it crashed on takeoff. At the time, I was in Fiji and the plane I was flying was a DC-10. The FAA grounded all DC-10s worldwide until they found the reason for the crash. For two weeks we were grounded. One afternoon I was sitting at the hotel bar sipping what they called "pork chops," which were just steins of beer. A gentleman sat beside me and that started a conversation that lasted the afternoon. He told me that his name was Bill Nieder. I looked at him and asked if he had ever put the shot for Kansas. He was a large man and replied in the affirmative. He sold tartan track surfaces and had attended a meeting of school representatives that morning. He shared that there were 28 in the room and he was the smallest man there. The Fijians are Melanesian and are very large and powerful. On three occasions, Nieder had set the world record in the shot put. What I remembered was that he had been runner up to Parry O'Brien and only won a silver medal at the 1956 Olympic Games. There they are again, another Trojan champion. No matter where we go in the world, we are reminded of the USC athletic standard of excellence.

It was fun and an honor to be a member of such a gifted athletic family. However, when they handed out the athletic genes, somehow they missed me. My grandfather on my mother's side was Canadian sprint champion, while living in Ontario. My mother was golf champion of her country club, as was my father, a scratch golfer. My father excelled in baseball in both high school and college. He played college football after never playing in high school. They were all just very gifted and it seemed to come naturally to them.

But athletics are so much more than just competing. They offer rewards in so many ways. Those of us who are Trojan fans of long standing have been amply blessed. Above all, USC athletics have provided memories. My memories include a track meet held between USC and Occidental College. USC had not been beaten in a dual meet for many years. In addition to world-record holder Gutowski, I remember Oxy's John Zetsman running the 440 and mile relay like the wind, with hair flowing in that wind. Zetsman ran a world record setting time with others in the mile relay. Walt Jennings threw the javelin. His javelin throw against USC fouled by a quarter inch. If he had not fouled, Oxy would have beaten USC. Instead, USC won 70-65. Later I met Zetsman as he flew for Continental out of our Houston domicile. Jennings, he was captain on the 727-200 out of Los Angeles and I flew with him for months. Again, a very small world and so many of those memories remind us of USC, which often serves as the center of our universe, whether we graduated or not.

Books by the Author

INITIATION to WRITING:

The author grew up in the Southern California bucolic ranching and oil town of Fillmore, California. At Fillmore High School, he wrote front-page articles for the town newspaper, the *Fillmore Herald*. He quarterbacked the varsity and wrote about what happened after each game.

In college, at the United States Air Force Academy, he wrote an essay on revamping the immigration system that was published by the Air Force. It was later-used in the governmental discussions leading up to the 1965 major legislation changing our immigration laws.

After finishing his fighter pilot career flying for NATO in Europe, he flew for 15 years as pilot for Continental Airlines, retiring early as a DC-10 Captain. For 34 years, he owned a truck and equipment rental business located in Ventura County, California (Cal U-Rent). While in the rental business and while a Board Director, he was Editor and Chief Writer for the *Conejo Business Times*, the newspaper of the Thousand Oaks-Westlake Village Regional Chamber of Commerce located in both Los Angeles and Ventura Counties of Southern California.

After retirement, he lived in Thousand Oaks, California as well as at a vacation home in the forested, mountain village of Pine, in Central Arizona. While there, he served as Editor and only writer for the Portal IV Homeowners Association's newsletter *Insight*.

CURRENT BOOKS:

The author began writing books late in life, after several careers involving piloting of aircraft and the running of a business. He has found writing to be exciting, educational, and very rewarding.

His first book was an unpublished *History of Hangar 99,* which was about the fraternal organization known as the QBs or Quiet Birdmen. The challenge for him was to find out the truth about the blending of three different histories of the national QB organization. Birdmen include about 20,000 nationally and included President George Herbert Walker Bush.

The author's first published book is *Why Johnny Came Marching Home*. Johnny was published and is available on Amazon.com. It is the story of the clandestine air wars that were fought in the skies over Laos, North Vietnam, and China during the Vietnam War. He was a fighter pilot heavily engaged in that conflict and returned from that war fully expecting that an author would write about what really had happened. His wait took 45 years and he finally became convinced that, if it was to be written at all, he would have to write it. His purpose was to tell why we lost the clandestine air wars fought in and over Laos, North Vietnam, the Gulf of Tonkin, and over China, which led to our defeat in the Vietnamese War itself.

He wanted to convey to the American public what life was like for a combat pilot in Southeast Asia. He also wanted other pilots who had participated, to find out what happened in the years that they did not participate in such a long war. In that, he sometimes got into the technical.

It took three years to write as it involved extensive research of the many declassified reports from agencies about the wars such as the USAF, DOD, CIA, NSA, USN, and the Pacific Air Forces (PACAF).

A reader may be interested to find out what happened in the battles in the skies that included severe losses against the forces of China and Russia, in addition to those from North Vietnam North Korea was also a participant. American fighter bombers attacked the most sophisticated heavily gunned, and heavily missiled air defense in the history of aerial warfare.

His second published book was also published and is available on Amazon.com. It is titled *Darkness @ Noon, Battling the Beast*. It is the story of the day-by-day fight against the Thomas Fire, which consumed so much of Southern California in 2017 and January of 2018. Due to the hellacious winds, the fire's start was explosive. At the time, it was the largest, single wildfire in the history of California. It involved the greatest assemblage of fire-fighting equipment, including over a thousand fire engines, in the history of California. It also involved the greatest usage of airborne fire-fighting in the then-history of the world.

The third published book is titled: *Westward Wagons – An American Family Journey*. In it the author portrays the life and travels of a family that emigrated from England and arrived to settle the Massachusetts Bay Colony. It details the many adventures of the family as it crossed the United States by railroad, stagecoach and finally, by covered wagon. It details many first-published accounts of the many battles fought and atrocities committed by the settlers, by the militias, and by the tribes. Much of the information came from private family documents and letters.

His fourth published book is titled: *Visions of a Just and Reformed Nation*. In it he details the divided state of our nation and what actions may be needed to heal the national wounds. He propose a Second Constitutional Convention to fix the many broken or wounded systems currently in-use by our government. He also presents the current state of many promising commercial ventures that could greatly enhance the economic strength of the United States.

83961299R00159